America's Management Challenge— Capitalizing on Change

America's Management Challenge— Capitalizing on Change

William B. Miller

Chilton Book Company
Radnor, Pennsylvania

Library of Congress Cataloging in Publication Data
Miller, William B., 1945–
  America's management challenge.

  Bibliography: p. 324
  Includes index.
  1. Management—United States. I. Title.
HD70.U5M43   1983   302.3′5   83-70785
ISBN 0-8019-7395-3

    1 2 3 4 5 6 7 8 9 0   2 1 0 9 8 7 6 5 4 3

Contents

The Corporation's New Management Team

Adjusting to Changed Environments

Facing Off Against the New Realities

Managing the Human Element

Turning Suggestions into Actions

Acknowledgments

I WISH TO THANK several people who were instrumental in converting this book from a wish into reality.

Val Faulkenburg typed the manuscript. Donna Ridgway conducted research and helped prepare the graphics for it. Their high level of skills and sense of quality made the project proceed very smoothly.

Many business and university colleagues read all or part of the manuscript. However, Michaela Cassidy deserves special recognition for the time she devoted to it and for the perceptiveness of her comments.

I am also grateful to the people at Chilton who provided valuable assistance in structuring the book and shaping the words as well as in critiquing the content.

Finally, there is one person whose continual encouragement and support were essential—my wife Karen. The book would not exist without her.

WILLIAM B. MILLER
June 1983

America's Management Challenge— Capitalizing on Change

"The old order changeth, yielding place to new."
—TENNYSON

Introduction

THIS BOOK is about change in the world of business. Corporate life is very different from what it used to be. Government regulation has mushroomed. The corporation has a whole new set of social responsibilities to go with its economic responsibilities. It's not even clear if making a profit is still socially acceptable!

The products and services picture is a kaleidoscope with a half-life of thirty seconds. Retailers change overnight from full-line department stores to discount operators to boutique environments to mail-order houses. If you don't like the financial services available to you from retail checking to investment banking, just wait a month or two until Congress changes the law again or Merrill Lynch offers a new service. Technology dominates many industries. Computers that look like type-writers are now more powerful than their million-dollar counterparts of a generation ago. Yet today's computer, state-of-the-art stereo receiver, or home electronic game probably will be obsolete in six months.

Commercial and retail customers have grown accustomed to variety. If Company A can't provide what they want, Company B will. And the price and quality level had better be acceptable, or Company C will step in. Managing a business enterprise under these circumstances is not easy. And, to add complexity—what if Company C is foreign? Many industries are wholly or partially dominated by foreign firms. Wristwatches, radios, automobiles for the retail consumer. Steel, machine tools, memory chips for the commercial customer. And foreign competition is continually increasing.

What about the changes in people? Most ten-year-old children know more about computers than do their parents. The work ethic is making

1

a comeback among young adults, we are told, but in the workplace, people with 32- and 36-hour work weeks demand job enrichment. The business magazines frequently feature articles on the decline in corporate loyalty among executives. The structure of work in society has changed so much, so rapidly, that many of us still find the statistics to be incredible: the 1950's family profile of working husband, housewife, and two children now describes less than 10 percent of the population. The two-career family has arrived, except when the husband stays home to do housework.

In addition, we don't know what is coming next. How much control will the government eventually have over U.S. business? Is the United Auto Workers (UAW) seat on Chrysler Corporation's Board of Directors a onetime response to an unusual situation or a harbinger of new labor-management relations? Word processing machines are already obsolete—the new term and function is Total Office Automation. The pace of change is accelerating, not slowing down. The future has arrived.

It has arrived because of change. Change is cumulative; when we have accumulated a certain amount, we recognize that a new era has arrived. Unfortunately, eras don't carry signs announcing themselves, so we have to figure out when we think one has arrived. We also have to figure out where it has arrived. Change is more rapid in some areas than others. It affects some businesses and individuals far more than others. Different industries and people truly live in different worlds. The worlds overlap where they must intersect in society, but the internal operations of each world are different. The world of commodity chemicals is different from the world of specialty electronics. Change affects both, but in different ways and at different rates. We must recognize this fact in our discussions. Different environments and eras will and must coexist. As a consequence, management approaches to dealing with change will not always be identical.

In this book, we will focus on business management—the process and the people. "Managing" carries its traditional implications of leadership, planning, organizing, decision making, directing others, external and internal communications, and so on. There are as many definitions of management as there are books on management. None of them is bad, but few of them convey all the essence of management. Good management is like sex appeal: it's hard to define, but you know it when you see it. We are going to worry about how to achieve it rather than about a precise definition of what it is.

Because change affects all parts of an organization, we will include all levels of management in our discussions. The chairman of the board and first-line supervisors are separated by a chasm that is wide at some places and narrow at others. The narrow places are the fundamental principles that apply to all managers. These principles, of course, are not immutable. After all, this book is about the changes in some of them. But they are largely common at some point in each company and environment, and we will discuss how to identify and implement them. Differences between levels of management also will be discussed. We cannot hope to eliminate all those differences, but we can try to get people to work together.

Non-management people are the production heart of a company, so they will not be ignored here; in fact, we will discuss the problems of managing the workforce in some detail. But our focus always will be management.

We will examine the ways in which management can be successful in the changing world. Success obviously includes professional success, i.e., effective performance in one's job so as to contribute to the success of the company. However, it also includes personal success. Why? Because one of the changes in many people's minds is in the relationship of professional and personal success. A simple equation of the two kinds of success is accepted by a continually decreasing number of people, irrespective of management rank. People are increasingly interested in self-fulfillment. Pessimists' claims to the contrary, this does not necessarily imply lack of interest in the success of the company. It actually can imply the opposite. There are many roads leading to professional success, many possible correct actions in any situation. Many people want to select the action that will directly and indirectly advance their personal success as well as professional success. By choosing this action, they actually become more committed to its success because of the personal stakes. Naturally, the process of determining the best course of action in this way can become more complex. That is one of the variables we will consider in our discussions of successful management.

Our discussions will be organized into a few major areas: the corporation itself, including its relationships with society; new responsibilities and characteristics of the corporation's management team; changing products, services, and customers; and management of a company's human resources. We will explore each area in depth. We will review the specifics of recent and future change, describe management strategies and operational practices, identify skills that will be required, and discuss how to acquire them. We will describe examples of companies and individuals that are already on the frontier and are coping successfully.

The arena will be the United States. There is a lot to learn from foreign companies, and for this reason they will be discussed extensively. But our objective is the improvement of U.S. management.

We will cover a variety of subjects. The chief executive officer's (CEO's) job carries many responsibilities, and we want to deal with as many of these as we can. We will discuss the fundamental principles guiding the relationships among the various responsibilities of management. Good management is similar to conducting a symphony orchestra. We will discuss the individual instruments and their players, but always in the context of the whole orchestra. This book is not a primer on the violin or the oboe. Those books exist and fulfill an essential purpose in the education of musicians. But there is a more advanced level, or simply different, if you prefer—playing in the orchestra versus performing solo.

Our approach, then, will be both extensive and intensive. We will provide broad coverage of the numerous problems facing modern management. We will review potential approaches and how to select from among the various alternatives. We will not spend much time on things that are unaffected or affected only slightly by change. We will describe them, of course, including their role in specific circumstances, but to elaborate on them would not be true to the purpose of this book. We want to deal with new things here, not (generally speaking) refinement of known things.

There are some issues that we will not pursue, most notably those that relate to corporate politics, gamesmanship, and in general, the seamier side of corporate life. Where these issues are significant factors and likely to be for some period of time, we will address them. Examples are such elements of foreign cultures as non-tariff barriers to imports or certain kinds of payments that would be bribery to us. To ignore them would be to construct a fairytale world. However, the majority of issues of unethical conduct are not deserving of discussion in a book on management. Unethical behavior, in personal and professional senses, always will be with us and probably always will be beneficial to some individuals and companies. But dissecting and analyzing it as a legitimate management tool is simply not within the scope of this book.

This is neither a "blue sky" book nor a book about the distant future. It is about the here and now. It is very concerned about change and the long-term effects thereof. It is very concerned about development of an understanding of what the future will hold and its meaning for management. It is very concerned about considering the long-term consequences of present actions.

But it is addressed to short-term actions: from now through the next five to ten years, approximately. This focus has a few implications. One is that we are dealing with real, observed change in the present and near future. We are not dealing with speculation about the far future or with potential but unlikely change. For example, it would not be reasonable to examine the possible effects of cataclysmic change—total breakdown of government, nuclear war, permanent cutoff of oil supplies from the Middle East, and so forth. Some events such as these possibly might occur in the next five or ten years, but forecasting them would be useless. Remaining sensitive to the possibility and being properly prepared, of course, is not useless and will be discussed here. Second, the five- to ten-year focus permits us to ignore such transient economic phenomena as short-lived booms or recessions. This is not a book to help you figure out when to buy stock and when to sell. However—and this is an important distinction—we clearly want to understand the basic forces influencing the U.S. economy and how managers should respond to them.

Another implication of our focus is a need for action. This book is not reference material to be placed on the bookshelf and consulted annually during the company's strategic planning process. Therefore, in this book we will formulate a total plan of action for management. Every good idea eventually degenerates into hard work, and we want to conclude the book with a firm plan for what to do after the last page has been read. Specific actions to take will be discussed throughout the book, of course, but they need to be integrated into a master plan that fits a particular company's circumstances and management talents. We will discuss how to do this. We also will discuss what to do when the going gets rough, since not everybody will agree on either the concepts for dealing with the changing world or the specific suggestions in this book.

Change is seldom easy to accept. It is even more difficult to adopt an active position regarding change than to take a reactive, defensive position. But it must be done if a business and its managers are to be successful. It can be done. This Introduction outlines how we're going to approach it. Now, let's get started with the real work.

The Challenge of Change

"Revolution—call it Progress; Progress—call it Tomorrow."
—VICTOR HUGO

Chapter 1

Evolution of the Corporation

MANAGEMENT of the modern corporation is the subject of this book. The implication, of course, is that management practices should be updated to reflect current realities. It is less obvious that the object of the management—the corporation—also has changed. As with any gradual change, the overall magnitude of the change is not readily apparent unless one considers the entire span of the event. Tracing the evolution of the corporation in the United States will add immeasurably to our understanding of the present.

In fact, we will see that many of the problems that business managers face today are the result of something other than changes in the external environment, for example, new technologies. They are caused instead by changes in the role and responsibilities of the corporation itself. To begin our process of identifying those changes, let's examine U.S. business in the days of Ben Franklin.

In the Beginning . . .

The United States always has been a bastion of business. By 1775 the thirteen colonies had more ironmaking and forging facilities than the whole of England and Wales. (In fact, the competition was so fierce that Parliament passed the Iron Act to restrict the colonials' activity; the Act was ignored.) In 1781 the Bank of North America was established in Philadelphia; other banks were established in short order. Traditional colonial businesses, for example, agriculture and trading, had been flourishing since the first settlers landed.

9

Corporation chartering is defined as licensing to do business under certain terms and conditions. Charters are granted by states to corporations on an equitable basis, i.e., meeting the terms and conditions entitles a corporation to a charter and the freedom to compete with other corporations. Chartering in this form took hold in the early 1800s as the individual states established their chartering capabilities. Before that time, chartering operated through favoritism, political rewards, and so on.

For nearly two centuries, or almost as long as the U.S. has been a nation, business has been recognized formally. It is an unwritten part of the Constitution and the Bill of Rights that a group of people may band together for their own economic interests; to create something of value out of land, money, labor, and materials; and to sell it to others.

The Result

During the 1800s business prospered. In many respects it was the heyday of pure capitalism. Not in the sense that benefits flowed to all members of society, as some proponents of capitalism would claim. But in the sense of individuals operating unfettered, wheeling and dealing with only their economic self-interest at heart—Economic Darwinism, survival of the fittest. The names of this era conjure up images of bigger-than-life beings: Commodore Vanderbilt, Jay Gould, Jim Fisk, Andrew Carnegie. Some businesses and individuals produced goods— textiles, steel, for example. Others provided services—river transportation, railroads. Still others manipulated money for their fortunes— initially other people's money and later, as they prospered, their own. The United States became the most efficient machine for the production of goods and services that the world had ever seen. Many people became very wealthy through the exercise of free enterprise. John Galt would have been right at home.

The Cloud

Unfortunately, the silver lining had a cloud around it. The business machine was an unqualified economic success in that it generated a net positive value for the country, but it was a social flop. It was what mathematicians call a "zero-sum game," which is a fancy way of saying that for every winner, there is a loser. There were big winners: the owners and managers of the capitalist enterprises. There were little winners: the customers for the best range of products and services that had ever been available to them. But there also were big losers: the workers and their families. The division of happiness and prosperity actually was not quite this clear, of course. Some owners suffered, and some workers did well. And, many people fit more than one category, e.g., workers were also consumers. Nevertheless, the statement is generally accurate. One of the recurring themes in U.S. business is the tendency of its leaders to kill the goose that lays the golden eggs, or at least to kill part of a flock of the geese. This happened in the late 1800s. The geese decided they needed some protection.

Labor unions were born at this time, starting with the Order of the Knights of Labor in 1869. In 1886 Samuel Gompers founded the American Federation of Labor. The railroad strike of 1877 kicked off two generations of sometimes brutal confrontations between workers and management. The century was closed out by the Homestead strike and lockout by Carnegie Steel Company, the forerunner of the U.S. Steel Corporation.

Public Action

Concurrent with the unrest of workers, the public began to move against the corporations. The public moves ponderously through its arm of action, legislative bodies, but it usually does move. One by one, states began passing laws to protect workers, such as the Massachusetts ten-hour day law for women and children, passed in 1874. Working conditions were by and large regulated by the states, not the federal government, but at least they were regulated. By the early 1900s almost all states had minimum ages for employment and other controls over abuse of workers. Enforcement was sometimes spotty, but the precedent was set. Federal legislation was slower in coming, being dependent upon evidence that states' legislation was nonexistent, ineffective, or inefficient. Not until Woodrow Wilson's term as President were laws passed setting minimum working conditions that, while an improvement over then-existing conditions, many of us today would regard as practically slave labor statutes.

Equal in importance to the legislation was the support of the judicial system. There was considerable effort by employers to have the courts toss out the laws as being unconstitutional infringements on the rights of employers. These challenges frequently were unsuccessful at the state level, although they met with more fortune at the federal level. Two separate child labor laws passed by Congress, in 1916 and 1919, were declared unconstitutional by the Supreme Court. The legitimacy of unions also was challenged repeatedly in court, with some limited (occasionally striking) success but with no overall victory. The unions stayed on the scene with the blessing of the judiciary.

More Victories

Corporations were getting the public's attention in more ways than through their mistreatment of workers. The corporations seemed to possess too much power. They were able to operate in ways that stifled competition. They appeared to be a law unto themselves, operating only for their own benefit in any manner they chose.

With the prevailing spirit to regulate corporations, it was not too difficult for Congress to pass the Interstate Commerce Act in 1887, regulating railroad charges, and the Sherman Antitrust Act in 1890. However, enforcement of the laws was a different matter. Within the hearts of most judges lay a strong pro-business sentiment. While not favoring child labor abuse and similar atrocities, they were disinclined to take a role in restricting business combinations and business dealings with customers. This attitude held up through the Supreme Court of the United States, which in 1895 upheld a nationwide sugar manufacturing monopoly on the grounds that interstate commerce was not affected. Ironically, the Sherman Antitrust Act actually was used against labor unions—the 1894 Pullman strike was broken through its application in jailing Eugene Debs.

During the first part of the twentieth century, though, things turned around. The Hepburn Act (1906) strengthened the Interstate Commerce Act. The Clayton Act (1914) supplemented the Sherman Antitrust Act by banning such specific business practices as predatory pricing, i.e., pricing solely to drive competition out of business. Federal legislation improving working conditions and formally legitimizing labor unions was passed. The Federal Reserve System was established in 1913. Governments started taking over utilities. Most large cities ran their own water departments. States established public service commissions to regulate utilities. Faced with the overwhelming popular support for such legislation, the courts fell into line. As has been observed, members of the courts read election returns. However the case is put, it is important for the courts not to be too out of step with the times, and so it was natural for them to take their place alongside the other guardians of the public welfare.

End of the First Cycle

Our history lesson has brought us up to the pre-World War I years. Since the turn of the century, regulation of corporations had been increasingly enacted by legislative bodies, upheld by the judicial system, and supported by the public. The principle had been established that the corporation is not to be trusted. What this meant, of course, is merely that corporations tend to act in their own self-interest, which ought not to be a startling revelation. With hindsight, some may wonder why it took so long to figure this out, since it would seem to be so basic.

Why have I called this the "End of the First Cycle"? Simply because it was the first significant move away from pure capitalism. It was a recognition that not enough members of society benefit from the kind of capitalism that was prevalent in the mid-1800s. This is neither good nor bad. It is merely the way things shook out. In a democracy, which the U.S. has in one form or another, a critical mass of citizens has to be supportive of an idea for it to exist and survive as a public policy. The idea of capitalism required a few changes in the late 1800s and early 1900s to be acceptable to enough people. This is why I refer to this time as the first cycle of capitalism in the U.S.

Another point on this topic: We should not ignore the power that was demonstrated by the public. If the first lesson of nineteenth century-style capitalism was that it had to be changed, the second lesson was that the people could change it. The change came from many directions. Individual voting and communication to legislative representatives helped. Special interest organizations such as the National Child Labor Committee were very powerful. The media publicized the causes—through both mass media such as newspapers and through such individual contributors as Upton Sinclair and Lincoln Steffens. The tools of transition in other words, were the same as they are today: individual action, special interest groups, and media support. The lesson to be learned is when all is said and done, the corporation and all other public institutions exist only in forms acceptable to the people.

The Next Step

The remainder of the first half of this century saw consolidation of the gains that had been made prior to World War I. The concept of government constraints on corporations was no longer a novelty. It was taken for granted that corporations should be restrained from exerting their maximum economic powers over individuals or smaller companies unable to defend themselves. In addition, the wartime agencies and boards with their virtually complete power over their respective areas, accustomed the public, business leaders, and the three branches of government to the notion of government shackles.

Of course, this time in our history was also a time of great industrial expansion. The mass-production automobile industry came into being, starting essentially in 1908 with Ford Motor Company's offering an automobile for one-third of the then-existing average price for new cars. By 1928 there were 26 million registered cars and trucks. The General Electric Company grew into one of the giants of industry. Radio broadcasting began in 1920. The telephone industry expanded and prospered. Many of the fundamental tools of everyday living today were brought to market in mass consumption form before the Great Depression began in 1929.

It is not my intent here to discuss either the Depression or World War II in any context other than the evolution of the role of the corporation in the U.S. Both the Depression and WWII affected the evolution. Many firms perished during the hard economic times, but many that survived were even stronger than they had been before. They knew how to weather adversity and they had a larger market share because of the demise of smaller competitors. Wars are among the best of times for industrial companies, so WWII made its contribution to the health of U.S. corporations.

By the 1950s the U.S. industrial juggernaut had reached a new level of competence. Airplanes and television were added to automobiles and radios as routine products. Thousands of consumer items were being manufactured and pushed out through retail marketing channels. Wartime production had increased the production skills and capacity of the basic industries—steel, rubber, chemicals, etc. Coolidge's observation that "the business of America is business" and Charles Wilson's belief that "what's good for the country is good for General Motors and vice versa" had never seemed so true. It seemed that the role of the corporation was to provide never-ending material prosperity for all members of society. The unspoken corollary was that all other problems would be worked out within the framework of this prosperity.

The Other Side

However, to retrace this territory from a different perspective, at the same time a wholly different series of events was occurring. Workers and their unions were obtaining additional legal protection. The Norris-LaGuardia Act (1932) strengthened the hands of unions, as did the National Labor Relations Act (1935). The Social Security system was established. The Minimum Wage Act was passed.

More controls were placed on business. The Securities and Exchange Commission was established in 1934 to regulate the securities markets. The Glass-Steagall Act (1933) and the Banking Act of 1935 increased federal control over banks. The powers of the Federal Reserve were increased. At the state level, additional controls were placed over utilities and other similar entities such as telephone companies.

Much of the legislation was part of Franklin Roosevelt's New Deal and was prompted by the excesses and errors of business in previous years. Nevertheless, the ideas took hold firmly in the U.S. business structure and were cemented in place by their apparent success. By the 1950s business and government, the latter acting on behalf of the downtrodden private citizens, had a working agreement that government could limit the rights of corporations to engage in economic exploitation of their workers or customers. It took a generation, but the principle was permanently implanted. The role of the corporation now had an important qualifier: the consent of the government in economic matters. In other words, expanding on my prior definition, the role of the corporation was to provide material prosperity within certain economic guidelines or constraints. Both sides were relatively happy. Business was prospering, and the individual citizen seemed adequately protected. So what happened next? Somehow, after only a few years of this Golden Age, we marched into another age, one that I think of as the "Total Well-Being Age."

The Total Well-Being Age

Up until this time, restraints on corporations' activities had existed primarily to protect the economic interests of the workers, for example, minimum wage laws, protection of union bargaining rights, and restrictive immigration laws. Additional protection for workers amounted only to elimination of the most barbaric working conditions and abuse of women and child labor. Well into this century, when the rights of labor unions had been firmly established in terms of wage negotiation, ten- and twelve-hour days still were commonplace, and unsafe, unsanitary work places were as much the rule as the exception. Things were better by the 1950s, but the principle was still economic protection.

We look back on the 1950s as a period of contentment. And they probably were. Although time turns the hue of history to gold, there was something soundly satisfactory about that period. People were making their way successfully, but without the frenzy of the 1920s. People and corporations—individually and as a team—were building a better life for each other.

Who can say what disturbed this delicate balance? Certainly a number of people believe that the death of John Kennedy forever destroyed a new mood, a new spirit in the citizens of the United States. Others will argue as vigorously that the Vietnam war was the villain.

There were too many things that changed between the 1950s and 1960s to chronicle them here. For the purposes of our discussion, let us examine the broader role of the corporation, in fact its new responsibility, in protecting the workers and other individuals. Over an amazingly short period of time, the corporation's role expanded almost beyond belief. On-the-job safety protection was mandated. We moved from a situation of daily risking of lives in unsafe work places to a thicket of rules and regulations.

Workers' health became a major concern. Laws were passed to compensate miners for black lung disease. Twenty- and thirty-year-old cases of asbestos exposure were tracked down. Stringent exposure laws and regulations were enacted. Cost/benefit tradeoffs were not an issue; even during the conservative times of 1981, the courts upheld the Occupational Safety and Health Administration (OSHA) in its position that a value could not be placed on employees' health.[1]

Environmental protection became a burning issue. The Congress decided to make the environment safe for mankind and almost every kind of living creature that was trying to coexist with industry.

Protection was extended beyond the work place to individuals who would purchase, use, or otherwise come into contact with a company's products. The licensing procedure for new drugs became so strict and time consuming that new drugs were improving hundreds of lives in other countries before they were available legally in the United States.

We greatly expanded controls over television advertising. Although many medical products could be purchased legally with no restrictions, the advertising for them became highly restricted. Advertising for products like tobacco and alcohol, which our puritan heritage has taught us are tools of the devil, became more controlled than ever before. We developed a concept of "fair" advertising.

These issues, and the others like them, are still very active. We have no end point or conclusion from which to develop a perspective. We are trying to write a history of a battle while sitting in the front-line trenches during the battle. However, it is clear that the country in the 1960s made the second great move away from pure capitalism. The corporations became responsible for not damaging any part of the well-being of the workers or the citizens that were affected by their activities. This time is what I call the Age of Total Well-Being. Its end point is somewhere in the future, but the direction is clear.

A Digression

Let us digress for a second to consider the plight of the poor corporation while all the additional controls were being implemented. Was the patient dying from the doctor's good intentions? Hardly. Business people today look back upon this period as the "go-go '60s." The times were very good for business. The tax climate was favorable. Wartime economies are always healthy. The electronics revolution was fully underway. Et cetera, et cetera. But, there also were opposing forces. Government was growing rapidly, and government is essentially unproductive, as it adds no real wealth to the economy. The seeds of inflation were being sown. The war wasn't that big as wars go. If you didn't know that the 1960s were a boom time, you might have trouble deducing it. But it doesn't matter. The times were good, business and its managers did well, and society did well. Is all well that ends well? Let's consider the next stage in the evolution of corporations.

Convergence of Ideas

Two ideas converged to form a third. The first idea was the extensive, apparently successful expansion of corporate responsibility along the lines we have reviewed. The second was the apparently neutral effect of this increased responsibility on the profit-making capability of corporations. Corporations made money in spite of the new responsibilities and constraints. By the late 1960s, a great amount of unfinished business remained on the agenda of the builders of the Great Society. Racism, poverty, and similar social problems had not yet been eradicated. So, a third idea arose: why not enlist the corporations in this effort? Or, more precisely, why not draft them? So we did.

The Third Stage

The second stage in the evolution of corporations was Total Well-Being. Before it had run its course, we added another stage. I don't have a name for this stage, but its hallmark is the active involvement of the corporation in solving the tough problems of our society. Consider, for example, racism. Various legal mechanisms had been attempted to outlaw discrimination and promote equal opportunity in education and job opportunities. By most quantitative measures, the approach wasn't working. Integration wasn't happening, minorities weren't being promoted, and so forth. So society invented "affirmative action." This concept simply says that a company will hire, train, and promote minorities and women until adequate assimilation is achieved. End of discussion. In addition, business expenses for discriminatory practices will be nondeductible under the tax laws. And the Feds won't do business with you if you don't have the right number of minorities. And . . . ad infinitum.

Let's take a less emotional example. Too many people are being killed and injured in automobile accidents. We have tried for years to educate the public in safe driving. We have tried economic incentives with insurance premiums. We have tried driver education classes in high schools. We have provided safety equipment such as seat belts. People insist on their right not to wear the belts and to kill themselves. So what do we do about it? Do we require wearing of belts? No. Do we make the car inoperable without the belts being fastened? We tried that, but the public outcry was so great that the politicians got the message. The solution? Make the car companies build idiot-proof products, cars that are much safer in collisions even if the driver is standing on his head or blind drunk. Not offer them as an option, but make them mandatory. We have come a long way as a society from the self-reliant frontier men and women who relied on nothing but their own skills.

There are countless other examples of this phenomenon. Companies have been granted permits to build new facilities on the condition that they provide pollution control equipment that would make the air cleaner than before they moved in. Adequate housing for low-income families is a problem. So, consider requiring construction firms to build low income housing along with their other developments and subsidize the low-income owners by proportionately raising the prices paid by people who do not qualify as low-income. The key word in that sentence is "requiring," i.e., pass a law. It's been done in California. What if you don't like the interest rates to be paid for mortgage money by poor people? Then, if you're the state official in charge of regulating savings and loan institutions, you require that below-market loans be made to poor people as a condition of approving a merger between two S&L's. It's also been done in California.

An Interpretation

Further detail on specific corporate responsibilities and appropriate actions is provided in later sections of this book. For now, let's just consider the point of an expanded role in society for the corporation. In some ways, the corporation is still responding to the well-being of the employees and the rest of society. However, it has a new more challenging role of taking the lead in some areas. For instance, in football terms, the corporation is definitely carrying the ball in the fight against racial discrimination. The modern U.S. corporation is actually in the vanguard of the attack on problems of society.

What do others think of this interpretation? Various surveys confirm a shift in attitudes of the general population that has been true for some time, and also a general reluctance by business to accept the shift.[2] This shouldn't be surprising. We have a reasonably representative democracy, and it is simply not likely that Congress, the executive branch, and the judiciary could have conspired to act against the will of the people for so long in such a dramatic fashion.

Peter Drucker, one of the most widely respected management authorities of all time, wrote in 1954 that the only legitimate goal of business was economic, to make a profit. He wrote in 1980 that corporations have become "carriers of social purpose, social values, social effectiveness."[3] He wasn't wrong in 1954—if anything, he was ahead of his time then, as he has always been. But, in less than thirty years, expectations have changed dramatically. Much more is expected of the corporation.

The Business Roundtable is an association of the chief executive officers of about two hundred of the nation's largest and most prestigious companies. In 1981, the group issued an official policy statement recommending that corporations consider the impact of their actions on society at large as well as on the shareholders.

Does this mean that U.S. business accepts the new role of the corporation? In a word—no. Many business people still see themselves as beleaguered by outside forces making impossible demands on the basis of ignorance and prejudice. They sincerely would prefer to return to the Good Old Days when the only goal was a profit.

The message of this chapter is simple. The Good Old Days are gone. The corporation has a new mission, a broader mission. It has been selected for this assignment because it is the only entity that can carry it out. It is the only institution that is simultaneously powerful and a net creator of wealth. Government can redistribute wealth but cannot create it. Small special interest groups can do neither. The corporation has the power and the wherewithal—it is the engine of our society. It has proven itself over and over again. To paraphrase Winston Churchill, it may not be the best system, but it's better than all the rest. This is the central truth—the new demands on business management and the corporation are a tribute to their effectiveness.

Having now taken a positive attitude, let us move on. Our next step is a study in frustration—dealing with the specific new demands of the multiple constituencies of the corporation.

"There is no greater enemy to those who would please
than expectation."
—MONTAIGNE

Chapter 2

Pleasing All the People
All the Time

AS WE HAVE SEEN, the role of the corporation has evolved into
something very different from the start made by the New England textile mill owners in the 1790s. The corporation is on the leading edge
of the fight for betterment of society. Its influence extends beyond its
workers and customers, to the home and hearth of every citizen. There
is no place it cannot or should not go, and in the process it meets up
with a number of strange companions. There are a lot of individuals
and organizations who want to assist the corporation in fulfilling its
social responsibilities. They are more than willing to provide advice on
corporate activities. In addition, where the corporation appears lax,
they'll be glad to help in defining the social responsibilities, in terms to
suit them.

Individuals championing causes and special interest groups always
have existed, and they always have been effective. However, the proliferation of the groups in recent years is a new phenomenon. Also, the
level of their credibility has increased. The credibility of special interest
groups not only equals that of corporations, but frequently surpasses
it. Ralph Nader often has appeared on lists of most-admired and most-
influential people.

The new reality is that corporations must assist the special interest
groups in achieving their valid objectives. The special interest groups
mirror society, and by helping them the corporations help society. In
this chapter we'll examine a few of these groups; we'll determine how
a corporation and its management team should act. And we'll discuss
the steps the corporation should take to implement its decisions.

The Environmentalists

Environmentalists have been one of the most visible special interest groups for the last twenty years. They also have had as much or more impact as any other group. By looking at a few case studies, we can learn a lot about the motives, behavior, and tactics of the environmentalists, and we can learn how to integrate business people into their world.

The Endangered Species Act provides protection for any species of living creature that is in imminent danger of extinction. The act was used to block construction of the multi-million dollar Tellico Dam, when it was discovered that the dam would result in destruction of the only remaining natural habitat of a small fish, the snail darter. The case became a cause célèbre for both sides of the issue. It incensed people who believed that any reasonable evaluation of the costs and benefits involved would have led to building the dam. Supporters of the snail darter lined up equally vigorously to defend the harmless little creature's right to live, and they eventually prevailed. The punch line came two years after the final decision was handed down. Snail darters were found in several other places; it turns out they really weren't close to extinction.

Air pollution abatement has been a goal of environmentalists. Laws and regulations have grown like weeds to compel reduced levels of noxious emissions, from utility plants to automobiles. The steel industry and the Environmental Protection Agency (EPA) have been at loggerheads for years over the cost of pollution controls in an industry that already is burdened severely by the cost structure of basic steelmaking operations. In 1978 the EPA commissioned a study by independent engineering consultants to determine the incremental costs of eliminating air pollutants. The study showed that costs rise dramatically, by multiples of ten or more, as air purity levels close to 100 percent purity are achieved. Eighty to ninety percent of the pollutants can be removed fairly inexpensively; the remainder are costly to get. These results, of course, aren't surprising. Neither, unfortunately, were the responses of the two parties in the issue. The steel spokesmen said that the report proved that pollution control costs are excessive for the benefits achieved. EPA spokesmen said that they were only obeying the law to enforce high standards, that they knew the costs would be high.

In the mid-1960s Southern California Edison embarked on a project to build a coal-burning power plant on the Kaiparowits plateau in southern Utah. By 1976, the company still required over 200 permits from more than forty federal, state, and local agencies. Various environmental groups had enlisted the help of, among others, the EPA and CBS's "60 Minutes" program to portray the plant in the worst possible light. The company cancelled the project.

Speaking of utilities and coal, a funny thing happened to U.S. industry on the way to pollution-free air. In 1955 coal supplied over 35 percent of the industrial energy in the United States. By 1976 the percentage was down to half that, as the pollution control laws had accomplished their objectives. What had we substituted? Oil and natural gas, of course; cleaner-burning fuels. Unfortunately, in 1974 we became painfully aware of our dependence on imported oil. So, in 1977 we acquired a new national goal, courtesy of the Federal Energy Administration (FEA): Coal was to return to 32 percent of industrial energy by 1985. At this point, it's not happening, but the goal was set. We were to have our cake and eat it too: Pollution control laws were not revised when the FEA set the coal usage goals.

The foregoing examples may seem to be an unusual way to state the case for corporate support of environmentalists. Not really. The test of a marriage is how well the spouses work out their difficulties; how they conquer adversity; how they adapt to changing, often unpleasant circumstances—not how happy they are when things are going well. Environmentalists are human. They are going to make mistakes. They are going to be overly zealous at times. Their tactics won't always be totally aboveboard. Changing events in the world will invalidate positions taken in the past and present.

But their hearts are in the right place. At least society thinks so. It's no more fair to judge them by their mistakes than to judge business overall by its failures. So my conclusion is business should support environmental objectives. Not simply by hopping on the bandwagon, although that certainly is better than tipping over the bandwagon. Get out in front of the issue. Become a leader in environmental causes that you pick. Choose ones that are consistent with personal and corporate interests.

Equal Employment Opportunity and Related Issues

This is the oldest special issue still in the forefront of our culture. It has its roots in the civil rights movement, which traces its origins back to pre-Civil war days. The Fourteenth Amendment to the Constitution was the first step in a long journey for minority groups in the United States.

The thirty years since the *Brown vs. Board of Education* school desegregation decision have seen a lot of progress on racial matters. However, the statistical prevalence of minorities in business at various levels has not seemed adequate to some observers in and out of the government. No one disputes that minority representation in the executive suites cannot be forced quite as easily (leaving aside the merits of either case) as the makeup of fourth graders in a classroom. But there the agreement stops. Disagreements over means to the end, allowable time for remedies to take effect, and the like have made for many acrimonious public and private sessions.

What is certain is that the government and interested parties are using any and all legal tactics available to promote equality of opportunity and result for minorities. The courts are obliging them by ever expanding the number of legal tactics.

In 1981 Westinghouse acquired Teleprompter Corporation. The Federal Communications Commission (FCC) had to approve the merger, which it did by a unanimous vote. As part of its approval, however, the commission ordered the companies to furnish detailed information in the next year about Teleprompter's minority employment practices. What has this got to do with the approval of a merger of two communications companies? Welcome to the new world.

Firestone Tire & Rubber Company is a well-established member of the corporate community. In 1980 the company was cited by the Labor Department for failing to develop an affirmative action program for a plant in Texas. Firestone was not charged with discrimination, but with failure to develop an adequate plan to increase the percentage of minorities and women in the plant. The company had a plan but they and the government were unable to reach agreement on what was acceptable for the contents of an affirmative action program. This is a little bit like a player in a poker game holding a pair being unable to agree with a player holding four of a kind. The winning hand—the government—barred Firestone from all federal contracts until the deficiency was corrected. Approximately $40 million of annual business for Firestone was involved, for 650 people at the plant. That works out to over $60,000 per person of potentially lost business. Evidently Firestone felt that the principle was worth the fight, but there is room for doubt.

Coca-Cola was boycotted by the Reverend Jesse Jackson's PUSH (People United to Save Humanity), a black activist organization, because of its perceived lack of support for blacks. In 1981 Coke announced that it would purchase more supplies from black-owned business; select a black for its board of directors; add more than thirty more black-owned Coke distributorships; and target various Coke business expenditures, such as advertising and banking, to black-owned organizations. The actual dollar value of this assistance probably wasn't significant; the additional effort or expense to use black individuals and companies rather than others certainly wasn't significant. But the principle, the foot in the door at Coca-Cola, was significant.

Heublein also has seen the handwriting on the wall. In 1982 the company worked out an agreement with the PUSH group. The company agreed to spend $180 million on black businesses over a five year period, in an attempt to create 9,000 new jobs in the black community. Significantly, the agreement was reached without a boycott or other overt action against the company.

These kinds of discussions and settlements are going to continue to take place. Each participant in one of these cases is going to win or lose, a little or lot. People are going to hang their hats on specific cases, such as the Bakke case (in which a white medical school applicant won a reverse discrimination lawsuit) and then be disappointed or pleased when subsequent cases are decided differently.

Better opportunity for minority employees and other citizens is eventually going to prevail. The opportunity will some day translate into statistical results that will make the government and special interest groups happy.

There will be some negative results, too. Some ground undoubtedly will be lost as people learn to work together in new ways. Any effort that does not go directly into producing goods or services will show up statistically as lower productivity. Whenever a person is added to a work force and that person's productivity is lower than the existing average, the new average will be lower. This is bound to happen. It is also impossible to separate from all the other effects on productivity, except in very unusual cases, and therefore it is not worth the worry. Better to concentrate on positive things.

What is the overall conclusion? Managers should move ahead to create better opportunities for minorities. Society has placed the signposts very clearly beside the road. Politics are volatile, and it is always possible to read things into transient ebbs and flow that aren't really there for the long term. There is absolutely no question which way the country is going on equal rights for minorities. Like rowing a boat on a meandering creek, you certainly can't tell your direction by where you're headed at the moment—but if you look over a long period of time, the direction is obvious. The companies that row with the current, not against it, will do well.

Consumerism

The consumer movement is a much more recent phenomenon than the civil rights movement, which predates it by more than a century. Its age belies its strength. Any manufacturer of consumer products can testify to the effectiveness of the consumer movement and the likelihood that it is here to stay.

The civil rights movement gained ground through a number of organizations such as the NAACP. Large, powerful organizations have also been beneficial to other movements. The Sierra Club has been very supportive of environmentalists' causes. The consumer movement matured in a different fashion. Individuals and small groups with specific consumer interests discovered that the structure of government is now tilted in favor of constraints and controls over corporations. The process of creating and staffing regulatory agencies is well understood by Congress. The executive branch is willing to do its duty. And the courts have, over the years, created numerous precedents for ruling in favor of special interest groups' rights.

Consumerism has also benefited from the concept of self-regulation. To ward off government intrusion, many industries have established their own watchdog groups to police the actions of corporate members and to take "independent" regulatory actions. The film-rating system of the Motion Picture Association of America is an example. Spinoffs of self-regulation, or actually precursors chronologically, are the independent regulatory associations that are supported and often financed by business. Better Business Bureaus are a case in point. Active consumerists know how to use both forms of self-regulation. Since a primary function is avoidance of government regulation, mention of the possibility of pursuing one's interests through government channels is enough to get serious attention from these organizations. The response is often faster and more effective than if the threat had been carried out.

The "kid vid" issue is an example of this approach. The federal government has certainly not been lax in its treatment of television networks regarding program and advertising material aimed at children. But their efforts have been overshadowed by the steps taken by the National Advertising Division of the Council of Better Business Bureaus. On several occasions this division has come down hard on advertising that conveys the message that usage of the advertiser's product would make a child superior to his or her peers. For this reason, it has been critical of advertising by Casper Fuzzy toys, Vistalite snare drums, and CBS magic cards. The division is sincerely trying to promote egalitarianism through advertising. Regardless of the merits of this approach—and it's not necessary to take sides here—it clearly is more radical than what government had previously proposed.

The Consumer Product Safety Commission (CPSC) was created by the government to deal with such problems as flammable children's sleepwear. It has identified and removed from the market highly dangerous children's toys. Its focus is not limited to products for children. It has reviewed such products as lawn mowers and chain saws, and acted as necessary to request manufacturers to correct defects or discontinue marketing of the products.

The CPSC has not been nearly so controversial as the National Highway Traffic Safety Administration (NHTSA). The NHTSA provides the means through which the government implements its charter to make cars safer rather than make drivers better. One of the interesting features of the NHTSA is that it has acquired a life of its own beyond its statutory authority. Its leaders have become champions of causes that are not yet in anybody's mind but their own. For example, the NHTSA published a book in 1980 called *The Car Book,* which evaluated various makes and models. The crash test evaluation used a standard for testing that was far beyond the standard required by law; this was the only test standard used. To repeat, the statutory standard was not mentioned at all. Naturally, most cars failed the tougher standard, and the NHTSA used the results to proclaim that most cars were unsafe according to its crash tests. You may agree or disagree with the NHTSA's conclusions—the point is that it staked them out in a strong advocacy position, hardly an unbiased agency balancing consumers' and manufacturers' needs.

Political winds affect organizations like the NHTSA, because the staffing is based largely on political considerations. However, the reality is that there are a number of other avenues for consumer advocates. Consider advertising alone. Suppose Federal Trade Commission (FTC) scrutiny were relaxed. Would things change much? No. The National Advertising Division of the Council of Better Business Bureaus also screens ads. Since 1971, approximately 40 percent of its reviews have led to modification or withdrawal of ads. What else? The Lanham Act and other legislation has been used successfully by private parties such as R. J. Reynolds Tobacco against competitors' advertising. The power of the federal agencies always lurks in the background, but normal political vicissitudes affecting the Feds' attitudes will not significantly detour the movement towards "fair advertising."

What can we learn from the CPSC, the NHTSA, and other matters discussed here? For one, business is not winning. In some cases, for some very good reasons: Every instance of marketing a dangerous child's toy puts a black cloud over all of business. Unfortunately, most issues are not this clear cut, and there is room for honest disagreement. But once again, business has managed to acquire an image of lack of care for the consumer. Whether the issue is safety or another issue, business is not out in front of the issue. How often do you see an ad that focuses on a consumer issue, such as a product's safety? Compare the number of this kind of ads with the number of the other kind of competitive-hype ads. They're selling the sizzle, not the steak, to use an old advertising slogan. But more and more people are buying the steak, not the sizzle. There will always be room for both in this world, but business is going to have to place a larger emphasis on the consumer issues in its design, production, and marketing of goods and services.

Unions

Are unions a special interest group? They were when they originated. They were a well-defined group of people with well-defined specific objectives that were a minority viewpoint in society. (I'm not sure if that's the definition of a special interest group, but it's close.) Unions grew until they represented over half of the industrial work force. Their demands grew more broad and began, naturally, to mirror the demands of the majority of the population. Maybe at one time they almost ceased to fit the mold of special interest groups. It doesn't matter, because their influence is on the wane now. Less than a quarter of those in the work force belongs to unions. As business goes through hard times, so do the workers and their unions. Therefore, we also find that the scope of the union demands has narrowed—not in the rhetoric, but in the actual contract negotiations. No longer is the sky the limit. No longer is labor reaching with both hands to get their piece of the action, to share the prosperity. They are retrenching, trying to preserve the gains of the past. The new demands, while made aggressively, are essentially defensive in nature—job security and the like.

What does this mean to the workers? And to unions, business management, society? We will explore the problems of human resource management in depth in later sections of the book, so let us confine ourselves here to a few specific observations regarding unions.

Unions have become a valuable resource to management. From their initial raison d'être of protection of workers, they have grown into bodies that provide stabilization of work forces through worker discipline and adherence to quasi-judicial procedures for resolving disagreements.

Even strikes are by and large non-violent. In addition, many union workers, their leaders, and members of management share the same economic goals. Only members of senior management can be truly independent of such goals. Middle and lower management share with union workers the same kind of economic frustration when times are bad. Perhaps not always in the same ways, but pain is pain, no matter what form it takes.

In tough times and times of uncertainty—change—the alternatives for workers and management are to work together with some degree of trust, or to pull apart and try to go one's own way alone. Both schools of thought exist on both sides of the bargaining table. There are people on each side who want to work together, and people on each side who don't trust each other. The people who favor cooperation are going to have to prevail. Not that the lamb is going to lie down with the lion. Human nature being what it is, simple mistrust of motives will be a brake on cooperation. However, companies can no longer afford the luxury of infighting. Most foreign competitors and a few well-managed U.S. companies have gotten over this hump. The counter-productive attitudes, whether at the work station or in the executives suites, are going to have to go. All this requires is a realization that all employees of a company have more in common than they do differences. Accomplishing this, of course, is complex, and is discussed in depth later in the book. For now, perhaps we can conclude that labels are not particularly meaningful in the case of unions, and that their special interests are more along the lines of normal differences among human beings than they are distinctions that warrant separation as a special interest group. Separation, in thought or action, would in many ways do more harm than good.

A Potpourri of Interests

The list of special interest groups is endless. Physically disadvantaged people have made their voices heard in some ways and are determined to accomplish more. Many individuals are concerned over noise at airports. Does that sound like a minor issue to you? Not if you are one of the 50 million people that the Federal Aviation Administration says are "substantially annoyed" by jet noise. Three sets of FAA regulations—1969, 1973, and 1976—limit the noise output of jet airplanes. Airlines have had to retrofit all the planes in their fleet and design new engines for new airplanes. Retrofitting an airplane engine costs several hundred thousand dollars. A new one costs millions. Noise regulation, like all regulations, has its pros and cons. The aircraft engine manufacturers haven't suffered.

Moral issues are favorite topics. It's easy to draw a crowd against obscenity in films or books. Violence on television is a popular topic. On a global note, the issue of what to do about South Africa has its own set of interested followers. In this country, treatment of the native population—the American Indians—caused upheavals in the judicial system when tribes were awarded huge settlements or large areas of land as a result of litigation.

You don't have to be in favor only of people with legitimate grievances. You can be a special interest group in favor of offensive people. In 1980 the California Supreme Court ordered a private hospital to reconsider the staff application of a physician who had been rejected because of his personal abrasiveness. The court noted that an abrasive person who was professionally competent still might be able to function in the hospital community. The justices didn't have any recommendations as to how.

The Outlook

We've looked at several special interest groups. What will happen to them in the future? Will the prevailing atmosphere of change be helpful or harmful to the special interest groups?

If the recent past is any indication, the number of groups will increase. The power of the existing groups will wax and wane, depending on such factors as their leadership, the general public climate, and current political forces. The scope of the issues will have greater depth and breadth. Depth, as the details of complex issues are worked out. Breadth, as the number of groups increases. Both breadth and depth as existing groups look toward new fields of battle. Bear one thing in mind—there is no such thing as a satisfied special interest group. This is true for several reasons. All organizations are like living organisms in that they have survival instincts. The leaders and staff have secure jobs; maintaining them is preferable to finding new ones in possibly less interesting fields. Also, there are always the extremists in organizations who can identify new evils to overcome. Then, followup action usually is required after initial victories have been won. Finally, there is the infusion of new talent. The newcomers need to have something to do. Even if they only make work for themselves, the organization lives on.

Let us step down a side road for a second. In discussing current and future special interest groups, I obviously haven't mentioned the women's movement. The movement is very important, but it is difficult to classify half the population as a special interest group. We are dealing here with nothing less than eliminating prejudice against half the members of our society by most of the other half. Such groups as the National Organization for Women (NOW) exist and play an effective part, but they are a subset of the women's movement, not the definition of it. The awesome breadth and complexity of individuals and their differences, spread across half the population and an innumerable variety of backgrounds, make it too simplistic, I think, to treat women as a special interest group or a minority.

Getting back to the main road, how will the special interest groups behave? In a sense, much as they have recently. By that, I mean they will use any number of tools at their disposal. Lawsuits, individual and in conjunction with the government. Lobbying for legislation. Actions through government executive and administrative agencies. Complaints to industry or independent regulatory and evaluative bodies. Mobilization of public opinion. Use of the media directly or indirectly (e.g., "60 Minutes"). Shareholder resolutions in annual meetings. At the moment, groups tend to use the approach with which they are most familiar or with which the issue is associated. For example, certain issues (like South Africa) are associated with shareholder resolutions, and resolutions are introduced each year at the annual meetings of the affected companies. The special interest groups are soon going to develop the capability to attack on all fronts. They, of course, already are better than most corporations at many of the tactics such as use of the media. Improvement of their skills will add to the corporations' discomfort.

Dealing with Special Interest Groups

We listed a few potential management actions to deal with particular special interest groups, such as consumer groups. Can we generalize from these experiences and develop a game plan for working with the special interest groups? In other words, are there any basic principles that we can apply?

Yes. First of all, management must recognize that society has blessed these special interest groups. In fact, it is likely that most people in society are either directly involved with such a group or have deep personal sympathies regarding one. With apologies to Abraham Maslow, there is a cultural "hierarchy of needs" operating here. The most basic needs in an industrial society are for the system to work well enough to feed, clothe, and shelter the citizens and keep them healthy. A chicken in every pot becomes the next goal—prosperity beyond mere survival. The U.S. is now in the Prosperity Phase. We are in the age of two television sets in every home. At this point it becomes acceptable to the national psyche to start paying attention to some of the little things that were passed over during the building of the industrial giant.

The general principles, therefore, are simple. Recognize that we are almost in the twenty-first century, not the eighteenth. Take advantage of the marvelous opportunity we have with the machine we have built to create wealth. Spread it around a little bit. To paraphrase Pogo, the special interest groups are us. We all will benefit.

Are there drawbacks to this? Sure, as there are to everything. The more things a corporation or an individual tries to do, the more likely priorities will be set poorly or resources incorrectly allocated. This is a challenge and no reason not to go forward. It does, however, place a premium on implementing the ideas effectively. How can we do this?

The Implementation Problem

Accepting the concept that the special interest groups are on the right track is half the battle. That leads you to take a number of logical actions that might not be pursued otherwise.

For one, understand the groups. Their objectives, approach, people. If you can, talk to them. Perhaps you can't—as maybe they won't be reasonable. But try. Study their tactics. Be realistic. Look at their true tactics. The tactic behind a lawsuit may not be judicial victory; it may be a delaying action calculated to increase your costs and change your mind.

Next, prepare a long-range plan for special interest groups. Know which ones are likely to affect your company. Approach it either from an issue or a group standpoint. The issue approach is probably cleaner and more intellectually appealing, but don't let that fool you. You are going to have to deal with people as well as issues, so learn about the groups. You may even be able to pick the groups that you work with on an issue.

Can you do this with the people you have? Probably not. So put some people on the payroll who understand the issues and the groups. This is somewhat a chicken-and-egg proposition, since you need the people to make an intelligent investigation, but you won't fully know what kind of people you need until the investigation is completed. The best bet is to acquire a small nucleus of well-rounded people. It goes without saying that they should generally be advocates of the causes. Not screaming extremists, certainly, but wolves in sheep's clothing will do you damage in the long run even though they may fit in better initially.

It helps to sort the issues and groups into three categories. The ones you support, the ones you don't support, and the ones whose goals you support, but not their means, people, or something else of significance. You know what to do with the first group, so let's discuss the second and third groups.

After you've picked your people, make your specific personnel assignments. Give the best people the toughest jobs.

Determine your position precisely, i.e., why you are in total or partial disagreement. If your position won't stand up to much scrutiny, perhaps it is better to abandon it. If it is a sound position, you need to communicate your message. Most tactics for doing so are available to both sides. Your tools are basically the same as the special interest groups. Use them. You may require some media experts, experienced attorneys, etc. These are all available—at a price, of course. The price may be high. That's okay. It makes you continually reevaluate your position and the value of maintaining it.

Know what winning is. This is also true if you are in the first category, supporting an issue or group. Unconditional surrender or mutual love are two possible definitions of winning, both unlikely to occur in the normal course of events. Set reasonable, attainable goals and monitor your progress towards them frequently. If necessary, change them—being a masochist isn't in your job description.

Take your long-range plan down to short-range actions. Again, this is important whether you are supporting a group, opposing it, or supporting it in a different way than it would like. Determine the actions required to meet your specific goals. Maybe the actions are the fight-fire-with-fire type, using the same tools available to the special interest groups (despite the description, presumably they are used more in support than in opposition). There are some additional tools available to corporations. Charitable contributions are an important one. Give money or services where both you and the recipient will feel good about it. Give either to special interest groups directly or to such public service groups as public broadcasting services. Corporations have lots of money relative to even the richest special interest groups. Use it wisely, but use it.

Don't let the political winds blow you over. If they're with you, make haste. If not, tack or wait for a better day.

The last rule—be ready for a hard time. If you oppose a special interest group, they'll fight you. But they'll at least expect it. If you support them, even a little bit, they'll be suspicious, and rightfully so. So, take your time, and suffer the slings and arrows. You will overcome.

"There is no good arguing with the inevitable."
—JAMES RUSSELL LOWELL

Chapter 3

Society's Great Expectations of Business

THE CORPORATION of the late twentieth century does multiple duty. It is responsible to its nominal constituency, the shareholders. The shareholders may or may not include members of management, a second constituency running the corporation to some extent for their personal benefit. (Although you would be hard pressed to find a dozen senior executives in the entire country who would admit publicly to being motivated by personal gain.) The special interest groups are a third constituency. They are an active force working for specific objectives and they must be dealt with on an individual issue or group basis. In the last chapter we examined some of the characteristics of these groups and the ways in which corporations can support their legitimate goals.

The fourth kind of constituency is diffused throughout society. It generally doesn't focus on specific issues through a formal organization. Individuals or informal small groups are responsible for action regarding the issues. One or more of the formal special interest groups may occasionally lend assistance, but they are not the driving force. The issues are broadly based, arising from the conscience of our culture, our code of moral values that runs like a strong current just beneath the surface, influencing the actions of all surface bodies. This code has developed as our industrial culture has matured and reached its current level of effectiveness.

The moral values reflect the U.S.'s historical preoccupation with the importance of people. They lead to such issues as corporate and personal liability for defective products. Corporate openness and honesty are encouraged. On the other hand, abuse of corporate power over indi-

33

viduals becomes an area for concern. And the rights of individuals to privacy, to a shield from the corporate eye, must be protected.

Simply listing the issues in this way helps us to realize how important they have become. Many of us have had personal experience with these issues. In this chapter we will look at them in detail, starting with their genesis in the success of U.S. business. We will look at their current impact on U.S. management. Then for each issue we will examine ways in which corporations can effectively cope with the expectations thrust upon them.

Broad Expectations

The effectiveness of production of goods and services has led to powerful expectations on the part of both retail and commercial customers. A full range of goods and services is the least of the expectations. For example, people expect to have clothing tailored in precise sizes in off-the-rack merchandise. In other countries, except where the U.S. influence has taken hold, all apparel is sold in only a few sizes. Styles here are different for every age group, fashion sense, social class, etc. And colors. Fabrics. Patterns. We take them for granted.

Transportation is an industry that affects both business and retail consumers. We all have needs to go places. Consider just air transportation. The U.S. cargo and passenger airline system is like no other in the world. We have almost as many major airlines as the rest of the world combined. You can ship anybody or anything to just about anywhere at just about any time of day that is convenient for you. And you can get it there almost immediately by using a package delivery company.

The same full range of services exists in the financial community. We are familiar with the blizzard of different services available to the average consumer. A variety of rates and maturities on savings accounts. Several different checking plans available at each bank. Or Savings and Loan. Or credit unions. Different ways of processing transactions—walk-in, drive-up windows, automated teller machines (ATMs). And on and on and on. It's even more true in the world of commercial banking. Services are tailored to individual customers. Sophisticated computerized account analysis services are offered to summarize and analyze a customer's dealings with an institution. Computerized cash management services. And more.

Speaking of computers, the situation is even more extreme. The United States is virtually the only country with an internally competitive computer industry that does not enjoy strong government support.

In fact, our government files lawsuits against successful companies when they become too successful. You can buy a computer to do almost anything you want—calculate your payroll, control your inventory, place your telephone calls, manage energy usage in your buildings, run your machine tools, etc. And at home it can play games with you or your children, manage your real estate investments, and do almost anything else that you ask.

In addition to the range of products and services, the availability is assumed. People don't stand in lines in the United States for a chance at one of the few scarce pieces of merchandise—except for post-Christmas sales! And often, if merchandise is unavailable, we give "rain checks" to customers so they can pick up the out-of-stock items on a future visit.

What have we sacrificed for this horn of plenty? Higher prices for the goods and services? No. The better merchandise obviously costs more than the cheap merchandise, but the price trend, if there is one, is in the other direction. Technology, production improvements, new materials, and similar advancements have kept prices well within the limits of reason. Has quality suffered? You might get an argument on this point, but generally the *potential* for acceptable quality has not decreased, although the *actual* quality levels are frequently a different story. There are a number of providers of goods and services who continue to provide reasonable quality at good prices. Other companies attempt to invoke a general theory of a necessary decline in quality in order to meet other customer expectations. More and more providers are using this theory, but they are running up against a wall of consumer resistance. The consumer's solution is to buy from other providers, often foreign companies. We will devote an entire chapter later to the quality problem. For now, let's just say that adequate evidence exists that quality does not have to suffer.

So we have high expectations for range, availability, price, and quality of our goods and services. How does this fit in with the overall economic picture of society? The answer is—fairly well. The United States still has the highest standard of living, on a purchasing power basis. Other major industrial nations range from about half to three-quarters of the U.S. standard of living in terms of purchasing power.[1] So, it is not surprising that the level of expectations for goods and services is high. It is merely a subset of the overall experience and expectation for a high standard of living. It also is not surprising that the U.S. is a pioneer in this respect. The overall level of expectations in other countries is not as high, so specific expectations for goods and services are not likely to be as high. This may change as their economies grow stronger. The U.S. is riding the crest of a long wave, and it remains to be seen if we can catch a new wave as the old one dies out.

Forecasting Future Expectations

We can read the future in the tea leaves of the present. The level of expectations has dimensions beyond breadth and depth. Our mass production society has found the way to mass produce individually varying items. In other words, our technology and management skills have developed to the point of achieving economies of scale while varying details of the products to suit individuals. The auto industry is an excellent example. It has long been held up as the premier example of mass production, but the black Model T disappeared a long time ago. In 1921 General Motors established its policy of producing a broad line of cars to cater to individual tastes and pocketbooks. Henry Ford was still making Muhammed go to the mountain for his limited range of vehicles. GM moved the mountain and has not looked back since. The automobile engineering and manufacturing process has evolved since then to the point where it is doubtful if any two cars on the road are identical, except for fleet operations. The options are staggering, as car salesmen are eager to point out. You practically can design your own car. Nobody else has one like it.

And your own computer. Or sawmill. As a business person, you also expect to be treated like an individual. This is perhaps the most profound result of the changing expectations of consumers and business people. The notion of gratification of individual needs has caught on. This notion has been a powerful incentive for improvement in goods and services, and it will continue to be. But it is a runaway freight train. It can't be easily controlled and it does a lot of damage to anything that gets in its way.

When Things Don't Work Out

Expectations are fine as long as they are being met. They are fine for the person whose expectations are gratified, and they are fine for the person doing the gratifying, who is being paid for the products or services. What happens when expectations can't be met, in the current atmosphere of high expectations?

Maybe the products or services just aren't up to expectations. Perhaps the seller and the buyer had a misunderstanding. On the other hand, perhaps there was no misunderstanding, but the seller simply did not deliver as advertised, intentionally or unintentionally. In the worst case, maybe the failure causes injury to the buyer—physical injury, mental injury, business injury, or any other kind. What should happen?

The rule used to be "caveat emptor"—let the buyer beware. In many cases now the rule is "caveat venditor"—let the seller beware. The liability picture has shifted. The engineer of the runaway train has to look out for objects on the tracks; it is no longer people's responsibility to stay off the tracks.

Product Liability

Let us now consider one facet of the problem: product liability. The basic principle is that companies are liable for something if their products are defective in some way so as to cause some kind of injury. That's about as clearly as the principle can be stated.

The principle and supporting law have undergone several changes, most of which have tended to strengthen the customer's case and weaken the manufacturer's. For many years, a major issue was the good faith efforts of manufacturers. As long as companies had taken reasonable care to ensure that their products weren't defective, it was difficult for a user to recover damages. In the early 1960s, this changed. Courts began to rule that companies could be held liable for a defective product whether or not they acted responsibly in producing it. Essentially, the courts said that a defective product is a defective product, regardless of how it came to be.

The law of averages also has been of no help to companies. Statistically speaking, a small percentage of almost every product made probably is going to be defective in some way. That knowledge, of course, is small comfort to the users of the defective items. The courts have agreed with the users.

The upshot is a "zero defects" standard by the legal system. Manufacturers simply are liable for any defects, regardless of their intent or their control systems to prevent defects. If a defect slips through, they are liable.

In addition, the law continues to change. A Los Angeles secretary named Judith Sindell set off a wave of paranoia by business management a couple of years ago when she won a landmark lawsuit. She felt that she had developed cancer because of DES, a drug her mother took during pregnancy. She had no idea which one of several possible drug manufacturers had made the actual drug taken by her mother, so she sued all the major manufacturers of the drug on the theory that one of them had probably made it. Her right to sue on those grounds was upheld by the California Supreme Court. The U.S. Supreme Court refused to overturn the decision, making the case a precedent for the whole country.

The law has also expanded in other ways. "Successor liability" has been increased. That is, the liability of a purchaser of a company for products manufactured by the acquired company before the acquisition. That seems fair, in a sense—the company still exists and should bear some responsibility. What if you buy some machines from a company rather than the company itself? Can users of products made from those machines, if the products were made before you bought the machines, sue you now because you own the machines? Yes, they can. In 1972 Patrick Bruno bought the equipment to make Sheridan die-cutting presses from Harris Corporation, which had previously bought them from Sheridan Co. He has since been sued for damages by workers injured by presses made by the equipment before he acquired it. Bruno has paid handsomely to settle such suits out of court. In addition, he has had great difficulty buying liability insurance, since the insurance companies are well aware of the trends in product liability.

Other Kinds of Liability

Product liability is a microcosm. The same trends are evident in other forms of liability. Exposure to dangerous chemicals has resulted in lawsuits by exposed workers. Asbestos settlements alone run to over $1 billion annually. Manville Corporation filed for bankruptcy because of asbestos lawsuits against it. Those companies that routinely use asbestos or other dangerous chemicals in their operations are being hit hard. BF Goodrich is one of these companies. Naturally it's been sued. There have been some novel twists in some of the lawsuits involving Goodrich. In one case, Goodrich itself was not sued, but over two hundred companies that supplied chemicals to Goodrich were sued, on the theory that a Goodrich worker had acquired cancer from one of the chemicals supplied to Goodrich. The courts permitted the suit. Supplier suits will probably continue—worker's compensation laws limit primary lawsuits in many states.

In another case, a person who lived over a mile from a Goodrich plant died from liver cancer. His wife sued on the basis that the fumes from the plant had caused the cancer. The dead person had not even worked for Goodrich or routinely been closer to the plant than home. She won, and the company settled rather than appeal the case.

Companies are becoming liable for anything that they do that causes injury—to customers, workers, or normally uninvolved citizens who come into contact with the company in some unfortunate way. Part of the trend undoubtedly is due to a feeling that injured persons should be compensated and in the absence of any government-sponsored program, the next best source of money is a company and its insurers. Part of it, too, is probably a genuine feeling that individual citizens come first in this country, that the U.S. is based on respect for the individual, and that injuries to individuals should be paid for by the injurer, especially if it isn't really a person, but an impersonal corporation.

How Big Is the Problem?

Liability is a growing concern of companies, as we have observed. Are there any quantitative ways to measure the size of the problem? Probably not—but there are some pieces of data that will enable us to make a general outline—not only of the current problem but of its potential future size.

Not all liability cases come to trial or even to litigation. However, the volume of litigation is one way to measure things. Figure 3–1 illustrates the volume of federal litigation over the last twenty years. Reading liability suits from this chart is not possible, so we have to rely on the opinions of attorneys and judges for the details. Many of them feel that not only has liability litigation kept up with the overall increase, but that it has actually surpassed it.

Another measure is the amount of insurance coverage for liability claims. Over $6 billion annually is currently paid by U.S. companies for liability coverage. The value of the coverage is over a trillion dollars![2] How much is a trillion dollars? Enough to give every person in the country over $4,000 in cash. Not everybody in the U.S. is going to make a liability claim, of course. However, people in the insurance industry have estimated that 25 million people are exposed to occupational danger in sufficient degree to warrant some future legal action. That's a big problem by anybody's definition.

Solving the Problem

The problem is big and getting bigger. What can be done about it? One possible answer is to reverse the practice of holding companies liable for virtually every injury that can be even remotely linked to them. Certainly the trend cannot continue or we'll have corporations liable for everything simply because they exist. But is stopping the trend enough? Don't we have to reverse now-existing legal precedents and now-established cultural practices in order to reduce significantly the burden of liability exposure of U.S. companies? Yes, we would have to do that. And, as Dizzy Dean used to say, there are two chances of that happening—slim and none.

Figure 3–1
Civil Cases Pending in Federal Courts
(in Thousands)

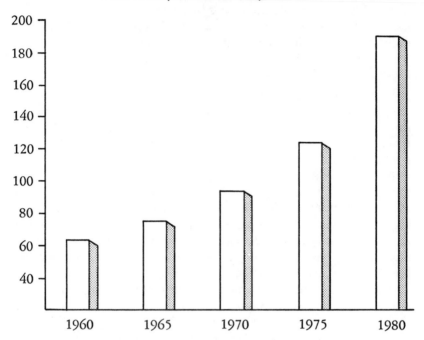

Source: Data from Federal Courts Administrative Office

So where are we? We live in an increasingly litigious society that has ever-expanding notions of corporate responsibility. All citizens will have to exercise their best judgment and their influence to reduce the number of frivolous liability claims. But we also have to accept human nature and the nature of our present society. That means being prepared and taking other management actions.

What actions? For a start, preventive measures. Management should thoroughly review all aspects of the company's operations and minimize the dangers to everyone involved. How do you provide incentives to do this? Simple—structure the compensation and promotion systems to reward the proper action.

Secondly, it's important to be prepared in case a problem should develop. Keep detailed records. Companies in certain industries have kept detailed records for decades. For instance, every section of the space shuttle's rocket casing can be traced back to the specific batch of steel used to make it, in case anything ever goes wrong. Some manufacturers of medical equipment maintain production and quality control records on every device they have ever made. Even small companies can do this. With the computer power available today, record-keeping can no longer be dismissed as too difficult or too time-consuming. What records to keep? When in doubt, keep it. That's the rule. The growing tendency is to put the burden of proof on the defendant, so don't think that the absence of records is a clever ploy—it may be, but it may also get the book thrown at you.

What if a problem does occur and you are faced with a potential liability action? Frankly, your best bet is to be totally aboveboard. There are going to be so many people after your hide that defending an indefensible position won't be any fun. Rule One is to identify the problem yourself. That gives you points for credibility and also a head start on the corrective action. If you can't manage that, at least be fully cooperative and, where possible, take the lead in definition and implementation of solutions. You may run into some extreme positions on the other side. Although at times it may not seem to be so, being in the right yourself rather championing your own wrong answer generally will work out better.

Dow Chemical started a program called "product stewardship." It involves babysitting Dow products all the way through to the consumer, even when Dow doesn't actually market the final product itself. The program allows Dow an additional measure of control over potential liability. It has been used to handle and pay for a recall of a product containing a Dow chemical, but packaged and marketed by a much smaller company. The smaller company never had a chance to consider whether it could afford the recall, since Dow took care of it. Everybody benefits from this kind of approach.

On the other hand, nobody benefits from the behavior by manufacturers of certain multiple-piece wheel rims used for truck tires. The tires can explode during the process of changing a tire, turning the pieces of the rims into deadly projectiles. Hundreds of accidents and deaths have occurred. There is a dispute between the rim makers and their opposition as to whether the rims are actually defective in design or after use, or whether their improper handling causes the explosions. Regardless of this issue, some other positions of the manufacturers are interesting. They successfully opposed a suggested warning label for the rims. They also hold that the death rate from the rims, estimated to be from a dozen to ninety annually, is so small as to be inconsequential. Maybe inconsequential to them, but not to the people handling the rims! There are, in case you are wondering, perfectly acceptable alternative products.

The behavior of these companies is clearly out of step with the times. They have fought hundreds of product liability lawsuits over this issue. You would think the effort and money could have been more usefully expended in assisting the victims of the accidents.

Executives' Responsibilities

Before moving on, let's consider one more aspect of corporate liability that directly affects business managers. This is the possibility of legal action against individuals rather than corporations. Some frustration on the part of victims and courts has developed when the individual perpetrators of illegal acts are shielded by the umbrella of the corporation. The corporation may be fined or punished in some other way, but the individuals go scot-free. This situation is changing. In 1975, a company president, based in Philadelphia, was held personally criminally liable for rodent contamination in the company's Baltimore food warehouse.[3] His subordinates on site, not he, had failed to correct the problem. But the jury found the president personally guilty even while accepting the evidence that he ordered the subordinates to correct the situation. Since then, other statutes and court cases have conformed to this precedent, although sparingly. The floodgates have not yet been thrown wide open, but a small trickle has commenced. There is not much doubt, given the direction of recent history, what the future will hold on this issue. Corporate management must step up to this liability problem. They are going to be held personally liable, and they must make certain that their personal positions, as well as the corporate position, are protected by measures such as we have described.

Other Aspects of Life in a Fishbowl

The corporate executive used to be the man in the grey flannel suit. The image of anonymity was cultivated assiduously. Sometimes the desire to stay out of the limelight backfired so that a reclusive individual became better known than his more visible colleagues. Howard Hughes is a case in point. However, most business people, even the leaders at the top, have successfully dodged the journalists, academicians, and others who would make them famous. How many people have heard of Daniel Ludwig? Especially as compared to, say, J. Paul Getty? Ludwig's industrial empire may be larger than the sum of the Getty and Hughes fortunes. It was all built from scratch, not on top of a large inheritance. Ludwig's exploits have been publicized more in recent years, but his name is still hardly a household word.

We have never lacked for charismatic or newsworthy business leaders who were frequently in the public eye, from Jim Fisk and Andrew Carnegie to Henry Ford II. The contributions of these individuals to the betterment of society has, sadly, been something short of spectacular. Society will not allow this to go on. Business leaders are being carried on the tide that is sweeping their corporations to the forefront of society's many battles. The chairmen and presidents of many companies already spend most of their time on external affairs, leaving day-to-day operation of their companies in the hands of the second- or third-in-command or, possibly, a team of senior executives. This trend will continue and extend to other members of management.

The form of management participation in external affairs is also likely to change. At present it is a rare executive who is a leader in one of the areas that we have identified as part of the corporation's new responsibilities. Most of the time spent in external affairs goes into government lobbying of some sort or other, civic or charitable activities, or gatherings with people from other companies. Far too much time is put into activities that are described as "educating the public about business." Too many business leaders cling to a dangerous illusion that the great unwashed masses would be more supportive if they understood business better. Surveys show that the public has an abysmal understanding of the accounting results of business—average return on sales, profit margins, etc.[4] But the public also understands in some vague way that business is doing all right. In contrast to business's success, several elements of society clearly are not doing all right, and it makes sense to get business involved with fixing the problems. Business leaders are overdue for their turn at the helm. If they neglect their responsibility, someone else will steer the ship and there will be little room for complaints about the heading.

Freedom of Information

The "right to know" almost has taken a place beside the rights to life, liberty, and the pursuit of happiness. Somebody got the idea a few years back that the government and business were hoarding information vital to the well-being of the populace and occasionally were engaging in outright deception. The opponents of this idea weren't helped when the Johnson and Nixon Administrations were caught with their hands in the cookie jar, or perhaps more appropriately, with their fingers on the erase switch of the tape recorder. A few well-publicized cases of bankrupt companies and penniless senior citizens who had lost their life savings similarly tied a can to business's tail.

Government reporting requirements increased significantly. The Securities and Exchange Commission (SEC) decided that investors and the public needed more information about publicly-traded companies, so they developed stringent annual reporting requirements, including such items as line-of-business profitability analyses. Companies naturally balked at providing some of this data publicly in forms available to competitors, but the SEC persisted and even strengthened the requirements. Information requirements for new stock issues also were increased.

Other government actions have also contributed to putting the corporate boudoir on public display. The Freedom of Information Act was intended to improve private citizens' access to government files, to avoid unpleasantries like the coverup of some Vietnam War information. Through an oversight (one hopes, anyway), confidential filings of business with government agencies were not clearly exempted. This has led to a running battle between citizens and companies or, in many cases, between one company and another that is trying to use the Act to gain access to confidential material that might help it at the expense of the first company. Sometimes the government even takes sides. As part of its government assistance program, Chrysler had to file public documents regarding some of its future product plans. The company was thus disclosing its strategy to Ford and General Motors as part of a program to get it back on its feet. Does that make any sense to you?

If it's any consolation, things are worse in other countries, notably Western Europe where the Common Market magicians have been hard at work. In 1980, the Dutch representative proposed a directive whereby multinational corporations would have to declare and discuss with European workers any contemplated actions in other countries that might substantially affect the workers. In a move that surprised many observers, the full European Commission passed the measure. In late 1982 the measure was amended to be more palatable to business, but it is clear that the idea is one whose time has come in Europe, at least in some form. It will be several years before the specific enabling legislation is passed, but the writing is on the wall.

What is the message here? It is this—the corporation is available for public inspection. Hours: twenty-four hours a day. Admission: free (actually paid for with tax collections). Please don't feed the executives. Anything else goes. Corporate managers have a permanent place in the limelight, and they had better get used to it.

New Constraints

All sorts of people are getting into the act of suggesting or telling corporations what to do. Community leaders across the nation have recently joined the parade, concerned over the behavior of corporations in the various local communities in which they operate. Even a large multinational corporation doesn't lead an amorphous existence. It has roots someplace, very likely many places, and it has to interact with the local citizenry.

In hard economic times, the corporation tends to interact by withdrawing. It lays off people, closes stores or branches, and in the worst scenario leaves an area totally. Rightly or wrongly, the locals often feel as though they've been had. They may have provided tax incentives or other motivators to the company in order to persuade it to join the community, and when the company leaves, they feel like a marriage promise turned out to be a one-night stand.

Europeans dealt with this situation many years ago by requiring advance notice of plant closings and other specific activities that differ by country. The idea is catching on in the U.S., led by Wisconsin and Maine, which passed the first laws regarding advance notice of plant closings and mandatory employee compensation after the closings. It will take a while, but there's a good chance all fifty states will have some form of such laws, or else we'll have a federal law to spare corporations the complexity of fifty different laws.

Generally speaking, communities are not going to be as free with their support of business. Fewer no-strings-attached incentives. Fewer zoning and other changes to accommodate business with no quid pro quo. Tighter restrictions on behavior. It is only through the experience of having a strong business influence in a community that the citizens realize that the roses came with thorns. Having been pricked a few times, communities are going to wear gloves and prune the branches more severely. Which, obviously, should not bother business management. Most of them honestly want to contribute to the welfare of a community. A few statutes supporting their moral rectitude should not be objectionable. The better companies will even take responsibility upon themselves to be better corporate citizens. While other companies were moving out of inner cities, IBM was moving in. The company has had a manufacturing plant in the Bedford-Stuyvesant section of Brooklyn for fifteen years. Two other computer companies, Digital Equipment Corporation and Control Data Corporation, have done the same thing, in poorer sections of Boston and Minneapolis, respectively.

From the Fishbowl into the Closet

While the corporations and their executives are being placed under spotlights, the employees are going underground. Privacy as an issue is in full flower and propagating rapidly as its seeds are borne on the winds of change. Workers are concerned about the contents of their personnel files and the distribution of the information. They are concerned about their credit files that may be checked by their employer or by other companies. Everyone is only too familiar with a couple of horror stories about undeserved poor credit ratings because of data errors.

Sweden has a law against processing sensitive payroll information in other countries. Norway requires a license in order to establish a computer data base containing personal information. The Council of Europe approved a treaty requiring privacy laws. The United States has passed laws to correct credit reporting abuses. In truth, the laws are not at all bad, although they are cumbersome to use. In other matters of privacy, we generally have adopted the honor system. Legislation has been spotty although impressive sounding at times.

Some corporations have gone fairly far in protecting their employees and others whose personal data they require. They may, for instance, collect no more than the minimal personal data to make a hiring decision or other decision, regardless of whether more data is permitted by law. They may permit employees to review their files. They may severely limit the information that can be given to outsiders. Even government inquiries may be required to have the proper authorization; no fishing allowed! They carefully limit what an insider can see to only the information required by that person for a specific purpose. They may refrain from psychological testing. Perhaps they neither use nor supply information to outside reference and credit bureaus; they perform their own investigation when necessary. Maybe they don't believe in worrying about what an employee does in his or her hours off the job unless, of course, it spills over into the job. They encourage employees to take positions, as private citizens, on public issues, even when their positions may not be the company's.

Can any corporation do all these things? IBM can and does. They are proof that nice guys don't finish last, that treating people with respect need not be accompanied by unreasonable costs.

The right-to-privacy issue is not so far advanced as others. Battles are still being fought over specific matters instead of over general principles that could lay the foundation for understanding and agreement. One of these days, though, things will all come together. More laws will be passed, agencies will be formed, and the ball will be rolling. The companies that have participated in the process and concurrently done the right thing by their employees and other people they affect will be a step ahead of the rest of the pack. They not only will know what to do; they will know how to do it efficiently. They will already have in place a satisfied workforce and customers who can go about their jobs while other companies fumble to catch up.

So the corporation is surrounded—by groups and private citizens pursuing their own interests in an environment of high expectations of the corporation. What can the corporation do? As we've seen, the interests are legitimate, and the only reasonable course is to attempt to satisfy them. Who should be responsible for this? Why, of course, the people who run the corporation. That brings us to an intriguing question for the next chapter.

The Corporation's
New Management Team

"In the long run every government is the exact symbol of its people with their wisdom and unwisdom."
—THOMAS CARLYLE

Chapter 4

Who Really Runs the Corporation?

OUR WINDOW on the world shows us that the way things work in the corporate world is not exactly the way most of us were taught. Actually, we knew that, but we weren't prepared for the real truth. Corporations and their management are buffeted from all sides, like a ship upon the ocean in a storm, and they must heed the power of the storm, use it to their advantage, not fight it. If they fight it, what happens? They usually lose because they are not fighting an issue, they're fighting society.

To the victors go the spoils. When society is victorious over the corporation, what does it gain? Power. That is the subject of this chapter—society's new involvement in the actual running of the corporation. In subsequent chapters we'll get into how the board of directors and specific management jobs must change.

Let's begin by discussing what it means for a corporation to "lose" to society.

The Meaning of "Losing to Society"

How can corporations lose? Litigation is the most obvious way and one of the most prevalent. Regulators—commissions, bureaus, agencies, departments—have their hands on the sceptre, too. In function they are close to the old time vigilantes. They generally are investigator, prosecutor, judge, and jury rolled into one body. There may be some administrative checks and balances. An appeals process may exist, either internally or through the federal judiciary, or both. But the odds are against dissuading the body from its intended course of action.

Why? In the internal appeals scenario, all opposition efforts must be coordinated with people within the body or with a functionary such as an administrative law judge who works with the body all the time. The alternative, the federal judiciary, doesn't really want to get involved, and consequently its decisions frequently uphold the rights of the bodies to deal with the matters. Also, unless your bank account is bottomless, it's difficult, because you customarily have to exhaust the internal appeals process before you can use the courts. The result is that the regulatory process is not an easy thing to challenge.

Which, by the way, is not necessarily bad, at least in the sense of being counter to the wishes of those who established the regulations, the Congress or state legislatures. Regulatory bodies do not just pop into existence on the whim of state governors or the White House. Their modes of operation are established by the legislation that creates them. If it is difficult to compromise with them or to alter their decisions, that's the way our elected representatives intended things to be. Sometimes they even defer to the expertise of the regulators and in the legislation state that the bodies will write their own operating procedures within broad guidelines.

Legislators can discharge their responsibilities in other ways. If they are disenchanted with business's response to an issue, they can change the law. This is another way that business can lose. Business can even win their case in the judicial system, only to have a new law passed that invalidates the decision, as long as it's not an issue of constitutionality.

How else can business lose? Boycotts. Strikes. Loss of confidence by investors, individual or institutional, and withdrawal of funds.

New ways to lose are being invented as you read this. Some will seem new, and some will seem like variations on old themes. Regardless, they all have one thing in common. Besides being onerous to the corporation, that is. They are all after-the-fact remedies. They are corrective action, or punishment or whatever term you prefer. Clearly it is intended that the corporation behave differently in the future but that is beyond the scope of the remedies. The remedy that is closest to affecting future action is regulation, but it is not really appropriate for dealing with specific situations and it cannot be made applicable to particular companies except in monopolistic industries. Legislation has the same drawbacks.

Through judicial action, a company can be compelled to refrain from conducting itself in the same illegal way again, but not from doing different things. One of the cornerstones of our legal system is the notion of judgment after the fact, i.e., you can't prosecute somebody for something he hasn't done yet.

This notion significantly restricts the exercise of the power that society has gained over corporations. What was needed, some people believed, was a way to have direct control over a corporation's future actions. Unfortunately for such dreamers, the board of directors runs the corporation. The directors are elected by the shareholders. Buying enough stock to elect board members would not be a practical solution for the number of corporations that would have to be affected. So the dreamers went back to the drawing boards. And they came up with an entirely unoriginal idea—putting government on the board of directors as part of the corporation's management team. The idea is as old as the first socialist society. But their methodology for pulling it off was brand new. And it worked!

The Government Gets Involved

In the late 1970s Bates Manufacturing Company was accused by the SEC of defrauding investors. The case proceeded in the normal tortuous way through the legal system until the proceedings culminated in a consent decree. A consent decree is a legal device whereby a company agrees not to engage in future violations of the law. Its real purpose is to give public notice that there might be some reason to suspect that the company would be a future lawbreaker, without having to prove that the company was guilty of a violation in the past. The advantages to the company are twofold. First, no conviction on its record. Two, no exorbitant legal fees spent in defending against prosecution. The benefits to the SEC are similar savings in legal effort, a victory that is not as good as a successful prosecution but a lot better than an unsuccessful prosecution, and the emotional satisfaction that derives from the modern-day Scarlet Letter worn by the corporation.

The SEC deals only with matters related to securities, but that umbrella covers a lot. It certainly covered the Bates case, in which the consent decree barred the company from future violations of securities laws. This scene has been repeated many hundreds of times in the hallowed halls of justice. What was different about the Bates case? Something happened in addition to the basic consent decree. The company also agreed to add to its board of directors three directors who were not employees or officers of Bates. These directors were to be acceptable to the SEC. Also, at the SEC's request, the company consented to form an audit committee of the board, a majority of which would be independent directors approved by the SEC.

Is the SEC now in the business of establishing the composition of the board of directors? Is it determining the ways in which the board carries out their responsibilities through committee assignments? Or is the Bates incident an isolated case? No, it's not an isolated case. Several years before the Bates case, Mattel, the giant toy manufacturer, was accused of improperly recording sales in order to inflate profits. For this impropriety and some additional minor infractions of the law, the company ended up with a consent decree requiring that complete control of the board of directors be given over to directors independent of company management. The independent directors had to be approved by the SEC and, in an additional twist in this case, also by the federal courts. For good measure, the SEC also required that an executive committee, composed entirely of independent directors, be formed.

One more example. Ormand Industries, an outdoor advertising company, agreed in a consent decree to three additional independent directors. The decree also required that the board appoint a special counsel, reporting to independent directors and the SEC, to investigate the SEC's allegations of illegal use of funds by corporate management. In other words, the company was directed to spend its own funds and time pursuing an investigation that the SEC thought might be useful. It was of no consequence whether the board of directors thought such an investigation would bear fruit. Nor was consideration given to the possibility that the SEC, not the company and its shareholders, ought to pay for the investigation.

Lessons

What is the point of discussing these cases? Simply this—under the guise of punishing transgressions of the law and avoiding future violations, the government is putting its own people on boards of directors and also telling the boards how to function. This is not necessarily good or bad. I am not painting a 1984 scenario of stifling Big Brother control. After consent decrees are entered, there is no ongoing direct link between the SEC and the new directors, new counsel, or whatever appointments are made. But the SEC's directors are made in the SEC's image. You can bet your last dollar that they are going to vote the right way. And they are going to vote on every issue before the board. Make no mistake: SEC-imposed directors are full-fledged directors. They participate in the development of strategic plans for the company. They make decisions on new products. They decide where to open new stores and new factories. They select outside lawyers and accountants. They determine the compensation of management. They even determine who should be in management. And they select new board members as vacancies arise. They do everything that any other board member does. However, their constituency isn't the shareholders. It's the government protecting the rights of the shareholders in its own way, and third parties not directly related to the corporation. Are all such directors puppets of the government? Of course not—no more than all other directors are automatically stooges of management. But it's likely that their loyalty will lie in different places. If not, what's the point in having them? The SEC is not engaging in a demonstration of futility.

The Trail of Bread Crumbs

We want to discuss the implications for corporate management of the increased government involvement. However, before we do so let's trace the history of this new development. In that way we will be able to understand better the sources of strength of the movement and its underlying philosophy.

In the 1960s the "counter culture" came into being. The Establishment became an object of scorn. College students railed against the Establishment, the Military-Industrial Complex, and in general, the symbols of stability in our society. Rebellion by idealistic young people is nothing new, but there was a new urgency and pervasiveness this time. The students were joined in varying but significant degrees by their professors and less-organized but equally concerned individual citizens. They were expressing their feelings in a way that was as new as the feelings themselves. Remember, this period was also the period in which the U.S. economic machine was creating individuality, as we discussed earlier. The synergy of the feelings and the manner of expression created a potent force.

The movement did not have a central focus. The Vietnam War, poverty, and other issues were involved. Business came in for its share of attention. It was perceived as the root of all evil or, at the least, an economic-oriented institution that had grown into a monster beyond control. It created social injustice, perpetuated poverty, and was responsible for most of the ills of the world. The feeling was not limited to liberal students and Marxist professors. Public confidence in business and business management fell to an all-time low.

In the late 1960s and early 1970s a series of events occurred that confirmed the pessimists' worst fears. The Penn Central railroad went off the tracks. Investigations disclosed indisputably poor performance by the board of directors and management. Equity Funding created millions of dollars of phony insurance policies and fooled the independent auditors. That a major scam could go undetected by outside auditors caused a fervor, although auditors had claimed all along that fraud perpetrated with management collusion was almost impossible to detect with normal audit procedures. In the National Student Marketing (NSM) case the accountants did their duty, exposing significant errors in NSM's reported income figures. The information was conveyed to the attorneys for NSM and the company with which it was to merge. They ignored the accountant's report, and the merger proceeded. Many investors lost a lot of money when NSM's stock price collapsed a few months later.

In a different kind of matter, the public was shocked to find out how many millions of dollars were being paid by U.S. corporations as bribes to secure overseas contracts. (ITT alone was responsible for almost $14 million of questionable payments from 1971 to 1975.) Payments were used to obtain services ranging from introductions to the right people, to expeditious handling of proposals and other documents, to outright decision making in favor of the briber. Corporations frequently tried to paint a picture of dealing with undeveloped, backward countries where the local morals, no matter how objectionable, had to be observed. Besides unfavorably playing on prejudice, the scenario was all too often laughable on the surface, since recipients of bribes were situated in such countries as Japan.

The problem was not confined to sensational cases. Although it is hard to believe, documented evidence exists that over 10 percent of major U.S. companies were engaged in serious illegal activities of one kind or another during the period.[1]

Some of the crimes were of the nature of reducing competition, for instance through price fixing. DuPont in 1970 had a division that produced dyes. So did several other companies. In 1970 DuPont wanted to raise prices on certain dyes, but they did not want to be left high and dry if the other companies held the line on prices. So they worked out an arrangement with their competition to raise prices industry-wide. The scheme was not uncovered until 1974, at which time the Justice Department brought an indictment of conspiracy to violate antitrust laws. The nine companies indicted all pleaded "no contest" and were fined.

Illegal political contributions have, unfortunately, been a way of life for many companies. For some reason, obeying the law seems to be difficult when a company is faced with the tantalizing prospect of buying a politician's favor or helping a friendly politician get elected. Firestone was engaged in this sort of thing throughout the 1960s, and until they were caught in the mid-1970s. The vice-president of finance was in charge of the scheme, which operated by reimbursing executives for forced personal political contributions. All the involved executives knew what was going on. The eventual settlement included a consent decree with the SEC. By the way, the vice-president also used the system to embezzle between half a million and a million dollars for his personal gain. Killing two birds with one stone, I suppose.

Other kinds of crimes abounded. Illegal kickbacks and rebates were common. Again, major companies were involved. Bethlehem Steel, in addition to producing steel, operates ship repair yards. The company pleaded guilty to bribing potential customers to give ship repair work to Bethlehem rather than to competitors. The scam was well-organized, known to a number of top executives and not particularly secret. A separate Swiss company was used to convert the money into cash, after which it was moved around in executive suitcases, just like in spy novels.

The portrait of U.S. business that emerges is not always a pleasing one; in fact, it can be rather ugly and disappointing. Or, possibly it merely illustrates that business executives have feet of clay, too. After all, West Point cadets were caught cheating on exams. Politicians are hardly examples to hold up to one's children. We are not a nation of miscreants, but it seems to be generally acceptable to do such things as steal paper clips from the office. Not that larceny on a large scale is verboten—it has been observed that we tend to admire the master criminals: the bigger the haul, the bigger the hero. Somehow, though, it didn't seem appropriate for business to be engaged in wholesale ripoffs. That disturbed people and something had to be done.

The SEC as White Knight

Into this corporate ethics vacuum rode the SEC. The securities statutes are remarkably vague and general about the SEC's powers. The SEC is empowered to enforce its conclusions through restraining orders or injunctions, administrative procedures (a nice phrase that means non-judicial, i.e., nobody other than the SEC has to approve its actions), or negotiated settlements such as consent decrees. The scope of the SEC's jurisdiction includes anything that can remotely be connected to public securities transactions. For instance, it includes accounting principles, since accounting reports are used by people who buy securities. The SEC can and does require filings with it, using accounting principles it prescribes, to report the information it deems useful to itself and other parties such as investors. This broad power is generally accepted because of history. The SEC was created in 1934 to correct the abuses in stock trading that had contributed to the market collapse. The public atmosphere then and since was supportive of broad powers instead of specific authority that possibly could be circumvented.

In the 1960s and 1970s the SEC determined that it had a duty to improve the performance of corporations' management. However, it was difficult to be effective. For example, many foreign bribes were not actually illegal under U.S. law. The SEC was reduced to prosecuting the few companies that had attempted to hide the bribes through improper accounting that had resulted in inaccurate reports to shareholders and the SEC. Ironically, the companies that openly admitted bribery were often technically guilty of no offense whatsoever. This was not a hypothetical situation. Many companies did account correctly for the foreign payments, and the SEC was unable to take any action against them.

Another hindrance was the lack of effective punitive measures for poor management performance. Fines or other financial punishment to a corporation appeared to make little sense if the object was to help the shareholders or others with financial interests in the corporation, since they would be the ultimate bearers of the punishment. Executives could be sent to jail or otherwise punished personally, if a strong enough case could be made, but that appeared to have many defects as an approach, not the least of which was the removal of good talent from the executive ranks of the accused corporation. This version of cutting off your nose to spite your face was not terribly appealing, since the SEC had no desire to go into the executive recruiting business.

In a nutshell, the SEC hit upon *preventive measures* as the solution to the problem. Since the board of directors was the ultimate authority in the corporation, all the Commission had to do was control the board. Of course, it was a complication that the SEC was not empowered by law to do any such thing. The traditions of law made it highly unlikely that the judicial system was going to take very kindly to the concept of removing duly-elected directors and/or adding non-elected directors. Judges are very touchy about due process. The way around the complication was consent decrees, which the SEC was empowered to negotiate with transgressors. After all, how could anyone argue that the SEC had exceeded its authority if a corporation voluntarily agreed to restructure its board? And if the courts wanted to put their oars in the water, so much the better: the corporation would have two masters to answer to. The courts were delighted, because they are always glad to have parties agree on a settlement rather than fight it out. Therefore, the consent decree became the Commission's main weapon. The message to corporations was, in effect, either agree to a consent decree or face protracted, expensive litigation accompanied by extensive publicity orchestrated by the SEC against the company. Human nature being what it is, most companies chose the former.

While all this was going on, of course, there was a lot of discussion among business managers, lawmakers, academics, and the public regarding this intrusion into corporate governance. Emerging from the discussions was a central fact: general agreement that the intrusion was justified. The holdouts, naturally, were business managers. But society had reached a turning point in its concept of the corporation. It was no longer to be left to itself. As Georges Clemenceau said that war was too important to be left to the generals, so society decided that business was too important to be left to the business managers. Monday-morning quarterbacking was out as the only remedy for poor team performance. The fans were going to play in the game and influence its outcome.

The Domino Effect

Once this conclusion was reached, the next steps were predictable. The SEC and other interested bodies began making pronouncements about the responsibilities and composition of all boards of directors, not just those where companies had done something questionable or wrong. The door had been opened. It was acceptable to challenge the results of the normal process of nominating and electing directors. Committee assignments and functions came under attack. Everybody had his or her own idea of what the board's responsibilities should be and how they should be discharged. No evidence was required to convict a company. If the board didn't have a certain composition and defined functions, it was assumed to be incapable of proper direction of the company—it was only a matter of time until the company did something illegal or immoral or both went the argument. In addition, pressures were put on private companies, which are not subject to the same SEC jurisdiction, to conform. A campaign was mounted to ballyhoo the SEC reforms of corporation management as the greatest thing since permanent press clothes. If the new rules of conduct were so reasonable, why shouldn't they be accepted by all companies?

The SEC with the general support of society began to develop a concept of "full fault" (as opposed in terminology to "no fault"). The main thesis was that corporate directors and officers were responsible for mistakes of the corporation and liable for punishment for the mistakes. Honest mistakes were not to be tolerated unless supported by mountains of evidence of supporting data of good intentions, nor were mistakes to be excused if they were made by lower-level management without the knowledge of the board. Management was literally not to be trusted. The directors had to "seek out the nature of corporate disclosures" since there might be "resistance on the part of management" to "full and fair disclosure" (National Telephone case).

The SEC was off and running with the ball. In fact, it was most of the way down the field! What were the legislative and judicial branches of our government doing?

The Role of Congress

In some ways Congress was responsive to the new mood. The Foreign Corrupt Practices Act of 1977 is a good example. The act was conceived as a reaction to the problem of foreign payoffs, but as enacted, most of its important provisions are in other areas of corporate governance. The law specifically makes directors liable for any deficiencies in a company's accounting recordkeeping and internal control systems. Not just *material* deficiencies, but any deficiencies. Another interesting aspect of this requirement is that it deals with subjects, e.g., detailed accounting systems, that boards have not historically been concerned with, and that very few board members are qualified to evaluate or even discuss. Yet the law makes no exception for lack of skills of directors nor does it allow for transfer of responsibility to lower-level officials, such as the corporate controller, when the board members are acting in good faith based on experience and empirical evidence. This statute moves the board—lock, stock and barrel—into the chief accountant's office. It makes the board responsible for a level of activity that previously was clearly the province of management. It moves them into procedural areas, whereas the board historically has been more concerned with policy matters. The interpretation of the law is taking some time, because the number of actual cases in the courts has been rather small. It will take several more years before we know if the courts will uphold the literal requirements of the law.

On the other hand, Congress has turned down various extreme proposals for reform in corporate governance. One involves the chartering of corporations. Corporations are currently chartered, that is, licensed to do business under certain terms and conditions, under state law. State laws differ a great deal. Delaware set out to revamp its laws entirely when corporate chartering became a competitive issue for states. The state simplified the laws and in other ways created a climate favorable to corporations. As a result, over half of the Fortune 500 largest industrial corporations are chartered in Delaware.

Ralph Nader and others have proposed federal chartering to impose a uniform set of standards. Congress has so far ignored the proposals. However, it is far from clear if this is because of the concept or because all the proposed model charters go beyond even the most strict existing state law in telling corporations how to conduct their business.

Some other legislative proposals are concerned with the composition of boards of directors. Various proposals for public directors, special interest directors, or merely independent directors have been made. These proposals all have in common the notion that boards should have a predetermined composition and that the composition should be decreed by law. So far Congress has not accepted these premises.

So Congress has joined the parade in spirit, but is not ready to take the same strong stance that the SEC has. On this critical issue—control of the board of directors—Congress has stayed on the sidelines. That could change, however, because Congress has been equally unwilling to challenge the SEC through legislation limiting its powers. More than likely, the individuals in Congress merely disagree on which way the wind is blowing. Once that becomes clear, Congress will take sides.

The Courts

The courts also have been a mixed blessing for American business. On the positive side (from the business standpoint), they have generally been reluctant to accept the idea that all mistakes are punishable, whether or not they were made while acting with good intentions. Good intentions means a couple of things. It means trying to do the right thing, having the proper motives, and so on. It also means doing the things that a prudent person would do in the same circumstances. It implies conducting investigations of facts, evaluating alternatives, soliciting other opinions, and generally taking the degree of precaution associated with the complexity and risk of a decision. The legal principle here is called "due diligence." The courts frequently have sided with defendants against the SEC, holding that the accused did in fact exercise due diligence in discharging his or her responsibilities. This has been true in such widely divergent matters as responsibility of board members and responsibility of public accountants to investors. The courts have simply been reluctant to impose a standard of "no mistakes" on corporate directors and management.

As with most things in this world, there is also the other side. The Delaware court system has long been favorable to business. However, in early 1981, the state's Supreme Court ruled that courts could not rely on a corporation's outside independent directors to be an objective source of opinion on whether a potential shareholder lawsuit had merit. Such directors had previously been relied on quite heavily by judges in all state and federal courts, since the directors appeared to be the best

source of both informed and independent judgment. The Delaware ruling strikes at the very heart of the concept of outside directors—it in
effect says that their judgment can't be trusted, that all potential liti-
gants must be given their days in court. It substitutes the judiciary for
outside directors. No one can argue with the judiciary's knowledge of
law. But we can make a case that the law needs a set of facts to which
to be applied, and the judiciary clearly will not be as well informed as
directors. The matter of independence is less clear cut. Judges are
human beings and have their prejudices. Some independent directors
are, and some aren't. Overall, it is hard to believe that courts can't
choose to rely on the opinions of the best informed impartial directors.
They probably will and just change the language in the opinions to
conform to the current rulings of higher courts.

In summary, the courts have been good followers, but not leaders
in the matter of changing corporation boards. They have been active
participants in the various consent decrees mentioned earlier, but have
not been in the front lines of the battle. It generally has not been the
way of the judiciary to break new ground in matters of corporate governance. We are reaching a point, however, where sufficient precedents
will have been established for judges to start imposing SEC-like remedies without the SEC or anyone else asking for them. This judicial activ-
ism is apparent in many other areas of our society and corporate governance is likely to get its turn. The few exceptions that have occurred
so far, where courts have been the leaders, will be looked at by histo-
rians as the first few bricks in the new structure.

Where Are We Headed?

We know the direction in which we are headed—increased government intervention in the board room. Our final destination and the
intermediate stages are not quite so certain, so let's examine some possibilities. Let's stay in the reasonably near future—such developments
as two-tier boards emulating some European countries are possible, but
only slightly, in the near future.

There are signs of additional constraints on the freedom of directors.
They already have been told how to perform some of their internal
functions, for example, creation and administration of audit committees. Dealing with outside professionals, specifically attorneys and independent accountants, is starting to come under attack. At the same time
the SEC is continuing its efforts, begun in a low-key way some time
ago, to enlist lawyers and accountants in its battle to control the board
of directors. The SEC has suggested that the duty of corporate attorneys

is to the corporation, not to its directors and management. Therefore, attorneys are obligated to disclose any potentially illegal action. Also, that communications between attorneys and corporation individuals do not enjoy attorney-client privileges of confidential communication. The first point is really not arguable except over how likely and serious the illegality has to be before reporting it. The second point has stirred up a hornet's nest of opposition. Courts have ruled various ways, so the issue is far from dead. The role of the independent accountant is similarly clouded, although with fewer thunderheads on the horizon. The SEC is constantly prodding accountants to be its watchdogs, using as its lever an implied threat to issue new accounting rules that would not be favored by the profession. The accountants don't seem to be quite as high on the hit list as some other groups, though, so they have received proportionately less attention. (In this regard, that is; they have taken plenty of heat in other areas.)

The SEC may or may not continue to be in the vanguard of the action. Its five members are political appointees, so the conscience of the commission changes over time according to political shifts. The chairman of the commission, although only one member, has a great deal of influence, so his or her political persuasions are important. But the SEC's year-to-year swings or lack of them are not important. The great machine has been set in motion and there is no turning back. Members of the judiciary have crossed the Rubicon, too, as we have noted. Legislative bodies are still on the shore, but the ships are ready to be launched.

Advice will continue to pour in from all quarters. University professors of government, law, and accounting will have their say. Representatives of these professions will continue to speak and write on the issues. Government individuals will contribute their two cents. Public interest groups and public spirited individuals will contribute. That leaves only one group, the people who would be most affected by all the proposals—directors and management. You would normally expect people in their positions to be the most vocal, but things haven't happened that way. Maybe it's a feeling of hopelessness or frustration on their part. Whatever the reasons, the silence must end. Business managers must make known their feelings.

But being outspoken is only the first step. At some point the parties will have to stop blowing their own horns and start working together. Extremists either will have to be shut out of the discussions or be forced to moderate their positions. Extreme solutions, such as some of the federal chartering legislation, are likely to happen only if unexpected extremes arise in the national mood. It would be to everybody's benefit, including that of business, to reach a consensus on practical changes in corporate governance. Even if all that results is codification of the existing situation, things would be better. A body of law is far preferable to a "law du jour" being made case by case by the SEC and the courts. Presumably, if some thought goes into it, we can do better than this. Maybe there are too many parties involved for each of them to go more than halfway—the phrase seems out of place—but the idea is sound: each party has to contribute willingly to a solution to be accepted by all.

This is not to say that all effort has to be a group effort. Clearly not—a committee never did anything useful. But working continually at cross-purposes has to cease. Independently, corporate boards of directors and management could start conducting themselves better. This also qualifies for the Going More Than Halfway Award. We are going to start working our way down the corporation in the next chapter, beginning with the board of directors, discussing exactly how they can carry out their new responsibilities and perform some of their new functions that we have touched upon. After that, we'll deal with management positions in the corporation.

"A wise man alters his purpose, but a fool perseveres in his folly."
—MABBE

Chapter 5

The Future Board of Directors

BY NOW, running the modern corporation probably seems like an impossible task. Things are changing so rapidly that it also seems that lessons learned yesterday become obsolete and have to be discarded in favor of even newer lessons. A board member is the Sisyphus of our times, pushing the boulder up the hill only to have it roll down again.

The task really isn't quite that hopeless. Standards are higher than ever before, and there is less room for mistakes, but boards of directors can still succeed. Their success is the subject of this chapter.

Like all change, the changes in boards will be different in different companies. Some will have to change quickly. For others the type of change will be more important than its speed. Regardless, the inevitability of change must be accepted along with the need to adopt an aggressive rather than a defensive posture. Then the board can focus on its mission: doing the right things, and doing those things right. What are the right things for the board of directors to be concerned with? Most authorities would answer the question with statements similar to the following. The board makes basic policy decisions. They establish the overall mission of the corporation and the strategies to carry it out. They allocate resources—primarily money and people. Part of the people allocation is determining the holders of the senior management positions. They evaluate and set the compensation of senior executives. Dealing with such outsiders as attorneys and accountants is required, sometimes in cooperation with management and sometimes not. They worry about the composition of the board—they nominate their future colleagues. They exercise a fiduciary responsibility to the shareholders to preserve the viability of the corporation and to provide a return on shareholders' investments. They are the ultimate bearers of responsibility for the corporation's legal and moral obligations.

There is nothing wrong with this list of activities for the board. Many boards, in fact, could benefit a great deal simply by using it as a template to identify their shortcomings. However, for other boards the list is not terribly helpful in practical terms. They need some additional guidance as to whether they are doing the right things as they try to adapt to change.

One implied activity is getting a reading of the future. An accurate fortune teller probably would be the most valuable member of many boards of directors. He or she could predict the next fad in litigation, the outcome of court decisions, or the next responsibility to be loaded onto the board by legislators. The board could concentrate on meeting their responsibilities rather than on wondering what the responsibilities are.

All kidding aside, making an educated guess about the future is one of the most important steps in changing the board. What are the company's future problems going to be? Certainly the traditional ones such as new products. But how about the new concerns that arise from responsibilities to government and shareholders? Which of the following will be significant? Obtaining new capital through equity offerings (SEC approval required)? Demonstrating compliance with the Foreign Corrupt Practices Act? Publishing accurate earnings projections for potential investors? Or myriad other possible issues. Books and other information sources can provide a good basic education in such matters, but managers need to examine their own companies carefully. It's useful to construct alternative scenarios and play each through as if it were a game. This sort of simulation approach can assist both in avoiding surprises and in ensuring consistency of your strategy with reality. If you are in the precious metals business, for example, it would serve you well to simulate the effects of such possible government policies as a return to the gold standard or stockpiling of precious metals for defense purposes. I don't mean just think about the consequences in a superficial sense. Everybody does that, and the results are on-again off-again bull and bear markets for metals. I mean develop a detailed contingency plan for important alternatives. Not *likely* alternatives—important ones. An unlikely alternative that would wipe you out or double your earnings is worth examining. I hear you saying, I can't afford to do that. The retort is trite but true: Can you afford not to do it?

Financial Responsibilities

Also near the head of the board's list of duties is the fiduciary responsibility in financial matters. If the corporation goes down the drain, not much else matters. Cash flow is the critical element over the short term. There is no such thing as operating at a deficit. If you can't pay your employees and your suppliers, you will have to close up shop. If operating earnings will not be adequate, the board will have to ensure that money can be raised through asset sales, deferral of debt payments or other bills, or acquisition of new funding through loans or sales of stock. Such activities to preserve adequate cash flow are a very poor use of the board's time, since management should have avoided the cash flow problems. But the overall fiduciary responsibility lies with the board.

Longer-term survival is more along the lines of what the board exists for. Specific strategies and tactics for this are delineated in later sections of the book. At the moment, let's discuss the board's responsibility to know how things are working out. How can boards measure financial success? Basically, the concept of profit was invented for this purpose. However, none of the currently accepted definitions of profit is satisfactory.

Let's pursue this thought further, since it bears on the functioning of the board. To understand what would be satisfactory, we have to return to the thought of corporate survival. The corporation needs to take in as much money as it pays out, not only on a month-to-month cash-flow basis, but on a sustained basis over a long period of time. For example, it needs to replace such assets as obsolete equipment. If outsiders have invested money in the corporation, then it clearly needs to pay them for the privilege of using their money. And so on—a simple concept: Take in as much as you pay out, making sure that you have indeed counted all the money that has to be paid out. If profit is the difference between amounts taken in and paid out, the required profit for survival is obvious—zero. In other words, if a company can accurately measure its non-immediate expenses such as depreciation, then over the long haul it can shoot for a profit of zero, i.e., for simply staying in business, supplying its customers, paying its employees, etc. Is this true? If so, it would seem to shatter a lot of theories about corporations. Well, it is true—for many corporations. If they're performing all their functions and providing for non-immediate expenses, why do they need any extra money? For growth? Investment in new business areas? Sometimes. But this rationale is very much overused.

Many corporations don't need to grow any more than an adult human being needs to grow. Maintenance of position is adequate.

Obviously there are exceptions to the above point. Growth may be a natural phenomenon for new industries such as electronics. It may be necessary for survival, if the competition is going to grow to a point where it can put you out of business. Physicists have a term for that situation: metastable. It means that you are marginally stable, but some external action could push you into instability. Clearly, if this is possible, a corporation ought to provide for it in its profit objectives. Otherwise, ambitious profit goals are probably no more than the personal goals of senior executives, and that can be dangerous.

If the corporation achieves its goals, it may mean that it overcharged its customers, leaving itself vulnerable to competition or to public censure. If it makes too much money, the excess may burn a hole in its pocket until it uses it for something that is not really right for the business but is fun for the people involved. The Bendix bid for Martin-Marietta in 1982 fits this description in many ways; Bendix, led by an egotistical William Agee, was sitting on a cash hoard and just itching to spend it. The resultant battle and takeover of Bendix by Allied was not one of U.S. business's finer moments. In general, profits that aren't earmarked for specific useful deeds are probably excessive.

Does that mean that all the U.S. corporations, or a majority of them, that report profits greater than zero are gouging society? Not at all. The accounting systems used to compute profits do not reflect reality. For many companies, depreciation charges do not begin to cover the cost of replacing their equipment. Profits are used in lieu of depreciation, to avoid eating the seed corn. For other companies, depreciation is overstated as a result of technological changes. Other problems also exist with financial statements. Foreign currency translations. Present value of liabilities in an inflationary economy. And many more. What is being done about the problems? The accounting rule makers and their brethren in government, business, and academia are working on solutions. However, the gestation period is not acceptable to corporations that have to measure their success now.

Boards of directors have to address this problem, and that is why we have spent so much time on it here. One of the board's fundamental responsibilities is corporate survival, for which it needs a decent measurement system. Board members cannot wait for the formal accounting rules to be issued. They have to design and implement a decent accounting and financial reporting system that accurately describes reality, not distorts it. This "shadow system" actually should be the basis for most key decisions. Since the other system exists and is in the public eye, it cannot be ignored, but compliance with it should be limited to statutory requirements.

Who Sits on the Board?

Before we pursue board activities any further, let's see who the players are. Who really sits on boards?

First, a few statistics and facts. Some of these are surprising, and some of them are about what you would expect. In the "surprising" category, given the hue and cry about director independence, is this one—approximately 90 percent of the boards of major corporations have a majority of outside (non-company) directors.[1] Not all outside directors are necessarily independent of management, of course. Independence, being a state of mind, is difficult to measure. Some indications of non-independence might be links through family, business connections, or previous employment with the company. Applying this test, the percentage drops, but still over half the major boards have a majority of independent outside directors.[2]

The inside directors are senior management individuals. Who are the outside directors? Usually other business persons. And, overwhelmingly, senior executives. In major corporations, over half the outside directors with business backgrounds were or are chairmen or presidents of corporations; most of the rest were or are executive or senior vice-presidents.[3]

About one in five major corporations has a minority-group member on the board.[4] Forty percent have at least one woman director.[5] (The percentages are much lower if all companies, including very small ones, are considered.) Although statistics aren't available, the consensus is that most boards with women and minorities have only one (of either). There are two ways of looking at the situation. The positive way is "progress." The negative way is "tokenism." The truth lies somewhere in between.

Which companies are role models? McDonnell Douglas and Beatrice Foods are publicly committed to having a majority of outside directors. Warner-Lambert is one of the few companies with more than one woman director and is looking for more. Who is still rowing against the tide? Minnesota Mining & Manufacturing (3M), an advanced company in many respects, has continually fought attempts to place a majority of outside directors on its board. The company might have historically valid reasons, but their stance raises the issue of their wisdom in expending resources in a battle that probably will be lost eventually. The direction of society is clear: expanding the makeup of boards is a high priority matter.

How Does the Board Function?

Let's get back to the functioning of the board. How does it perform its activities? Not "how" in an effectiveness sense, but in a process sense. What are the mechanisms through which it conducts its activities?

At one time the board convened as a "committee of the whole" to conduct business. The entire board discussed every matter on the agenda. As issues have become more complex and more time-consuming, the committee approach has evolved. Directors are assigned to committees that deal with such specific matters as the external audit report, executive compensation, or nominating new directors. Assignments are made on the basis of interest, skills, or absence of conflicts of interest (e.g., executives of the company would not sit on the executive compensation committee). The committee approach has proven to be quite effective. There is no evidence yet that the committee structure will not work in the future. However, a few storm clouds can be seen on the horizon. The growing tendency to view all directors as liable for actions of the board, for example, is inconsistent with separation of duties by committee. Committees may instead be forced to evolve into bodies that merely do staff work for the entire board to review thoroughly in the decision-making process. Regardless of whether this or another direction develops, the board should think through its internal assignments very carefully.

How often should the board meet? Whenever is necessary! And what information should it have? Whatever is necessary! Seriously, though, precise answers to these questions are impossible, so we will offer some preferences and the reasoning behind them. Monthly meetings are probably the most popular choice, followed by quarterly meetings with exceptions in busy times such as fiscal year end. These preferences, unfortunately, are based less on necessity than on feelings that more-frequent meetings would tie the hands of management and less-frequent meetings would leave the directors open to charges of inattention to the corporation. If we look at the reality of how events occur, a fixed calendar of meetings provides no advantage except a feeling of comfort. A few companies have experimented with the idea of calling the next board meeting at the conclusion of each meeting, when members can determine with some logic the best time to reconvene. It seems to have worked well in making efficient use of the directors' time and focusing on issues at the right time.

The information question is equally serious. Most discussions of the topic have attempted to describe by formulas or by example the information that the board needs.[6] These discussions usually are accompanied by horror stories of what happened when the CEO failed to provide adequate information to the board and subsequently made a horrible mistake that could have been headed off by the board if they had known. The real mistake lies in focusing on the information per se. The key is who decides what information is needed. Putting one individual in charge of that decision is presumptuous. Putting the CEO in charge of it is putting the fox in the chicken coop. Only board members can decide what information they need. Individuals may have individual needs. Can you imagine a person in the position of a board member, overseeing an entire corporation, being dependent on someone else's idea of what he or she should see? Yet this is exactly the situation in 99 percent of U.S. board rooms. Board members simply must take the initiative and state their information requirements.

Does this mean that the board is going to come into conflict with management? Yes—more than ever before. Part of it is natural and inevitable, because the board provides a check-and-balance system for management. Occasionally they are going to rub a little too closely together and some sparks will fly. Another part of the conflict is not so healthy. A very serious problem has developed with definition of responsibilities. So far the problem has received the same attention as the Emperor's new clothes—everybody wants to believe that there is not a problem, or only a minor one, and so they do. Believe me, the problem is not minor. In its most simple form, it is as follows. Who is in charge of the corporation? The board or management? When push comes to shove, who is really responsible for ensuring that it sets and meets reasonable long-term and short-term goals?

Most of the literature on the subject says, as we have said here, that the board has the ultimate authority. If that is the case, perhaps the best and most highly paid people should be on the board. The average individual compensation for the top three or four executives in major U.S. corporations is close to $300,000 annually.[7] Directors are lucky to make 10 percent of that.[8] Are the executives being paid that much to carry out someone else's decisions? Of course not. They, not the board, are really running the corporation. They know it, and their career goals are to be CEO or chairman of their own company, not a director of another company. They know where the power lies. Is there something wrong with the concept of the board as we and others have stated it? No, and even if there were, it wouldn't matter—society is moving towards more responsibility and liability for the board. So something has to give. My crystal ball is no better than anyone else's, but I see the role of directors continuing to grow in stature. It will become an acceptable career path and the compensation will be much improved. Boards will be accepted as the overall guiding bodies for corporations. Dual responsibilities will disappear: people will be able to be on the board and in management, but not in positions of power in both places. Connecticut General, now part of CIGNA, and some others already have separated the roles of chairman and CEO. Other companies are considering going further and limiting management participation on the board to the CEO. Specific companies will experience differing amounts of pain as they progress, but progress they will. They have little choice.

Strategic Planning

Strategic planning is the process of figuring out what you want to be when you grow up and how to achieve it. The customers and markets you want to serve. The products to offer. Acquisition and allocation of resources. Financial rewards. Role in the local and national community. Reputation. Whatever is important to the company. As I mentioned, a little later in the book we will deal with strategic planning techniques and answers in specific industries and companies. The board's role is our immediate concern.

There are two kinds of roles that the board plays—participative and administrative. The participative role is the more important, although few corporations treat it that way. The wealth and diversity of experience on the average board are staggering. Channeling the experience into the planning process is one of the most valuable services that the board can perform. Each board member will possess expertise and opinions in certain areas. It is his or her duty to put them on the table and ensure that they are completely utilized in the preparation of a plan. This may take place in several ways. If properly conceived, there is an initial phase to every strategic planning cycle when ideas are sought from many sources, including the board. As the plan takes shape, some of these sources should be able to lay hands on the partially finished object and mold it to suit some of their desires. The board should be one of the artisans. Finally, the last-minute touchup and polishing must be done, and again the board should be involved. As planning may be a frequent occurrence in our rapidly changing world, the cycle should be repeated as often as necessary.

The administrative roles are primarily procedural in nature, to ensure that the planning process in fact takes place and is well-controlled. The board will not usually directly employ the planning staff, but they must ensure that the planning is performed through a disciplined process. A formal planning department may or may not exist. If one does, the board's task is a little easier. Regardless, the objective is the same: assurance that an open-minded, thorough planning process is being followed. Many strategic plans are no more than yesterday's plans with today's dates. Other plans are elaborate rationalizations of the CEO's prejudices. Others are simply inadequate explorations of the possibilities or poor analyses of facts. The board must challenge all apparent or real deficiencies in the planning process.

Texas Instruments is one of the world's most successful electronics companies (despite their problems with home computers). Managers are given both operating and strategic assignments, differentiated so that the longer term nature of strategy is preserved. Various levels of management are involved continually in formulation and execution of strategy; strategic plans are organized, budgeted, and summarized once a year for the entire corporation. Board members play an active part in all aspects of strategic planning. They interact with management and they also share their ideas. The counsel of the board is so important that a separate advisory group of six independent citizens, not on the board, was formed to advise the board on key issues that might affect the company's future. Texas Instruments is one of the few companies that takes seriously the notion of understanding the relevance of external influences.

Incidentally, TI also does many of the other things that we have discussed regarding boards of directors. The board has a majority of outside directors. These directors are expected to become involved with the corporation in ways other than board meetings. For example, they attend normal management meetings, visit TI operating locations, and contact individual TI managers as they wish to acquire information they need. They are compensated well—up to $100,000 annually. TI has learned how to make the board an effective part of the company without stifling management.

Public Issues

The board can find itself bumping up against public issues, those involving social responsibility of corporations. Some are legal issues that can be addressed crisply, but many are not. The purely moral issues affect boards most directly when they appear as shareholder resolutions at annual meetings. The number of such resolutions has been steadily increasing to a current number of a couple hundred per year.[9] The most popular issues by far have involved dealing with foreign governments perceived as repressive or otherwise undesirable, e.g., South Africa. Nuclear issues also have been popular. Numerous others, including consumer issues, have received scattered support.

It is not likely that shareholder resolutions will ever be eliminated. They are an effective symbol, a way of putting a corporation on public display. They are also one of the few tools available to individuals who are unable to reach agreement with corporate management and still wish to state their points. Generally, however, it would be preferable for corporations to be able to deal with the issues in some other way. The board is right in the middle of the action, and consequently their involvement is a part of their duty.

Boards have some choices in handling public issues. One is to prevent stonewalling by corporate management. Directors can insist on opening a dialogue with the dissident shareholders. Such dialogue may lead to withdrawal or modification of resolutions. The three major television networks were faced a few years ago with shareholder resolutions on women and minorities in their programming. After discussion, the resolutions were withdrawn. Discussions between Exxon and shareholders led to a different conclusion: a modified resolution which was then supported by Exxon management (it passed).

Sometimes the best course of action is to correct the problem that sparked the resolution. Several companies have tightened their policies regarding South Africa. Citibank will no longer make loans to the South African government. A General Motors chairman once described shareholder resolutions as an attempt to challenge the entire system of U.S. corporate management. Under a different chairman, GM has sponsored affirmative action proposals in South Africa. Times have changed, and so have the better boards.

The Outside Specialists

We previously outlined some of the issues regarding outside specialists—attorneys, accountants, etc.—and the government, especially the SEC. There are a couple of issues involving only the board and these individuals. The major issue with outsiders and the board is the conflict-of-interest possibility when outside specialists sit on the board. The accountants' rules of ethics bar them from sitting on boards, but nobody else's conscience is quite that strong. Consequently, attorneys, investment bankers, consultants (except in accounting firms), and all other kinds of "independent" professionals sit on boards of companies that frequently use their services. Unless all these professionals have overnight attacks of probity, the situation will continue. Boards can only make the best of it by trying to keep their afflicted members in line, with maybe a little fake now and then to keep them on their toes. If your lawyer is on your board, suggest that the company evaluate other law firms to see if they could provide better service at a lower fee. Such diversions can liven up otherwise dull board meetings.

Directors also might get in trouble for not soliciting information and not heeding advice. They are supposed to pay attention to the independent outsiders, such as accountants. The outside accountants may have better access to information and people in the company than any other group, especially if they are doing a full audit, as they do for publicly-traded companies. In these days of concern over rising audit fees and increasing competition among public accounting firms, the accountants are driven to do everything they can to help the corporation improve its internal operations. They'll get some of the credit, and fee pressure will ease because the accountant will have fewer snarls to untangle. Directors should pick their brains carefully, not necessarily as a separate assignment (which would mean extra fees), but as a debriefing after the audit. Ask them tough and sensitive questions—in private, without management present. Don't forget to ask about your people. The external auditors can generally recognize talent—they are in a people business, and their stock in trade is people. They have very definite biases, but these are plainly seen. Take the biases into account and you can get some pretty useful information.

The lawyers are a slightly different story. They have limited direct access to information not directly involved with a specific assignment. Their usefulness is confined to matters of law, which is not to demean it. Pay careful attention to what they say, and don't get possibilities mixed up with probabilities. Also, bear in mind that they have to separate their roles of personal counsel and corporate counsel. If they don't always seem to understand the difference, you certainly should. In many cases, their own rules of ethics would prohibit them from filling both roles where the interests of the two parties might be different. If you have need for a personal counsel, you had best retain a firm other than the corporate attorneys. In addition, as we said briefly in the previous chapter, it is not good practice to bare your soul to the attorneys unless you are certain the communication is privileged.

Avoiding Going to Jail or the Poorhouse

As we observed earlier, criminal and civil liability of individual directors apparently is going to be on the legal hit parade in the 1980s. Directors have an obligation to the corporation, the board, and themselves to stay out of this kind of trouble. The individual director has to take and defend the position he or she believes is legally correct. The ultimate defense is notifying the authorities. This can be difficult in the lynch-mob atmosphere that often accompanies controversial actions. The "If you're not with me, you're against me" mentality tends to prevail. It's easy to cave in, but not always wise. Louis Cabot was on the board of the Penn Central during its unscheduled journey into infamy. He was an outspoken advocate of changes in the way the Penn Central board operated. His position was documented in writing. As a result, he ended up as one of the few individuals whose reputation was not scarred by the railroad's collapse. But he took chances in doing so. He stayed on the board and tried to correct things from the inside. A noble attempt, but one that is not unquestionably always the best. He could have been seen as part of the problem rather than as part of the solution. One's commitment to one's beliefs can be misinterpreted when one continues to be associated with the wrong kind of people.

Even the most cautious person may find himself or herself on the wrong end of a lawsuit or prosecution. What then? Get a good lawyer! By then, of course, you are in trouble, but some precautions can limit the potential risk. Directors and officers (D&O) insurance coverage should be carried. If it is not available in the required amounts, directors should seriously consider how committed they are to their directorships. There just aren't very many precedents yet in the field of individual liability for directors, and you don't want to be the case that breaks new ground for expansion of liability. Where state laws permit, look into the possibility of indemnification by the corporation for damages and attorneys' fees. It's possible in some states, but not in others.

In general, bear in mind that being a director is no longer a Sunday stroll. It's a steeplechase where the obstacles aren't known in advance. Be alert and be careful.

Finding and Evaluating Directors

You have accepted an assignment on the Nominating Committee of the board. Two directors have unacceptable time pressures and are not going to stand for reelection. You have six months to come up with two new individuals who will be satisfactory to the board, management, shareholders, and interested outsiders. How should you proceed?

Presumably you have learned enough by now that you are not going to start calling friends of yours or of other directors. You are first going to figure out what skills are needed. Then you will go through a process which is a little bit like the annual professional football draft of college players. Each team knows what its weaknesses are. The scouts know what the players can do. The draft is a simple matching process with an element of intrigue in outfoxing the competition.

Determining your weaknesses starts with the corporation's future plans and known problem areas. Areas where additional strength on the board would be welcome should be obvious. Maybe strategic planning for diversification. Or experience in managing high technology or maintaining market share in a declining industry. Perhaps you need skills to attack problems. Legal skills. Or, more likely, specific legal skills such as securities law. Accounting skills. Skills in government relations. Whatever is required. Peabody Coal Company chose as a director and Chief Executive Officer Roderick Hills, former SEC chairman. Crown Zellerbach selected as a director Dorothy M. Simon, research vice-president at Avco. The Xerox board chose Vernon Jordan, then-president of the National Urban League. Each of these individuals brought skills and background that were needed by the companies.

IBM believes that its relationships with the federal government are important. Many of its board members and key executives are equally at home at corporate headquarters or in the White House. Several, including Nicholas deB. Katzenbach, have held Cabinet-level appointments. The closeness between the company and the government may strike some people as an interlocking relationship right out of *Captains and the Kings*. In reality, however, government and business are so intertwined that we are all better off if they get to know one another. By its closeness, IBM is certainly attuned to key issues better than most other companies.

Speaking of people, how do you find them? Aren't directors' jobs the pinnacle of business success, for which only a few individuals are qualified? Let's put things in perspective. There are approximately 10,000 SEC-registered companies, with an average board size of thirteen people.[10] That's 130,000 seats, not even counting subsidiaries that have their own boards.

What do the numbers mean? They mean that air at the board level is not so rarefied after all. Directors' jobs are held by ordinary people, high achievers certainly—but not necessarily superstars. You're not going to be able to zip by the local McDonald's and pick up a couple of directors. But they're available and can be located without using the FBI. Normal acquisition practices, such as using executive recruiters, can be followed. In many cases directors can be located more easily than executives for such key positions as data processing. Naturally, you'll want to consider many backgrounds besides business for your directors. It makes good sense and it also makes the search easier by expanding the pool of potential people.

The final step is the actual election of directors by the shareholders. Legal requirements for disclosure to the stockholders of background information on director candidates are minimal and most companies do no more than legally required. However, a few companies have gone far beyond the legal requirements for years. Esmark and Dow Chemical both believe that informed stockholders are in the best interests of the company. They routinely provide detailed information with their proxy material in order to enable the voters to make intelligent decisions. This will happen more in the future. Not only does it lead to better decisions, but it defuses any potential charge against the board of railroading through unqualified candidates.

How Are They Doing?

We've described a number of things that directors should do and how they should do them. But how do directors know if they are doing a good job? The only external evaluation of directors is a negative one, for example, they can get sued for poor performance. The SEC doesn't give awards to good directors. Pretend you're a director (or maybe you are). Unless the absence of a lawsuit is sufficient to give you peace of mind, you need a way to evaluate yourself. Here are some pertinent questions.

How is your background knowledge? Of the company. Of all board and key management matters in the past. Of the positions of the SEC and other important bodies. Of the special interest groups that interact with the company. Of general trends in society.

Are you prepared for meetings? Do you speak up when the agenda does not include all appropriate issues, or when adequate discussion time or materials are not available? Are you well-informed from company or external sources? Do you think through all matters and encourage others to do the same? Do your positions always reflect rectitude rather than expediency? Do you consider all issues for which you are qualified, not ducking any, including committee assignments?

Are you personally honest, not using the position for any unethical or illegal gain? Do you avoid conflict of interest situations with the board and your other responsibilities and/or directorships? Can you make tough decisions? While doing so, can you remain pleasant and a contributing member of the board?

Does the board pass your personal test of relevance? Is it concentrating on the right issues? Are you comfortable with the division of responsibilities between the board and management?

If you can answer all the questions in the affirmative, you are in pretty good shape. If not, you have some thinking to do. You might want to read some technical material on the behavior of boards, such as the American Bar Association's discussion of legal responsibilities or the SEC's pronouncements. Or you might just want to look inside yourself and evaluate your motives and needs. Whichever you do, or both, it's important to determine whether being a director is suitable for you and if it is, how to start acting like one.

To summarize, today's directors have a lot of things on their minds. New responsibilities such as satisfying the public's social conscience. New approaches to known responsibilities such as strategic planning and filling board vacancies. Are directors alone in the world? In some matters, yes; nobody else in the corporation can provide much help in selecting new board members. But in most activities, directors can get help from other people in management. For this to be possible, of course, the overall organization and people in management must also be attuned to change. The next chapter shows how that can be accomplished.

"Genius does what it must, and talent does what it can."
—BULWER-LYTTON

Chapter 6

Changing the Manager's Job

THE BOARD OF DIRECTORS is the summit of the mountain. Under it lies the management of the corporation. It is not always clear where the division between the two is, but worrying about it is as fruitless as worrying about where the snow line on a mountain will be during the next storm. It will be obvious when it occurs; there isn't anything that can be done about it except prepare; and there is plenty of mountain for everybody on both sides of the line. It is time for us to move down the mountain to the ranks of management. As change affects the board, so it also affects management. Some change comes laterally to management and some comes downhill from the board. It is our task to meld the two kinds of change into a cohesive plan for the future.

Management cannot be effective in the future on an ad hoc basis. "Be prepared" is more than the Boy Scout motto. It is good business sense. The first step requires preparing the people to face the future. This includes defining job functions correctly, establishing the proper corporate organization, developing and planning career paths, and making the right personnel assignments.

New Positions

New times call for new jobs. Each new demand on the corporation can be traced through to new functions that it creates within the corporation. For example, the increased role of government has spawned corporate jobs that essentially involve only dealing with the government. Many corporations maintain offices in Washington, D.C., for this

80

purpose. Lobbyists are on the payroll, often exclusively, sometimes shared with other companies. Some managers have responsibility for government liaison on specific issues. All major government contractors have ongoing communication with their contracting agencies. The companies work on both existing and potential contracts. They also stay in touch with their legislative representatives and the committees that affect them, including the committee staffs, who are often the power behind the throne. Because of their extensive experience, the defense contractors often do this better than anyone else (except perhaps the special interest groups and other non-corporate bodies that also are trying to influence the government). They focus on three things: a formal presence in government offices, frequent contact, and a structured, well-disciplined approach to dealing with government officials. The assault on the government's coffers is organized and directed with military precision. Not surprising, given the people's backgrounds and those with whom they deal, but it works. These companies are a model for how to deal with the government.

The professional service firms (attorneys and so forth) with clients who interact with the government also maintain Washington offices. They have their own staff of experts with ties into the government. Smart companies take advantage of both their expertise and their contacts. Of the two, the contacts are the more important. Knowing where to go can be essential. And doing business with friends is always easier.

State governments, of course, can't be neglected. California and New York are larger than many countries. They can be attacked in much the same way as the Feds. Smaller states may not have the horsepower, but they have something else—a close-knit family atmosphere. You really can be shut out in smaller states if you don't know the right person.

Dealing with government is one of the new realities that change job descriptions. What others are there? Public relations has changed dramatically since the entry of the corporation into public life. Companies have hired professional press agents. They are learning how to apply makeup to hide blemishes, how to behave on stage, and which side looks better to the camera. The PR person is no longer a washout from a newspaper or the advertising business. In fact, the title has changed along with the status, with many companies calling their position corporate communications or external affairs. The position is usually a vice-presidency, but that's nothing new—it always was, to impress the people being spoken to. What's new is that the job has really grown up to true vice-presidential level. Communication with the outside world has become very important. Companies not only want people in these positions who won't drop the ball, they want help from them in coaching other executives who are appearing more and more in public, voluntarily or otherwise, for example, as an invited witness at a Senate hearing. Companies are running training programs on going public and using outside firms to assist in such endeavors.

Public Interest Managers

Public interest issues are creating jobs of their own. Using the concept that the best approach is a direct approach, companies are sweeping all responsibilities related to an issue under one individual or function. They give the function broad powers in dealing with external bodies and internal company departments. A steel company may have a pollution control officer, for example, who deals with government agencies, the news media, and internal engineering and manufacturing functions. Some of these positions will fade away as public opinion changes or problems are permanently corrected. Others will remain as a way of life. Allied Corporation, one of the largest chemical producers, has a vice-president of environmental affairs at the corporate level and a director at appropriate divisions. Other chemical concerns, including Monsanto and parts of W. R. Grace, also have highly placed environmental officials. The people typically are involved in everything from diagnostic reviews to cleanup operations after an accident. The companies' continued battles with environmentalists indicate that there are still areas of disagreement, but the new jobs are a step in the right direction. If your company is facing important public interest issues, perhaps you need a public interest manager.

Executive Specialists

Jobs are changing in other ways, too. It used to be that there wasn't room on the executive floor for the technical specialist. There were plenty of executives who had started their careers in technical positions, and there were a few members of top management who were still fairly competent technically in the design of their products. But the latter were rare, and their counterparts, technicians in areas other than engineering, were confined to lower-level positions. Then the world started getting very complicated and very competitive. Technical executives are still far from common, but their names are going on more office doors every day. They are not displacing other executives. They are supplementing them. In many cases their management skills are barely passable—it's hard to be all things to all people. What they bring to the party is needed knowledge and expertise in technical areas.

The needs are not the same for all companies. Executive marketing specialists may be required for the company to react to changing customer desires. Achieving acceptable levels of quality has been difficult for many companies. (Later we will discuss solutions to this problem in some depth.) Commitment to raising quality levels can be demonstrated by placing a quality specialist at the highest echelons of the corporation. General Motors has recently done this. Whether GM actually can improve the quality of the products is another question. What's important here is that the problem is highly visible.

Another new kind of executive specialist is the operations expert. In every company there are aspects of internal operations that are critical to the success of the company. Traditionally, companies have had one or two senior operations executives who oversee many operating functions, for example, manufacturing, distribution or store operations for a retailer, or back office operations for a bank. This is not likely to change. However, we will see subsets of operations being elevated in importance out of proportion to their organizational equivalents. Certain departments will be recognized as important for cost control, or as the critical link in the production chain, or as vital in some other way. Their selection will not always be obvious. Regarding cost control, for example, the critical department probably will not be the one with the largest costs. It instead will be the one where excessive costs could do the most damage or where cost reduction most likely can be achieved. Logistics costs are a prime example. Rising transportation costs and the 1980 deregulation legislation have created both the incentive and the means to control transportation costs. Some companies have created high-level transportation executives. General Electric is one that has discovered the person more than justifies the $75,000 salary.

The energy specialist is a mixture of technical specialist and operations specialist. No one needs to be told that energy conservation is important. Planning, conservation, acquisition, and other aspects of energy management have become high level concerns at many companies, leading to high level positions. R. J. Reynolds, for one, created a full-time position of energy manager for the corporation.

Specialists in administrative areas also will prevail. In some companies this may be the personnel function, which has grown up to be Employee Administration or something similar. The laws and regulations governing the function have become quite complex. Fulfilling both the company's needs for the right people and employees' frequently expressed needs for the right job has become a challenging and frustrating proposition. The person who can do this well will have a high-level job. Another example is the data processing function, now called information services or the like. Many companies, such as Lockheed, have already made this position a vice-presidential one, and the trend will continue so long as companies require central information processing and planning functions. Most incumbents in these positions will have technical backgrounds and be expected to contribute technical expertise to the management of the corporation in the context of top management-level discussions. They will take their place alongside such other departments as finance and marketing, long recognized as key functions.

In summary, the executive specialist is not a new concept, but we are going to see more of such individuals. Rabbit-like proliferation is not likely, because there will not be dozens of critical specialties in each corporation (although across the whole of corporate society, dozens will pop up). But there will be several in each company to assist in permanently altering the organization chart.

A variation on this theme is a traditional executive function that has a larger technical component than in the past. "Technical" does not necessarily mean computerized. It means specialized. It means that general management knowledge and experience will not in itself suffice. Such knowledge and experience is invaluable, but it has to be combined with a detailed knowledge of a subject area. Planning is such an area. Practical experience and technical knowledge both are essential. We will see more and more examples of companies placing all strategic planning responsibilities under a senior corporate executive possessing the requisite skills. Xerox calls their position vice-president and chief strategy officer. No matter what the title or the specific function, the future will hold more of the same—executive positions requiring more technical strength at senior levels for key activities.

One final idea here, one that perhaps is not really an executive specialty. Except that I happen to think it is. It goes by the name of Futurism. It is not astrology, and you are not likely to see its practitioners on the cover of the *National Enquirer*. It is a serious endeavor. The objective is to make an informed guess about what the future will hold. It is multi-disciplinary, drawing on data from every segment of society and the company. The information can be very useful in strategic planning. The essence of futurism is the absence of straight-line extrapolation from the present. Anybody can do that. The trick is to identify key trends or to see the truly new things that are going to happen—the next color television or airplane or political event like the oil embargo. We are not talking about extra-sensory perception, so no single individual is going to be right all the time. Companies are experimenting with futurists, however. John Naisbitt, an entrepreneur, established a trend identification firm in 1973. ARCO has an internal group called issues managers. I think we'll see more of firms and of individuals specializing in futurism. Their impact will be gradual. The futurists don't seem to fit the business mold, in appearance or thought patterns, but the good ones are hard-headed realists in addition to being bright and perceptive. One of these days they'll foresee the next transistor and gain a lot of publicity. Then every corporation will have one.

Unconventional Approaches to Organization

The new jobs and functions discussed above are going to make a lot of difference in the corporations of the future. But the individuals in these jobs are going to need a way to work together to improve their and the company's effectiveness. A planned method of working together is called organization. We are going to examine some new kinds of organization.

Organizational effectiveness certainly sounds like a worthy objective. It rolls nicely off the tongue. What does it mean? It means bringing the right skills to bear on a problem. Putting in the right people at the right time. It means accountability for activities—unambiguous responsibilities. It requires a measurement system, or at least the capacity for one. The measurement system only has to be facilitated by the organization; it need not be part of it. And, of course, results. Organizational effectiveness means results.

The criteria sound like they could be applied equally well to a military unit. Not surprisingly, the military model of management organization is the most popular today in U.S. business. When corporations started taking hold in this country, the military had been around for centuries with an effective organization using a hierarchy of line officers supported by staff functions. Corporations borrowed both the concept and the terminology. The terms line and staff are still used to denote the differences between operating (in the military, combat) functions and support services. The military model was and is psychologically appealing, the more so as you move higher up the organization. It is predicated on a hierarchy in which subordinates take orders unhesitatingly from superiors. This fit the autocratic style of the entrepreneurial founders of many corporations. It lives on today because giving orders is a lot easier for many managers than rationally explaining a course of action to those who must carry it out. Very few companies operate under combat conditions of urgency for which the military model of quick unquestioning obedience was developed, but this point seems to have been overlooked by many managers.

These are alternatives to the hierarchical military model. One that we will see more of in the future involves increased and more sophisticated use of staff services. Managers in line positions will draw on improved analytical resources to provide them with better information for decision making. Some of these resources will be found in the executive specialists that we just discussed. Others will be traditional support departments, such as financial analysis, operating with a broader charter and better tools, such as personal computers. Line departments may employ staff people such as operations analysts.

Certain staff functions always have been viewed as organizational equals of the line departments; they were staff only because they weren't directly involved with the product or service of the company. The finance function is perhaps the best known of these. We can expect elements of such functions, perhaps the accounting or controllership function, to play a stronger role in many companies. This is an outgrowth of the need for better information, better procedures, better people, etc., for performance of the line functions. The line functions that have to be performed are not going to change very much over time. Companies will be competitive by changing how the functions are performed and the staff support they receive. The improved use of staff, then, is hardly a choice; it's a necessity.

Matrix Management

Of course, there are some other ways to mold the same clay. Matrix management is perhaps the opposite of the military model. Rather than patching the military model with staff until the original line structure is unrecognizable, many companies would do well to take a look at something fundamentally different. Patching an organization is no different from patching rust spots on an automobile. When it's required continuously, there are some problems under the surface. Matrix management is not a super-staff organization. But it may be worth considering for companies that can't seem to stop the organizational rust with staff patches.

Matrix management, like all great ideas, was born when someone realized that in certain situations theory was fatally inconsistent with reality. The someone was the aerospace industry several decades ago. Their reality was that 99-$\frac{44}{100}$ percent of their business was project-oriented. They were making mostly tangible products, e.g., missiles and aircraft. They had some research assignments. Everything they did had a starting point and an ending point with a fixed product in between. Contracts were signed for, let's say, 100 aircraft to be delivered over a specified 36-month period. They had several contracts going at any one time and had to manage all of them. A perfect project-management environment? Perfect for a project-oriented management organization as is used in construction projects? No—for the following reason. Unlike construction projects, which take place at separate and independent sites, many production-type functions were shared by the aircraft programs. It would have been prohibitively expensive to build a separate factory with duplicate equipment for each aircraft program. They had to share facilities.

Separate programs (aerospace terminology) or projects sharing common functional areas. Organization theorists could have spent a lot of time and several research grants sweating over this problem. The aerospace company leaders simply appointed program managers to go along with their functional managers. The functional managers continued to manage their functional areas such as accounting, fabrication, and the other shared areas. The program managers watched over their programs as they progressed through the functional areas. Every person who was not a program or functional manager had two bosses (Figure 6–1). Matrix management of this sort was a simple and direct approach that violated many tenets of organization. But it worked— actually for the very reason that theorists thought it would not work. The major argument against the matrix was the two-boss concept. But it's normal in life to be responding to conflicting demands. The military model is actually the unnatural approach. People thrived in the matrix environment as long as they weren't measured by non-matrix standards, i.e., by the standards of only one of the bosses.

Why will we see more of the matrix in the future? Because of its ability to accommodate change. A program or project in the matrix can be a product or service of the company. It can also be an important customer or anything else that should be tracked separately. Functional areas can be run by their managers for maximum efficiency. Program managers can be provided with staff assistance appropriate for the specifics of their programs. Functional requirements—staffing, equipment, budget—can be determined by consulting the program managers. Best of all, when programs are born, die, or change, the organization automatically reacts in the right way. Change is no longer an external influence to be fought. Instead, change, manifested in the life cycle of programs, is baked into the organization.

When is the matrix not appropriate? When the two dimensions— programs and functions—really do not need to be in balance. In 1982, for example, Texas Instruments revamped its matrix organization. The functional efficiences had become much less important than the management planning and control for specific programs and products. So,

Figure 6–1
Matrix Management

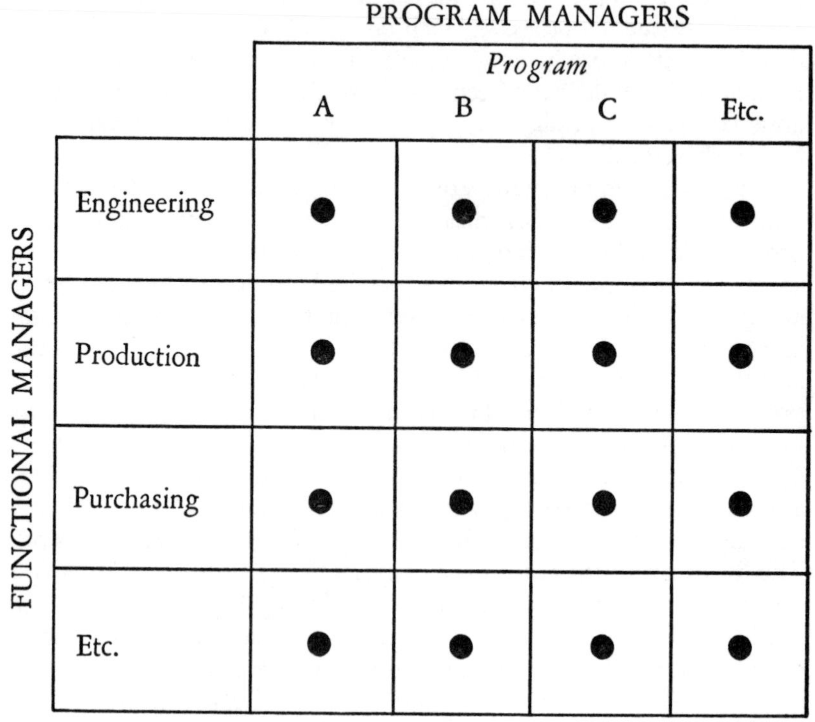

PROGRAM MANAGERS

| | | *Program* | | |
	A	B	C	Etc.
Engineering	●	●	●	●
Production	●	●	●	●
Purchasing	●	●	●	●
Etc.	●	●	●	●

FUNCTIONAL MANAGERS

● Employee with two bosses—Functional Manager and
Program Manager

after almost ten years of matrix management, TI significantly reduced the functional responsibilities of the matrix and strengthened the program units called PCCs (product customer centers).

No new idea will gain overnight popularity, and this is true for the matrix approach. However, we would have cause to worry if no firm outside the aerospace industry had adopted it. We might have missed something that made its application unique to aerospace. That hasn't been true. We've already discussed Texas Instruments. Companies like General Electric and Citibank also have implemented matrix approaches successfully. The incidence of its use is still too low to be called a trend, but the demands of the future are such that this will change. Either that, or companies will skip the conventional matrix and go right to the next form of organization, which we'll discuss next.

The Ultimate Matrix

There are two dimensions to the matrix organization, and its stability depends on both of them. In the normal matrix, change is slow and confined to the program dimension. The functional dimension may evolve over some period of time, perhaps even adding or deleting functions, but wholesale change is not part of the rules. If both dimensions are changing rapidly, the whole thing dissolves into anarchy. If you have such an environment where stable functional areas cannot be depended on to exist in a support role over a long period of time, then you are approaching a need for task force management. A task force is an organizational entity that has the program characteristics of transience, but requires specialized skills that are not found in the functional areas or need to be controlled so tightly that the functional control must give way. The task force manager becomes the dominant or sole manager, building the team that is required for the project. When the project is completed, the team dissolves and returns to functional areas or moves on to other task force assignments. In *Future Shock,* Alvin Toffler coined the term "adhocracy" to describe a business operated on the basis of transient task forces. The closest that we come to it in today's world is the construction industry consisting of many separate projects. However, the projects all are basically the same, whereas in its element, task force management can deal with a variety of problems. It has been used sparingly in this country by business, although such government agencies as NASA have found it to be very effective. Where it has been tried in business, it has been effective. New products have been conceived and brought successfully to market through task force management, for example, Litton's microwave oven. Texas Instruments, as it evolves from pure matrix management, is going to try this approach in a limited fashion for its product research program. As the world continues to change and the pace of change increases in many industries, task force management will be attempted more frequently. It will eventually take its place alongside other organization approaches, as a legitimate tool to be used in the right circumstances.

New Structures

The new approaches to organization that we have been discussing provide a skeletal framework for the company. Specific organization structures are needed to put some meat on the bones. Many aspects of the organization of the future will be the same as they are now. Companies always will need accounting departments, whether they exist in a traditional hierarchical organization, program-oriented matrix organization, or a transient task force organization. There will always be an accounting manager. The same is true for the other key functional elements of a business. The building blocks remain the same, although they can be arranged in a variety of ways.

The future will show us some interesting new arrangements of the blocks. One particularly interesting arrangement is a synergistic combination of the top blocks of a corporation into an office of the president or an office of the chairman. The top functions have become so complex that one person rarely is able to master the critical elements of strategy, operations, and finance. This is normally dealt with by ensuring that top-flight people hold the posts of chairman, chief executive officer, president or chief operating officer, chief financial officer, executive vice-presidents, and heads of operating divisions. The tasks are thereby mastered, with the tradeoff that the functions are splintered among a number of people, creating a need for informal coordination. The coordination is effective in some companies and less so at others. In addition, informal coordination has a drawback of leaving people somewhat uncertain of where they stand. Cliques tend to form with no legitimacy attached to them by the organization chart.

The office of the chairman takes care of these problems by requiring formal interaction. The key senior executives, whose titles normally don't change, are assigned to the office of the chairman or of the president. Duties can be shared and coordination more easily achieved through the formalization of working together. Only people who work well together are asked to do so, so the clique problem is solved by admitting to it. Top management infighting and scrambling for promotions to the top spot are also reduced because the lines of succession are clearer. The few people in the office of the chairman have the best shot at the top, and the people beneath them now have a new goal to strive for. The more goals, the less fighting over them.

The office of the chairman is not for everybody. In some companies one or two individuals really can do the top job all by themselves. In others, the informal coordination works. In still others, the top people are afraid of relinquishing authority. But some corporations have opted for the structure. Avon Products decided to do their calling with a three-person office of the chairman. GAF Corporation created a seven-person office of the chairman to include virtually all senior executives. Penney's has four people in their office of the chairman—the chairman, vice-chairman, chief financial officer, and vice-president of merchandising. They also have a fourteen-person management committee that assists in making key decisions.

The complexity and importance of the new issues driving the corporation affect the levels of other jobs besides the top ones. We touched briefly on this point during our discussion of executive specialists, but let's emphasize it here. Additional senior positions, usually vice-presidential level, are being created. This creates "span of control" problems. The span of control of any one individual varies, but more than six or seven people reporting directly to another person becomes burdensome and inefficient. The office of the chairman can help with this problem. Whereas one chairman can handle, let's say, seven executives, an office of the chairman consisting of three people can handle twenty-one executives, which is a lot of vice-presidents. Such structures will help to cope with the proliferation of vice-presidential positions. For the same reason we will see the very senior executives taking on general titles so as to expand the kind of positions that can report to them without looking funny. Functions that would appear illogical under a vice-president—finance look fine under a vice-president—administration or simply an executive vice-president. This title creep is real, but it's usually based on a true need to develop better structures, not on executive emotions.

Middle Management Changes

A similar phenomenon has occurred with business units of a corporation. In the 1960s and 1970s corporations began pushing profit-and-loss responsibility further down into the organization. Product lines that once were consolidated under one management team became separate divisions with their own management. Growth contributed to this situation. New divisions were established for new product lines or markets, then were continued when they were successful rather than folded into other divisions. Acquisitions were left to operate as independent divisions. International expansion created more divisions. For tax and other reasons, a subsidiary was formed for each country; in many countries, two or more (split by marketing and manufacturing, or some other way) were created. The subsidiaries had their own management.

Companies with twenty or more divisions became commonplace. How do you manage twenty or more divisions, each with its own president? You create another layer of management between the divisions and the parent company. Each person in the new layer watches over several of the divisions, maybe a few large divisions or a larger number of smaller divisions. The divisions are grouped in some logical manner, perhaps by product, e.g., chemicals, or geography, or customer socio-economic level (department store groups). The most common name for the groups of divisions is "groups," and the heads of the groups are called group executives. General Electric invented the term Strategic Business Units for their top-level groups, and the terminology is starting to catch on. Whatever it's called, it's popular—over 60 percent of the Fortune 500 use the group structure.[1]

The primary advantage of the group structure is its obvious necessity in maintaining a reasonable span of control for executives. The disadvantages in theory are few; in practice, many. If improperly implemented, the group level of management does very little. The operating decisions are in the divisions where they would have been anyway, but the strategic decisions are placed at the corporate level. Very few benefits are derived, and good management talent in the group executives is wasted.

However, when correctly implemented, the group is more than the sum of its parts. Most financial and operating decisions can be made at the group level. Strategic direction can be determined at the group level, to be coordinated with other groups. The division heads just do not have all the authority they would as heads of independent companies. Attempting to perpetuate the image that division heads are mini-CEOs has caused much of the problem with divisions in group structures. They are not, any more than the group executives have full autonomy. What is important is that in some areas the division heads do have essentially complete authority. The division executives need to have areas that they are responsible for with little second-guessing by the group and corporate parent. As long as the number of such areas is reasonable and it increases up the executive ladder (i.e., a group executive has more such freedom than a division head), most executives will not be concerned with the few areas in which they do not have total control. The ones who are concerned ought to find a smaller company in which they can be chairman or CEO.

What does the future hold? We will see better implementation of the group structure. We will also see the principle of individual authority carried to lower and lower levels in corporations. The principle is not different at worker level than at executive level. The people who function well with responsibility and authority should be given some, carefully carved out to provide areas of autonomy. The areas will be smaller as you move down the ladder, but that's all right. The arrangement is not for all people, and it should not be imposed blindly. However, it can be successful, even within relatively small environments such as a simple manufacturing plant. A plant can be organized, for example, along product lines with each product line having engineering, production, financial, and other functions to support it. Each product group can have its own profit and loss statement. Both Burroughs Corporation and General Motors have used this approach, with a half dozen or more groups per plant.

Career Paths for the Future

We have moved around a lot of the traditional blocks in designing our new organization structures, or at least in highlighting some of the important changes that the future will be imposing on us. Individuals have very personal needs to understand how the new structures relate to them. Their career paths depend on such understanding. Trying to operate without it would be like trying to drive across the country on the interstate highway system by using a 1937 road map.

Career paths have changed in two ways. One is the plethora of careers. The new variety of top-level executive positions will provide career paths throughout the organization. There no longer will be a narrow neck in the bottle through which all top management aspirants have to pass. An engineering career or quality control or environmental interests do not have to be abandoned to reach the executive floors. An analytical person who is neither very good at line management nor very interested in it can do quite well in a top staff position. People with low boredom thresholds can seek out companies that have chosen to implement matrix management or task force management, where their jobs and exposures change frequently.

The career broadening naturally will affect educational backgrounds. There will be less dominance by a few fields. Some of the corporation's new responsibilities will be best handled by people with liberal arts and political science degrees, which are currently about as popular in corporations as copies of *Das Kapital* on manager's bookshelves. Technical degrees always have been popular, but in the last two decades primarily as undergraduate degrees followed by MBA degrees. The usefulness of a business education is difficult to deny, especially at executive levels, but the overwhelming emphasis on the MBA has about run its course. There will be a re-emergence of technical backgrounds. Occasionally we will see such signs of the times as attorneys in the chairman's office. Irving Shapiro, an attorney, was elected chairman and CEO of DuPont, a chemical company. That would not have happened a generation ago.

Mark Twain said, "It is difference of opinion that makes horse races." As DuPont needed a leader with a legal background, so other companies may need something different. Some may need a very broad person, who knows a little about a lot of things. Such a person would fit in an environment which had a balance of concerns facing it instead of one or two critical concerns. Companies change with the times, and requirements for leaders change. Nabisco had four different types of people in charge from 1945 to 1980. The first three were specialists, in production, marketing, and finance. The company by then had expanded into a broad spectrum of markets, modernized production facilities, and put its financial house in order. They still faced a number of challenges, but no one thing was likely to be their undoing. The subsequent chairman of the board had broad experience in a number of areas, since the breadth appeared to be what was called for.

In summary, careers are going to be more varied than in the past. From the courses taken in school to the position that a person retires from, he or she will have had opportunities for unparalleled variety. Careers must be helped along, to work for both the employee's and company's advantage. Unfortunately, extensive career planning never has worked and probably never will. You can't feed facts about a person and his or her background into the corporate computer and get in return a career profile for the next twenty years. People have an inability to be reduced to numbers. They change over time; the company changes; and the rest of the world changes. Companies can, however, put into place a system or process that allows people to move wherever and however is best for them and the company. Part of the system is starting with the right base—encouraging the different educational and work backgrounds that will contribute best to the company's future. Another part is providing appropriate assignments and rotation out of them for high achievers or persons who turn out not to fit the assignments. Managers can be evaluated on how well they develop subordinates. Congruency of goals is important. If the employee and the company have conflicting goals, then in the long run neither will be happy. The goal message isn't easily conveyed, and at times positively incorrect goals can be accidentally communicated. Let's take one common error: measuring achievement by short-term operating results and rewarding successful persons with promotions to new jobs. The individuals eventually reach lofty positions where the future of all or a part of the organization is in their hands, but all they know how to do is produce immediate results. Worse yet, they've always been rewarded for sacrificing the future to the short term. It's no surprise at all that many of them fail. They sometimes fail while producing spectacular quarterly profits. Eventually, of course, the corporate organism is too sick to be squeezed for more profits. By then, things are in very bad shape and usually a major turnaround effort with wholesale management changes is in order. When this happens, it is only partly the fault of the individuals. Most of the blame lies with the people who established the career progression and reward systems.

Some firms handle career planning well. Jewel Companies, the $4-billion retailer based in Chicago, does most of the good things described in the previous paragraph. Financial success has been one result. Another result has been a cadre of young top management. At the very top, the veterans have a history of moving out before normal retirement age. The most recent CEO retired at age 52. He has gone on to another career as a director of a dozen other corporations and foundations. Jewel tries very hard to keep people interested in their jobs and part of that is keeping opportunities available. When even the CEO has a career path planned for himself, you know the matter is taken seriously.

We have a good idea by now of the corporation's new responsibilities, how to attack them, and how the management team can be structured. But there are also other things to worry about. One of them is the changing nature of products and services and the companies that provide them, e.g., the emergence of high technology companies. Dealing with these changes is an essential part of the modern manager's responsibilities. The next section discusses how success can be achieved.

Adjusting to Changed Environments

"Each age is a dream that is dying, or one that is coming to birth."
—O'SHAUGHNESSY

Chapter 7

Shifting Foundations of Industry

IT WAS FUNNY when it began. Cheap—and inexpensive—Japanese products for the U.S. consumer. Jokes about the products being made from American beer cans. But people bought the products because they were a decent value for the low price. I remember riding around Los Angeles in the late 1960s in a business associate's new Toyota Corolla. The car was small, boxy, and generally unlike anything made in the U.S. But it was built well, reliable, and miserly with a gallon of gas. My friend had never before had a foreign automobile, but she swore she was never going back to U.S. cars. She was not alone in California—even then imports had 20 percent of the market.

The impact of foreign manufacturers has been profound and lasting. A permanent shift in the industrial foundation of the world has taken place. In this chapter we are going to describe a few such shifts and explore some theories for the occurrence of the shifts. Then we will discuss the management problems created for specific victims of the shift, the steel and rubber industries. We will see how to overcome the problems, or at least to survive the effect of them. This will lead us into understanding some fundamental rules for succeeding in business under tough conditions.

The Changes

In the last quarter century, autos and other consumer products were appearing with "Made in Japan" labels on them. Some basic industrial products also started appearing in volume from overseas producers. The German steel industry essentially was rebuilt after World War II. It was out-producing the U.S. steelmakers. Textiles and downstream apparel manufacturing were in a dozen countries, all producing for the U.S. market. Developing nations discovered that mining was an ideal use of low-paid unskilled labor, of which they had plenty and the U.S. had little. The commodity chemical industry, which in many cases simply refines natural deposits of chemicals that are mined from the ground, underwent a similar fate.

Within U.S. industry some equally momentous things were happening. The corner grocery store was disappearing under the onslaught of the supermarket chains. Consolidation and shakeout were two names for the same game, the game in which the number of companies in an industry shrunk from dozens or hundreds to only a few. Technological advances made their mark. The impact of the transistor, invented by Bell Labs, was felt across the nation as the vacuum tube industry was permanently short-circuited.

While all this was going on, little attention was paid by the public, academia, or even business, except as they were directly and personally affected. It was left to the next generation to discern a pattern in the shifts in our industry and that of our counterparts on foreign shores.

The pattern provides a very persuasive view of the world. In its unadorned version, it and the logic behind it are as follows. Effective competition requires competitive pricing, which requires low costs. Foreign producers in many cases had lower labor costs than the U.S. In other cases they had newer equipment that could produce more goods at lower cost. Their equipment was new after WWII, replacing destroyed equipment, often paid for with U.S. assistance. Foreign producers were also subsidized in many ways by their governments. In the U.S., things were different. Achievement of low costs came through economies of scale. Big was better. Only industrial giants could create the volume to drive costs and prices down. Only they could make the large profits required to develop and harness new technology. Consequently, the only U.S. companies to survive were large ones that were not vulnerable to the specific advantages that favored foreign firms.

This pattern is still the conventional wisdom to explain the ill health and demise of some U.S. industries and the robust success of others. It is quite self-serving, but it is also clearly based on common sense and immutable laws of economics. Is it correct? Let's answer the question by reviewing some other theories that take a much broader view of events. They do not so much support or invalidate the conventional wisdom as they provide a fundamental model explaining why the conclusions of the conventional wisdom, if not the reasoning, may be sound. The theories raise the issue of life cycles of industries and the societies that they support.

The Nature of Industrial Economies

Do fundamental laws govern entire economies over long periods of time? A Russian economist named Kondratieff thought so. In 1926 he observed that economic activity over the previous 150 years had occurred in three waves that crested in 1814, 1873, and 1920. The cycle between crests, which consisted of economic deterioration until a trough was reached followed by growth to the next peak, lasted fifty or sixty years. He virtually predicted economic decline in the late 1920s and 1930s, to be followed again by a period of prosperity. The Great Depression and subsequent post-WWII economic growth have brought attention to Kondratieff's analyses.

Kondratieff was a better data gatherer than theoretician. He really didn't have any ideas about why the waves occurred as they did. Harvard economist Joseph Schumpeter thought Kondratieff was onto something and explained the waves in terms of industrial innovation. Innovation leads to prosperity until the innovation matures and stagnates. Great innovations like the railroad system powered each of the three waves observed by Kondratieff. Jay Forrester of the Massachusetts Institute of Technology has built computer models of industrial economies which unintentionally (i.e., as a by-product, not a planned part of the model) generated Kondratieff-like waves of approximately forty-five to sixty years duration. His analysis of the behavior led him to conclude that waves are geared to new ideas and subsequent capital investment. During the upward swing of a wave, capital investment increases and, in fact, fuels the rest of the economy. In the latter years of an upswing, capital investment becomes excessive as the "me-too" approach continues beyond the rational point. Eventually the brakes are applied after excess industrial capacity has been put in place. The shock causes a recession that continues right on into a depression as people react to the recession by pulling their horns in further. The economy goes into a tailspin because there is no force to introduce new types of capital expenditures and get it back on track. Eventually, there is a need for new capital investment and an acceptance of new ideas, so the cycle begins anew. Interestingly enough, although his explanations differ from those of Schumpeter, the timing of Forrester's cycles is the same. He sees the 1980s as potentially the peak of a wave or the start of a decline, unless something is done to halt the cycle. This timing applies primarily to the United States and its partners in the current stage of development. Other countries may well be in different parts of the cycle, which helps to explain why certain of their industries are thriving while the same industries in the U.S. are gasping for breath.

There is quite a bit of controversy about the Kondratieff waves or long waves, as they are also called. Many economists dismiss the patterns of upswings and downswings as statistical aberrations. They argue that technology, management styles, and other factors have changed so much in two hundred years that a fixed cycle is laughable. The counterargument is that people drive the basic cycles in history, and people are famous for repeating the mistakes of previous generations. It is no accident that the upswing and downswing periods of the waves each coincide with approximately the span between human generations.

Some Confirming Facts About Cycles

An ounce of facts is worth a pound of theory. In an economy as large as ours, there ought to be some facts regarding cycles. What kind of facts would we be looking for? Something to indicate growing or maturing industries, possibly. Some data that indicated diminishing returns from maturing or dying industries and accelerated benefits from growing industries.

Such data exists. Consider a group of industries that once were the backbone of the U.S. economy: automobiles, steel, rubber, basic chemicals, textiles, mining, and the like. For the last ten years, their capital investment growth rate actually has been about twice the average for all industries.[1] But growth rates in both profits and output not only were below the average for all industries over the same time period but actually declined. There are many reasons for this. Automakers and steelmakers would claim that their capital expenditures for safety and pollution controls are a drag on returns. However, certainly a large part of the investment must be for useful things. And not all U.S. managers in these industries can be incompetent. Could it be that the U.S. manufacturers are in an unfavorable part of their cycles?

Consider a group of technology-driven industries: electonics, computers, aerospace, communication equipment, etc. Their investment rates over the last ten years was half again, i.e., 150 percent, of the old basic industries' and about three times the average for all industries.[2] Their output growth rates were five times the average of all industries, while the growth rate of the basic industries was negative. Quite a contrast! Just better managers? Not likely—the business climate probably helped. These companies are in the growth part of their cycles.

Cycles: A Summary

Does it matter who is right? Whether or not long waves exist? Yes and no. By that I mean that the key is understanding the facts and arguments, not the conclusions. The discipline that is forced upon us by the long-wave theories is to think in fifty-year time frames. If we do that, we probably will come to some interesting conclusions. For example, industries have a life cycle of growth, maturity, and death. There may be mini-cycles of regeneration within the main cycle. Industries are linked to other industries, as leaders or followers. Their fortunes move in lock step; their management decisions do too. Auto industry capital investment will lead to steel industry capital investment, as sure as night follows day. If we understand where we are in the life cycle of an industry, we can do a much better job of managing. If we look at a number of industries, we can estimate overall economic performance. We can gauge, for example, whether the economy overall is going through major upheaval or moving smoothly in a certain direction. We can extrapolate downward to the effects on our own companies, for instance, on the availability of venture capital in light of the needs of other companies in society. This long wave or Kondratieff-type thinking hardly binds us to the deterministic conclusions of the devotees of the theories, but it should help us deal better with our own situations.

We are going to look into some aspects of managing in different stages of life cycles. Before we do, however, let's spend a little time on some topics that are political in nature but deeply affect all businesses. Over the last decade they have had at least as much to do with the shifts in business activities as the long wave or any other economic theories.

The Oil Problem

The Arabs really got our attention in 1974 and they seem intent on keeping it. The oil embargo and subsequent periodic shortages have caused a number of economic and political distortions. The politics are beyond the scope of this book, except in one very important way. The sooner we all learn to live with the oil situation, the better off we will be. Living with it is primarily an economic adjustment. Since U.S. business is the main contributor to our success or failure in this regard, management skills are, perhaps unfortunately, related to the oil situation.

The oil problem often is referred to as the energy problem. And, in many ways it is. However, in some other respects it has to do strictly with oil. That, after all, is the commodity that currently the industrial world cannot do without but that is not under their control. The pumpers of the oil hold all the aces. Industrial power also has come to the companies that assist the oil countries in getting their black gold out of the ground, as well as provide most of the transportation and distribution mechanisms to put the oil into the tanks of the users.

Time for some statistics. In 1981, eight of the ten largest industrial companies in the world were oil companies—names like Exxon, Shell, Mobil, Texaco—the friendly neighborhood gasoline stations. Twenty of the largest fifty were oil companies. More than one-half of the top fifty's annual sales (over 650 billion dollars) was in the hands of the oil companies.[3] But, you say, that's because the prices from their suppliers are so high and they simply are passing the costs along after adding a reasonable profit. There is no point in arguing over what is reasonable, but here are some facts. In 1981, 40 percent—almost half—of the total profits of all the top fifty companies in the world came from the eight oil companies that were in the top ten. Eight companies—16 percent of fifty—produced 40 percent of the profits.[4] In 1982, six of the top ten largest industrial companies in the U.S. were oil companies (not even including DuPont/Conoco). They had almost 30 percent of the profits of all the fifty largest companies. Six of the fifty—12 percent—produced 30 percent of the profits.

There are, of course, many ways to measure profits. How about return on equity? Returns above 20 percent have become common in the oil industry. The truly huge international oil companies are a bit sensitive about profits and have kept their returns slightly below 20 percent, but they've done a lot better than you and I have in our savings accounts. And not over short periods; these numbers hold over five or more years. (Returns declined in 1982—so did inflation—but still were better than most of U.S. business'.) The point here is not that the profits are too high; I know how to measure only numbers, not moral values. But the amount of money being taken in by the oil companies and redistributed as they use their profits is staggering and has led to some restructuring of business in this country and others.

Before pursuing that point, let's talk about the oil-producing countries. The primary inflow of money has been to them. The Arabs mostly, but also Mexico, Venezuela and some others. Most of the money has gone right back out again as the countries have attempted to make life better for their citizens and to build economies that will survive when the only thing left under the desert floor is rock. Their needs have taxed the resources of even the largest companies. They need roads, airports, power plants, telephones, utilities, banking systems—

you name it. Instant affluence. The jury is still out on whether a country can leapfrog centuries technologically and survive the social and cultural adjustments. But they're trying and in the process are altering the business structure of the world. The companies that can support them get rich and big and play the tune for the others to dance. There are some disturbing implications in this for the U.S. Much of U.S. business sells products and services oriented toward a very different style of living than exists in the oil countries. Except for such companies as Bechtel and ITT that have always operated extensively in numerous countries at various economic levels, we often are not qualified to provide the goods and services needed in the oil countries. U.S. businesses are having to fight hard for every victory, and it is likely that this will continue. Success comes only to those who carve out a niche for their products or who modify their products to fit the different environments. As a nation we do the former far better than the latter. We are so accustomed to being and having the best that it is difficult to accept modifying products to suit someone else. If we are going to be big players in the oil countries, this will have to change. We will need to accept that the environments are different but not necessarily backward. "The customer is always right" will have to reappear as a meaningful slogan.

While other countries are scrambling to supply them, the oil countries are building their own industries. Their banks already are drawing significant amounts of funds away from other institutions. Their airlines are competition for our airlines. We will review this situation in depth later on, but it provides a sense of urgency to our industries that need to gain footholds in their countries. The sword of competition cuts both ways, and it will definitely be cutting into our industries. If we do not strike back on their territory, we will be a net loser.

Ripples in the United States

Like a stone thrown into a pond, the oil crisis has created ripples that affect people near and far from the original action. U.S. business has been changed as much or more than that of the international scene. Stripped of most of their foreign wellhead profits, the major oil companies have turned to refining and distribution for profits. Gasoline stations once were loss leaders, but no more. The companies and independent operators have found that customers are not very sensitive to a difference in price of a few cents a gallon. Overall, the big increase in prices in the last decade has altered buying habits, but at any particular time many customers do not appear to be sensitive to the few cents that are the difference to the oil companies between good profits and great profits.

The amount of money being made by the refiners and distributors of petroleum derivatives makes them natural targets for suppliers. The oil people are willing to spend money to make more money, so the combination works for both. The lesson also extends to the drilling operations in the U.S., which are mammoth and growing larger to off-set the loss of overseas operations. Suppliers of drilling technology, rigs, and other equipment recently have been in boom times, as have the providers of goods and services to the communities in which drilling is performed.

Of course, 1982 saw the collapse of the oil boom (at least relative to its previous strength) and a weakening of the oil cartel. The first half of our oil lesson was that the balance of power had shifted permanently away from the oil-consuming countries. The second half of the lesson is that the world oil situation has not yet stabilized to where oil-related economic events can be predicted with much certainty.

The point of our discussions of economic cycles and the oil business is not simply to chronicle the external forces that influence or could influence U.S. business. If we wanted to do that, we would have to add the world agriculture situation, dependence on foreign suppliers of key minerals, nuclear power, and many other issues. Rather, our point is simply to demonstrate that some fundamental forces are at work in our economy so that we can determine how to deal with them, not in a sense of specific rules, but in the sense of basic principles. Let's start with an example, then move on to the principles after we've seen them in action.

The Steel Story

The steel industry apparently has been the victim of fundamental economic changes. It is certainly a classic case of an industry in trouble. In an environment of adequate worldwide growth, the U.S. steel busi-ness has been characterized by low average returns and individual com-panies racking up annual losses in the hundreds of millions of dollars. The scenario is well known. Not only does it fit the stereotype of out-moded production facilities and management techniques compared to other countries, such as Japan, it was the model for the stereotype. We are not going to engage in additional post-mortems here. Instead we are going to look for some ways out of the mess in which the steel industry finds itself. The results should be instructive to other industries that may be worrying about the same plight.

One solution is to concentrate on a peripheral but essential part of the business. In the minds of many people, the steel business is associated with sweating men working with giant ladles of white-hot molten steel. That's the basic steelmaking process. There are several later steps, from casting through rolling to producing the finished sheet, coil, tube, bar, or wire stock. But even the finished products are not much good to anyone at that point. What can you do with a three-foot wide coil of steel that weighs a ton? Answer: somebody "slits" it and cuts it to the right length for you. The big steel companies used to do that for their customers, charging them a healthy price. Then independent businesses called steel service centers opened, buying the steel products from the mills and custom cutting them for the end users. They offered reasonable prices and immeasurably better customer service than the mills where management understood steelmaking, not customers. Earle Jorgensen built his service center business into one that earns almost 20 percent return on equity.

Another possibility is to select a single product or a limited range of products that can be produced more cheaply by themselves than as part of a full range of products. Small mills, known as mini-mills, recycle scrap steel without going through the costly basic steelmaking process. Their product range is limited, but companies have earned over 30 percent on equity with this approach. Nucor is one of them.

Do you always have to succeed through an end run? Or is there a way to be successful and still be in the mainstream? In the case of steel, can you be heavily in the basic steelmaking business and make money? Yes. Concentrating on cost control is effective. Simply keeping costs down leads to better profit margins and better prices for customers. Through this strategy Inland Steel frequently has been able to outperform such giants of the industry as U.S. Steel, who are supposed to be enjoying economies of scale. Inland's profitability (return on equity) has even been better than that of companies like Bell & Howell, which is theoretically in a much "easier" industry.

So success is possible. As we noted earlier, however, the industry overall is sick, and its return per invested dollar simply is not keeping pace with other industries. Is there hope for the industry as a whole, especially for basic steelmaking? Many companies do not think so and have been diversifying out of the steel business. Armco, once solely a steel company, now derives only a third of its sales from steel. U.S. Steel is big in chemicals and in early 1982 bought Marathon Oil Company. They clearly are giving up. (By the way, U.S. Steel's non-steel operations tend to make the profitability picture for steel look better than it really is when company averages are calculated.) Conversely, Bethlehem Steel is committed to basic steel and is backing it up with over $300 million of new capital investment in steel facilities.

The success of Bethlehem's investment moves and Inland's cost-control mentality will depend on whether they can make it through the down part of the industrial cycle. Basic steelmakers in the United States have not been able to take the big leap in technological or management advances that others, such as the Japanese, have. Instead they have made minor improvements, complained about government policies, and diversified out of steel. The innovation and risk taking that characterize young industries have not been there. Until those qualities return, the industry will continue to die, fulfilling Forrester's prediction about the behavior of mature industries. Conditions such as demand for steel and other countries' capacity will determine whether it is a slow or a fast death. But it will be death unless the companies (including the workers and their unions) can quickly change their attitude.

Where the Rubber Meets the Road

Rubber has many uses, but in the United States the rubber industry is synonymous with the tire industry. The industry has been beset by problems as severe as steel's, but of different origins (at least partially). The prolonged slump of the U.S. automobile industry has driven many tire makers to the wall. However, it is far from clear if the cure is better than the disease. In good times the auto industry is a very tough negotiator on prices. As the old quip goes, the tire makers lose a little on each tire, but make it up in volume. There is intense competition at both the wholesale and retail level. Foreign manufacturers have not been much of a threat. Michelin, Pirelli and others threw a real scare into U.S. rubber companies when the radial tire fad first hit, but the U.S. makers bounced back nicely with competitive products. The real problem with the foreigners is that they exacerbate a bad situation; the U.S. manufacturers can ill afford to lose any market share to them, no matter how little.

The bottom line of the problem has been recent industry average returns on equity of 5 percent to 10 percent, with several companies periodically hovering near zero.[5] A number of small companies have gone out of business. But among the shattered shells of companies that slumped with autos stand a few tire companies that have done well.

Goodyear is the giant of the industry. They recognized the potential of radial tires in the early 1970s and built new plants specially designed to produce high volumes of mass-market radial tires. BF Goodrich decided not to take on Goodyear. They set out to distinguish themselves from the rest of the industry, positioning the company as performance tire specialists. The strategy worked. Goodrich T/A's and others became the tires of choice for sports and muscle cars. They withdrew from the low-margin business of supplying tires for new cars. They have used their strategy to become one of the more profitable tire makers. Cooper Tire did a similar thing, focusing totally on the replacement market and staying with a majority of bias-ply tires, instead of jumping into the crowded radial market in which Goodyear was beating everybody else with high volume production in modern plants. The result was 22 percent return on equity in 1981.

Uniroyal took a different approach, going after cost control with a vengeance. They closed obsolete plants. They reduced inventories. Workers took pay cuts. The pruning was effective. The company moved from a $121 million-loss in 1979 to a $45-million profit in 1981. Other companies have followed suit. Armstrong Rubber and Firestone have begun to take costs seriously, having seen the writing on the wall.

General Tire in the late 1970s had about the best financial results of the tire companies. However, it was done with mirrors, or, more prosaically, with rockets and broadcasting. Its Aerojet General and RKO divisions recently have produced 40 percent of its sales and almost all its profits. The diversification has been their source of survival.

What does the future hold? As long as there are cars, there will be market segments with different types of customers. If you're huge—Goodyear—you can pursue the masses. Otherwise, specializing in certain kinds of tires would appear to be an excellent way to survive. As would cost control. Diversification? Perhaps, but that's survival only in the corporate sense. It's playing basketball rather than football because you don't do well at football and don't want to try any more. It's not really the same as surviving in the tire business.

Succeeding Where Others Haven't

Are there some common elements in the successes we have described? Genius, perhaps, or luck? Let's leave out diversification as a strategy for now. Diversification was running away from the fight in the cases we have examined. Perhaps the right thing to do, but it does not teach us how to fight better.

There are two common threads that wind their way through our discussions and are present in the hundreds of other cases that we could have reviewed. They are low cost and product differentiation. Nucor and Goodrich. Uniroyal and Jorgensen. Goodyear, focusing on a big new market and driving down costs with high volumes. You have to give the customer something different, or the same thing as everyone else at lower cost, or both.

Companies accomplish this first through the overall management direction. A company has to understand itself, its competitors, and its markets and customers. Honest evaluations are essential. Then it has to segment its products and markets by the characteristics that pop out during the evaluations. You have to identify crowded markets, uncrowded markets, unfilled needs, me-too products, and unique products—potential and actual. After you've decided what to go after, it's important to assign clearcut responsibilities for success, whether it is measured by profit, market share, return on investment, or something else.

Above all, you need technical competence. The long and the short of it are that you can't achieve market success with financial people or public relations people. They're important, but they don't design, sell, make, or deliver the product. You need analytical skills, for instance in market research. You need production control and manufacturing skills. Marketing and sales management skills. Engineering or the equivalent product design skills in your business. You may need good project management if you are contemplating bringing out an entirely new product. In other words, someone is going to have to do the work and they are going to have to do it well.

Adversity is one of the best teachers. We learned the fundamentals of coping with it from the steel and rubber industries. Next it is important to understand the details of applying the principles. That's our next topic.

"A good scare is worth more than good advice."
—E.S. HOWE

Chapter 8

Managing in Difficult Situations

LIKE THE TECTONIC PLATES under the surface of the planet, the fundamental economic structure of U.S. business is shifting and producing quakes on the surface. In the previous chapter we discussed how industries once thought to be anchored in bedrock are now floating away on underground currents. We explored management's predicament in two troubled industries—steel and rubber—and identified successful management strategies. There are management challenges as well in other industries. We would like now to explore these difficult situations and amplify on our previous comments. As with steel and rubber, the examples are not ends in themselves, put here merely to describe idiosyncrasies of specific industries. Instead, they are springboards for advancing our knowledge and understanding of how to manage in the world of the future when difficult situations are likely to be the rule, not the exception.

What Qualifies as Difficult?

What is a difficult situation? Probably every CEO whose company is not making the desired earnings would regard the situation as difficult. Some such problems are due to the national economy, guessing incorrectly on fashion trends, or other transient factors. We are not talking about this kind of problem. We are talking about fundamental problems leading to chronic low profitability. Webster's definition of "fundamental" is: "of or relating to essential structure, function, or facts." Not bad—in fact, it might have been written with the corporate world in mind. Another way of looking at it is the severity of the prob-

111

lem over time. If it is not amenable to a quick fix by throwing money or people at it, it may well be a fundamental problem. It does not matter whether it was created by external influences, internal decisions, or a combination. The key to attracting our interest is the fundamental nature of the problem and, logically enough, the solution. Our real interest is the solutions, but you don't find important new management concepts applied to minor problems.

Why look at profitability? Because continued low profitability threatens viability. As we discussed much earlier, the accounting systems used today do not measure profitability as all income of funds less all expenditures (including current provisions for future expenses). It's certainly not clear that this would be the best or even a good definition of profitability. However, it would be more understandable than the current situation where profitability, sometimes substantial, is required for mere survival because of the design of accounting systems. Regardless, we are stuck with the current systems in which low profitability year after year is a danger signal.

How do companies get stuck in a trap of low profitability? Can't their management see the situations developing and take corrective action before they get out of hand? That issue and others like it are part and parcel of this chapter. However, let's run down a list of things that can give companies severe headaches. We won't analyze them at this point, but they'll help to set the stage for the next step.

Foreign competition certainly has left its share of U.S. companies in corporate Boot Hill. No problem is more fundamental than another company having a better product at a lower price. Demographics are another more subtle enemy. Changes in income distribution, housing patterns, numbers in the work force and other population-related factors will strongly affect most industries, especially those that deal directly with the public. Speaking of the public, their tastes change. Lifestyles change. Status symbols change. Cigars once were enjoyed by a large segment of the population, but the industry has been going down in flames for the past decade.

Cost structure has been the undoing of many companies. Too much bank debt. Uncompetitive labor costs. Too much expensive material in the product, or expensive machines to produce it. Or the opposite—penny pinching. Outmoded equipment and facilities. Insufficient research and development (R&D) spending—one day you wake up to realize you have only old products and the cupboard is bare.

Those are examples of things that are fundamental problems. Let's consider one of the affected industries.

Television's Twilight Zone

The recent history of the U.S. television industry has been brought to us in living color—red for red ink. After a great start that saw a dozen U.S. companies jump into television manufacturing, the gentlemen from the Far East walked in and took over the industry. First were the Japanese, then came the Koreans and others. Over 50,000 U.S. jobs in television manufacturing moved overseas. By 1975, half of the domestic producers of televisions got out of the business or subsidized it with earnings from other parts of their companies. The indisputable cause of the debacle was low prices. The Japanese simply underpriced the U.S.-made sets. Whether the victory was a fair one is a hotly debated point.

On one side of the table are the Japanese who argue that their lower wage rates and superior efficiency enable them to turn out television sets at lower cost than U.S. manufacturers. On the other side are the U.S. manufacturers who fervently believe that the Japanese are "dumping" television sets, that is selling them below cost or at least for below what they sell for in Japan. They point to specific examples in which the identical set sells in the U.S. for half the retail price in Japan. They describe the rigid tariff and non-tariff barriers that limit television imports in Japan to almost zero. They explain the economic benefits of the assistance of the Japanese government to Japanese manufacturers. They accuse the Japanese of going so far as to falsify prices on import documents.

To make a long story short, the U.S. government was never satisfied enough with the U.S. manufacturers' charges to take substantial action against the Japanese, although some minor penalties were applied and some import volume agreements (quotas by another name) were reached in 1977. The skirmishes in the battle took place over an eight year period. The actions of the U.S. manufacturers during that time, in addition to complaining to the government, are quite interesting.

In the early 1970s Zenith was the market leader by a large margin. As the leader, they were hurt severely by the imports. Zenith moved to the forefront of the legal battle against the Japanese. RCA instead took up the production challenge. They moved some costly assembly operations to Mexico, redesigned their products for lower costs, licensed patented Japanese technology, and moved heavily into automation in U.S. manufacturing. By 1979 they had overtaken Zenith and were the market leader. Zenith tried to do some of these things, but their preoccupation with the legal battle cost them dearly. In addition, they made some big mistakes such as overestimating the color television market by 30 percent and pouring money into a redesigned picture tube that never met expectations. A well-run company, Zenith eventually saw the light and began to do many of the things that RCA had done. They are now once again respectable, but probably will never regain their earlier dominance.

Lessons? Don't take your eye off the ball. Don't put all your eggs in a basket held by someone else. And don't forget that it's impossible to create a low-cost product in a courtroom.

Soft Drinks: What to Do When the Kids Grow Up

The late teens-early twenties population will be declining through the rest of this century.[1] That group has traditionally been the big consumers of soft drinks. Population moves in cycles, of course, and the trend will reverse. After 2000, there will once again be growth towards a substantial group in this age range. However, treading water for the next twenty years does not sound like a corporate strategy that many companies would like to embrace. What can the soft-drink companies do?

Enter an old friend, diversification. PepsiCo figured out a while ago what was going to happen. Less than half of their sales are now from beverages. They are still No. 2 behind Coca-Cola and taking the soft-drink business seriously, but they also understand reality. Is this running away, as we characterized other diversification efforts? Probably not. Fighting over an increasing or stable market is one thing; fighting hard to be the big fish in a pond that is being drained is something else.

Dr Pepper was in an entirely different set of circumstances. They were going to be eaten by one of the bigger fishes, so they decided to find their own little spot in the pond where they wouldn't be bothered. They pushed a different-tasting drink that certainly couldn't be confused with a cola. Or with anything else, for that matter. Then they just went quietly about the business of acquiring customers who liked the taste and not worrying about the ones that didn't. By 1980 a rather startling thing had happened. Sales of Dr Pepper, regular and diet, had catapulted the company into third place behind Coke and Pepsi. Sort of like the Nash Rambler sneaking up behind GM and Ford. Seven-Up had fallen to fourth place. Dr Pepper has since decided to expand aggressively into other soft-drink areas, except colas, and go after a much larger market share, an interesting change of direction. Their plan is to continue to stay out of Coke's and Pepsi's line of fire, but to grow in the remaining third of the market. They bought Canada Dry in 1982 after earlier acquiring the marketing rights to Welch's soft drinks.

What happened to Seven-Up? They were so intent on looking ahead of them that they forgot to look behind. The attempt to lure away cola drinkers failed while other companies succeeded in wetting the palates of the non-cola drinkers. They simply did not establish adequate differentiation in the consumer's mind or taste buds. The existence of other products that people either preferred or found interchangeable was too much for them. They finally were acquired by Philip Morris, who plans to do for the company what they did after buying Miller Brewing (they brought out Lite beer, improved Miller's marketing, and moved the company from nowhere to second place behind Anheuser-Busch). Like, a low-caffeine cola, has been their first significant new product; others will come later.

Royal Crown Cola is a perennial follower, being fifth behind Seven-Up. They've had their share of breakthroughs—first decaffeinated cola, first diet cola, and first use of 16-ounce returnable bottles. Nevertheless, the company has not been able to turn its innovations into great success. They proved that differentiation is not much good if you're ahead of your time or unable to get the message to your customers.

We come now to the granddaddy of the soft-drink companies—Coca-Cola. Coke had not diversified much through the mid-1970s; over 80 percent of its earnings came from soft drinks. Since then it has diversified into other food areas as well as into other businesses, often unrelated, such as water purification equipment and movies (Columbia Pictures, acquired in 1982). By and large, however, the company has remained committed to the soft-drink business. It is depending heavily on overseas sales to make up for the coming decrease in the U.S. market size. In this country they have introduced Diet Coke, their first new product since 1886 to carry the Coke name. They are remaining competitive by improving relations with their bottlers, focusing more on differences among local markets, and letting bottlers participate in decisions affecting them. They are orienting advertising more toward the mature adult market. In general, Coke has gone back to acting like a hungry company that wants the business and no longer takes success for granted.

We've presented five different companies, from which five different pictures emerge. RC Cola is the passive company in the group. The others have all done something besides just wait for the ax to fall. Seven-Up sold out to a better marketer, but even that should get them some credit. When the world is changing, you have to change with it. You may be wrong, but at least you have a chance of success; standing still guarantees failure.

The Graying of the Silver Screen

The movie theater industry is either a horror show or a tragic drama, depending on how pessimistic you are. Not the movie industry—they're doing well. There have never been more places to show movies: theaters, network and local television, cable television, cassette and videodisc players. Which, of course, is exactly the problem for the theaters. The movie industry's gain is the theaters' loss.

The theater owners have been through this before. In the twenty years after WWII, when television was reaching into every household, the number of public theater screens fell by 35 percent.[2] Then the theater owners got hold of themselves and realized they were shutting down unprofitable large theaters with several hundred seats. They started building smaller theaters with several screens under one roof to share the cost, and the number of screens increased almost to what it had been, although seating capacity was lower. General Cinema Corporation was the leader in this drive, parlaying the strategy into 20 percent returns with average annual earnings increases of the same magnitude.

Things are likely to be different in the future. Even the Motion Picture Association of America, the association of movie companies, expects a downturn soon, perhaps as severe as the last one in terms of percent reduction in screens. The National Association of Theater Owners also concedes that some dark screens are likely. What can be done? Three things. First, owners must recognize that the movie theater is merely a distribution mechanism for movies. Technology is the carrier of death for all such media. The theater owners will have to change with technological changes if they perceive that they are in the business of bringing movies to audiences, not in the business of operating theaters. They will become involved in cable companies and the like. Moviemakers (e.g., Columbia and MCA), cable companies (e.g., Home Box Office), and home video equipment manufacturers (e.g., RCA) already are getting together with joint ventures and licensing agreements. If the theater owners don't get involved, they'll be left in the dark forever.

Second, theater owners should take advantage of the inherent advantages of showing movies in a theater. The size of the screen, the fun of being with other people, getting away from home—all these are valid attractions of movie theaters. Such advantages as first access to top films should be used while they exist, because they will be lost as the other media become more important. In fact, maybe new popular films won't be important. Landmark Theater Corp. built a chain of thirty-six theaters nationwide based on showing film classics, obscure foreign films, and the like. Product differentiation at its best.

Third, movie theaters should cater to the movie buffs—the 25 percent of the population who buy 85 percent of the tickets.[3] Too many theaters now exploit these customers rather than pamper them. That will change as the theater owners realize where their best interests lie. Perhaps reserved seating, quantity discounts, better food, and other amenities will be offered. Only through such differentiation will their theaters survive.

The Challenge for Aluminum

Aluminum is a different story. A generation ago it was the metal of the future. Lightweight. Strong. Not susceptible to rust. The sleak dream cars in the 1950s auto shows had aluminum bodies and glistened like spaceships under the bright stage lights.

Much of the optimism came to pass, although not precisely as forecasted. Cans and other containers grew to take up almost a quarter of all aluminum usage. Aluminum became popular for aircraft parts and to a lesser extent for ground transportation. As long as gasoline remained plentiful and cheap, the incentive to build lighter cars did not exist, so automobiles were not a good market for aluminum. By the time gas prices rose, plastics were a better alternative. The result—today the average car's weight is less than 5 percent aluminum.[4] Construction, including housing, was a stronger market than expected for aluminum, and eventually grew to be second only to containers. Overall, the industry grew solidly, if not explosively, for twenty years. By 1980 over three-billion pounds of aluminum were used annually in containers, primarily beverage cans.[5]

Unfortunately, certain business successes carry with them the elements of their own destruction. Success in market penetration eventually leads to market saturation. Case in point: Over 80 percent of all beverage cans now are made of aluminum.[6] Forecasts for the aluminum industry for the rest of this century are for growth rates in the range of one-third to one-half the rates of the previous two decades.[7] The conditions are ideal for strategic planning.

Reynolds Metals perhaps is the best known of the large aluminum producers, having created a household word out of their aluminum foil product. They believe strongly that the growth forecasts for aluminum are incorrect or at least do not apply to their company. They are bullish on the use of aluminum in the auto, communications, and energy industries. Alcoa shares much of their enthusiasm, believing that the amount of aluminum in the average car could increase to four or five times what it is now. But Reynolds and Alcoa also have high hopes for international markets, where proportionate usage of aluminum is far lower than in the United States.

The marketing hopes and plans are all well and good. However, profitability has to do with costs as well as sales revenues. Increasing attention must be paid to costs. The companies in the aluminum industry differ widely in their rates of return, and a high priority item for the companies lower in the rankings must be to catch up. The industry as a whole should also shore up the average rate of return compared to other industries if it wants to continue to attract investment dollars.[8] Another compelling reason to cut costs is competition from non-aluminum products. Such materials as plastics, layers of glass fibers or other "composite" materials will continue to be popular in auto bodies and even aircraft. From 1977 to 1982, use of aluminum in autos increased by 20 percent, while use of plastics increased by 35 percent.[9] In addition, some of the uncontrollable costs of making aluminum, such as energy costs, are going to rise more steeply than those of competitive products. Aluminum will need to watch its costs to even remain in the game, let alone raise its rates of return. There are few signs yet that this message has penetrated to the people who run the companies.

The Malnourished Supermarket Business

Let's take up a more appetizing subject: food. The wheel has come back around for the big supermarket chains. They showed little remorse in driving out the small stores, like lions feeding on helpless rabbits. Well, the rabbits are now gone, and all the lions have left to eat is each other. Their strategies for surviving this unpleasant scenario are interesting.

Before we discuss them, though, let's review some financial aspects of the business in order to see how much flexibility our supermarket friends have. There is a myth, perpetuated even by business publications that ought to know better, that supermarkets are only barely profitable. This myth is founded on the low profits as a percent of sales, typically in the 1 percent range, that supermarkets make. Those margins simply reflect the fact that a very large amount of merchandise is moved through stores with relatively little markup over cost. But— here is the key—the investment capital required to make the money is relatively small, so the returns on investment are quite respectable. The returns on equity for the top five supermarket chains average over 20 percent, which is very good and better, for example, than that for the top five department stores.[10] It's a profitable business, and the lions have a lot of money to figure out ways to eat each other.

The ways they have chosen reflect U.S. business at its best in the display of imagination and diversity. The superstore concept is one way to get the customers in your door and, once they're there, sell them a lot of goods. Safeway stores now have pharmacies, bookstores, and housewares. Ralphs and Kroger have sit-down eating. The Pathmark chain has major appliances, including televisions, and auto maintenance products. Are these the wave of the future? Probably not. They will be popular for a while, as the superdrugstores were ten to fifteen years ago. But the concept will be abused, the popularity will fade, and eventually the superstores will survive only if they give good value, the only reason anything survives after the novelty wears off.

Stratification according to consumer socioeconomic levels is another approach. At the high end of the market are the gourmet supermarkets that feature octopus and lobster in an environment of carpeted floors and soft lighting. At the bottom are the self-serve warehouse stores. In between are the generic foods that your local market now stocks in recognition of the fact that brand loyalty has declined almost 20 percent in the past decade.[11]

And the supermarkets haven't forgotten cost reduction. Energy is a big expense, considering lighting, food freezers and coolers, and fuel for truck fleets. Entire store heating and cooling systems are being replaced as the savings from redesigned systems exceed the replacement costs. As wages rise, controlling labor costs will become more important. The single biggest factor in this area will be automated checkout, using scanners and electronic terminals, combined with automated inventory control and materials handling. Errors also will be reduced, since customers usually report checkers' overcharges but not undercharges. And, finally, the technology will be a competitive tool. Properly implemented, the automatic checking devices are a real boon to the customer by speeding checkout and providing itemized receipts. Improperly implemented, they have a number of well-publicized drawbacks that frighten the consumer into believing the store is shortchanging him or her. Resistance will fade as more and more stores do it right.

Transportation Emancipation

Supermarkets have been honing their competitive skills for three decades. The trucking and railroad industries have considerably less experience with competition. Regulation and restriction of competition go back nearly a century to the 1887 Interstate Commerce Act. In 1980 separate pieces of federal legislation gave new freedom to the rail and trucking industries. The environment of increased competition has been exhilarating to some companies and terrifying to others. Let's examine the trucking industry first.

Truckers have two new degrees of freedom: services to offer and rates to charge. Previously, the Interstate Commerce Commission (ICC) decided which companies would be allowed to compete in a market or over a route. They also determined the rates that could be charged; the rate manual was so comprehensive and complex that few companies were able to put it on modern, large computers! The ICC's authority, while not eliminated entirely, has been reduced such that the trucking industry resembles normal U.S. industry in terms of competition. The truckers' response has been twofold. First, they geared up for competition through cost-cutting. Labor costs were high—over $17 an hour for Teamsters Union employees—and have been targets for reduction or stabilization. Yellow Freight System and others worked with the Teamsters Union to establish more competitive labor rates in some positions. The second thrust of the trucking companies was marketing, attempting to differentiate themselves from other companies through price, services offered, or quality of service. Here they learned an important lesson. Marketing schemes that can be easily copied by competitors are worthless. It costs money to do anything different, so why do it if your competition will merely copy you if it works? You have to pick something that requires substantial investment, the unique skills of your people, or something else that provides a barrier. The airlines have never learned this, with rare exceptions, and continue to compete through suicidal price-cutting rather than examining the entire package being purchased by the customer. The truckers learned the same lesson and are trying to apply it in practice.

The railroad business either has become fun again or become a nightmare, depending on your love for competition. The same freedom to set rates under limited ICC review was granted to the railroads. They too embarked on marketing and cost-cutting strategies. But their strategies had a slightly different twist because the railroads own their tracks while the highways are provided by the public to truckers. The tracks and associated switching operations are high-cost items that are fixed in location. Great efficiencies are possible in selecting shipping routes that you own, and great marketing advantages accrue to the company that owns a large system. Hence, mergers and acquisitions emerge as a way to successfully implement strategies of either low-cost operation or customer orientation or both.

In the future, the industry is going to be dominated by large railroads and a few clever small operators. However, another turn of the regulation wheel is likely. Things will reach a point where the survivors have won and have large market shares with virtually no competition for hauling commodities that do not lend themselves to truck or air transport (can you imagine a Boeing 767 full of coal?). We will then be in the situation of the 1880s that led to regulation to curb the abuse of the natural monopoly of the railroads. Until then, though, life will be fun for the railroad people.

Truck Makers

We are moving towards the inevitable in a chapter on difficult situations—a discussion of the auto industry. Let's do our calisthenics and warm up for the big issue by talking about the truck makers. Not vans and pickup trucks, but the real things—the 18-wheelers on which the tires are higher than the doors on your car, and their medium-size brothers.

The history of the truck manufacturers is tied to the history of the trucking and railroad industries. As the road system improved in this country, trucks became a viable alternative to rail shipments. Government policies encouraged this by such policies as not allowing railroads to depreciate trackage. The interstate highway system effectively became a license to print money for the truckers and the truck makers. Regulation created a very benign environment for the trucking industry: Rules were fixed and major barriers to new entrants kept competition down. The truck business more than quadrupled from the 1950s through the 1970s.

The world has changed. Several things have hit the truck makers at once, many of the same things that hit the trucking industry. The unshackling of the railroads. Deregulation, which has forced truckers to look closely at costs and often decide against a new $90,000 truck (the average price these days). The price of gasoline and diesel fuel. The saturation of the trucking market.

Not surprisingly, the result is that the truck makers recently have not been doing very well. White Motor went bankrupt. Some truck divisions of other companies would have gone under if they had been independent companies. Yet there were exceptions. The company that makes Peterbilt trucks, one of the premium quality trucks, has been running average returns on equity close to 20 percent. So has the maker of Kenworth trucks, another high quality heavy truck. Just as prices for luxury homes hold up better than middle-market homes, so the market has held up for these premium-priced, high quality trucks. Are Peter-bilt and Kenworth going to knock each other off? Not likely—they're both made by the same company, Paccar. Not a bad strategy, to own two of the best truck lines made in the U.S. It's easy to perceive the distinction between the two lines so that customers do not have identical Kenworth and Peterbilt trucks to choose from. And it's tough for the competition.

It's going to get tougher. The likes of Mercedes-Benz and Volvo are moving into the market, in many cases by acquiring failing U.S. companies or truck operations. They understand building quality products to meet customers' needs. The truck manufacturing business is no longer a license to print money; instead, a fool and his printing press are soon parted. Only the smart will survive.

Designing Strategies: The Questions to Ask

What have we learned about the principles of managing during a period of adversity and applying the principles to specific situations?

We still have the twin strategies of product differentiation and low cost/low price provision of the product or service. However, we can see now that these principles apply primarily in saturated or low-growth markets. Both the soft drink and the aluminum industries believe that substantial markets exist in countries other than the United States. If there are plenty of customers to go around, the market can be shared by competitors who do not need to differentiate their products or their prices. New markets are not always in new locations. They may be new uses for the same products. The makers of seltzer and club soda, facing a stable market as consumers switched from mixed drinks to wine, have been able to position their products as cheaper alternatives to the expensive sparkling waters, which are enjoying an increasing market. To many people, carbonated water is carbonated water and the mixers are suitable. So the principle is this: expand the market where possible; it's easier than fighting over a saturated market.

But what if you have no choice? How do you differentiate your product? Basically, by putting yourself in the shoes of the customer and seeing yourself through the customer's eyes. Only in this way can you develop real "market awareness" and become sensitive to the truly important factors in customers' decisions. For example, is the customer paying for a better-performing product or for the after-the-sale service? Is the customer shopping in your store because of your merchandise or because the store environment is pleasant? Banking with you because you offer high-interest checking or because the teller lines are never too long? Obviously, most selling situations consist of balancing a set of customer needs, but the way you balance them is critical. Who are your customers? What is their income level? What are their tastes? The inability to walk the line between deep discounting and selling junk has driven many low-market discounters to the wall. Market surveys don't necessarily help. (Remember the Edsel?) They're a tool that can be useful. The key is awareness of customer desires, especially as they change. Mini-generations now exist; people five years apart in age have value differences as sharp as once were common only across entire generations.

After you have designed your products to be different, be sure to communicate the differences. Through packaging design. Advertising. The communication—marketing—is a specialty in itself. Maybe your product really is not the merchandise but the distribution system or the store itself. Don Fisher built The Gap chain of stores by offering selection—almost every size and style of Levi's—at competitive prices. The idea of a store where you could find what you wanted caught on.

What if there aren't any available market niches? Or if you simply aren't very good at, or possibly not interested in, marketing and you'd rather be price-competitive through lower costs. What can you do? It's a good idea to fine tune your production or service delivery operations to squeeze out the last penny. But do something else first. Think about big changes. Think the unobvious. Whatever the most common ways of doing things in your industry are—think about changing them. The most common elements are very likely the ones that no one has ever thought about changing because things are always done that way in your industry. If your industry is always vertically integrated, consider purchasing semi-finished products. Leasing rather than buying facilities or equipment. Employing subcontractors rather than permanent personnel. Regional rather than central warehouses. Consult the people who make the product or deliver the service. They may know how to cut costs, as long as it doesn't involve eliminating their jobs. Maybe you should have fewer models or customer options or should price them differently (the more differentiated the product the more you can charge for it). Pricing is an art in itself, but it seldom will keep you alive if you are doing other things wrong; it will help you get the most that you can for your products, however.

And, while you are doing everything else, think about where your company is positioned in its life cycle and vis-à-vis the world economy. Try to understand what your expectations should be. In other words, develop a framework within which you can operate. If you don't like the answer, that's a different matter which we'll discuss later in our chapter on corporate strategy. For now, just establish the environment where you're trying to compete.

When in doubt as to how to achieve differentiation or low cost, try thinking back over the examples in this chapter. They're hardly exhaustive, but they contain many ideas that may be transferable to your environment.

Autos—The King of Difficult Situations

This example is a little different from the rest, in that it isn't clear that the patient is going to survive. Let's attempt to do a thorough, if relatively brief, analysis of the problems faced by the U.S. auto industry and the potential solutions, if any, to the problems.

Maybe a good place to start is with the stereotypes of the auto industries of the major countries. German cars are known for their high quality, spirited performance, and high prices. British cars are tradition-bound, fun to drive, unreliable, and manufactured with low quality. French cars are weird, often funny-looking, and generally out of the mainstream in the U.S. Swedish cars are dependable, of high quality, and a bit pricey. Japanese cars are good low-to-mid-range cars, efficient, reliable, offering good value for the money. Italian cars are exotic, high priced, with spotty quality. U.S. cars are good-sized, inefficient, made poorly, and generally overpriced for the value received.

There are limitations on one-sentence characterizations of the entire automobile industry of a country, but these are consistent with opinions of groups as widely diverse as the general public and editors of car magazines. What would the stereotypes tell you about sales if they were accurate? Presumably that Japanese and German cars were doing well, Swedish fairly well, Italians well in limited markets, and French, British and U.S. cars not so well. That is more or less what has happened in the U.S. market in the last fifteen or twenty years; so maybe the stereotypes aren't so deficient after all.

The problem has been recognized as serious for some time, or so we have been told by U.S. auto executives. What in fact has been or is being done?

The down-sizing effort that GM began in the mid-1970s has continued to the extent that U.S. cars are no longer outrageously larger than their foreign counterparts. Very few eight-cylinder engines are made any more. There has been some movement on costs, including some significant concessions by the United Auto Workers (UAW) union. Capital spending and product development programs have been pared back down to reality. Quality control recently has been given some emphasis.

The result is the hemorrhaging of the U.S. auto companies has been only mildly abated. Imports are up to an all-time high, nearly 30 percent, limited only by informal voluntary quotas. More than two-thirds of the imports are Japanese. American cars are twice as likely to be recalled as Japanese cars. The inescapable conclusion is that the approach isn't working. Let's apply the principles we've learned and see if we can understand why.

In terms of product differentiation, all the U.S. automakers have done is copy the imports, from the econoboxes to the Mercedes look-alikes. The originality and imagination belong to imports, from Volkswagen for its Rabbit up to Mercedes for its turbocharged diesel performance cars. Quality continues to plague the U.S. automakers. The Plymouth Horizon, one of the new breed from Chrysler, received the second worst rating in the entire history of one car magazine's owner surveys, primarily for the quality of workmanship and the like.[12] GM has "quality circles," but a friend of mine bought a new, top-of-the-line Buick and during the first rainstorm a week later the windshield leaked and the wipers failed to work.

What are the U.S. makers doing about costs? The fact is that Japanese cars have at least a ten to fifteen percent cost advantage.[13] (There have been virtually no charges of dumping or predatory pricing against the Japanese automakers.) Labor rates for Japanese auto workers account for some of the difference, but their management costs are also much lower. The countries that do not have cost advantages—Germany, for example—are positioned at the high end of the market where customers are not particularly price-sensitive.

What do the U.S. automakers have to do to get back into the game? Taking one thing at a time, they need meaningful product differentiation. They will need to regain the lead in engineering, product design, and styling. They are beginning to add such features as turbocharging and advanced electronics, but the competition is on the second and third generations of such improvements. U.S. automakers need to get out in front.

They will have to rethink their car lines and models that fit the markets of the past but not today's markets. Not minor tinkering, but major rethinking. The Japanese have structured their lines for today's market, not the 1940s. Do the major car lines of GM still have their places or should an entire marque be scrapped? In some recent cases less than $100 (total) separated the Chevy-Olds-Pontiac-Buick versions of the same car. Is a world without Buicks really unthinkable?

They will have to deal with changing lifestyles. People are keeping cars 30 percent longer than in 1970.[14] People also have been conditioned through dashed expectations to look beyond advertising claims. The foreign carmakers cooperated by not engaging in exaggerated advertising. While the U.S. makers continued to use advertising to convince customers of a car's quality, the foreigners simply built quality cars. Guess which worked better!

We could go on and on. The lessons that other industries have learned have not taken root in the auto business. Perhaps it's because some factors, like the fuel economy requirements, really did hit the U.S. makers harder than the rest of the world (because of gasoline being cheap here for so long). Perhaps it's the periodic upturns in the business that are straws for people to cling to if they are so inclined. Perhaps it's the poor labor-management relations that make it difficult for either side to admit a significant responsibility for fixing the problem. Whatever the reason, it's time to stop using it as an excuse. The auto companies have no lack of talented people with good intentions, and it would be unfair to say that they couldn't turn things around or that some of the ideas we have discussed here aren't also being discussed in Detroit. The discussions must be turned into action—that's the challenge facing the U.S. automakers in the rest of this decade. It's a sobering challenge. And perhaps an interesting example to use in a book on management—an example of failure instead of success. But if anything can bring home to U.S. executives the bankruptcy of past management practices, it may be the failure of the U.S. auto industry.

"Truth is simply the opinion that has survived."
—OSCAR WILDE

Chapter 9

Products vs. Services

THE SEPARATION of product and service industries is traditional in management circles. Since general management principles are obviously applicable in all kinds of industries, I suspect that many people would have some difficulty in articulating the hard and fast management differences in service vs. product industries. Clearly, in the absence of a product, one does not require engineering and manufacturing skills. But are not similar skills required, called by other names? Perhaps. However, as Tevye observed in *Fiddler on the Roof*, tradition is difficult to overcome. Our objective in this chapter will be to apply some logic to the situation and describe the true differences that may exist in management of service industries. Our approach will be the same as in the previous two chapters—identification of management principles through discussion of specific industries and companies. But first, let's cover some background material about service industries.

The Myth of Service Industry Growth

Anyone who has not been a hermit for the last thirty years has witnessed the growth of service industries. If the significance of the phenomenon was not fully appreciated, the business press took care of that by constantly emphasizing the growth of the service sector of the U.S. economy. There were even some predictions that we would evolve into an entirely service-oriented economy, leaving production of goods to the less-advanced countries of the world. A couple of facts seemed to escape the prognosticators responsible for these ideas. First, the growth of a service economy doesn't result in fewer goods produced. Virtually

127

every service business uses products in its operation, from banking to airlines to auto repair. The products have to come from somewhere and clearly, the production capacity of other countries could not replace the awesome capacity of the United States. The second fact, of course, is that the management and technological skills do not exist to produce the goods wholly in other countries even if the production capacity existed. Products are continually becoming more complex, not less, demanding higher levels of skills to make them. If the production processes are automated, someone has to make the machines. Overall, we are going to continue to have a robust goods-producing sector of our economy for a long time. It will exist for its own sake and to support the service sector.

By the way, you may be asking, what precisely is the service sector? Many business analysts would have a tough time giving consistent answers. We all can agree that such businesses as dry-cleaning establishments and travel agencies are service businesses. Lawyers and doctors are in service businesses. But how about the airline industry? It's also called part of the transportation industry, with railroads, trucking, buses, etc. Are they service businesses? How about banking? Real estate? Insurance? Some of these seem like service businesses, but others seem to have products and processes that resemble a manufacturer. Is a department store in the service industry? Or, in general, retailers who sell products, not services? The local supermarket? Hotels? Seems likely. Public utilities, like the telephone, gas, and electric companies? Isn't electricity a product? Or natural gas? And where do we classify all government functions, from federal to state to local governments?

When you read headlines that say 70–75 percent of all U.S. jobs are now in the service sector, which of the above industries are they talking about? The answer is—all of them. The number is close to 55 percent if public sector jobs are given their own separate category and over 70 percent if all of the work force jobs are considered.[1] That seems to put things in a different light. After all, the country always has had retailers, hotels, and most of the businesses that we call service businesses. The businesses always have used products extensively and always will. Maybe the 75 percent number is a form of sensationalism that leaves an unfortunate impression of explosive growth in the service sector? Yes—that's true. The share of service sector jobs when Harry Truman left office was just under 60 percent.[2] The actual increase in the share of jobs held by service businesses has been less than 1 percent annually. So the structure of the economy has not changed radically, and the underlying dependence on goods has not disappeared. But the service sector has expanded.

Why has there been a gradual shift to a larger position in the economy for service jobs? Part of the reason clearly is the movement of some jobs overseas—television and auto manufacturing, for example. Part is the addition of new jobs to cope with new technology—the computer people, "information specialists," the users of such information. Part is the growth of professional services from attorneys and accountants. Another part is a cultural evolution, movement up a commercial "hierarchy of needs," to borrow the phrase again from Abraham Maslow. Service industries recently have tended to use goods/products for reasons beyond survival and economic self-sufficiency. The goods became elements of luxury or desire rather than necessity, and the service jobs expanded to accommodate these needs.

What are the implications in this analysis for the future of service businesses? And what are the unique aspects of management, if any? The financial world provides our first example.

Financial Services

Financial services is a broad appellation. To most consumers it includes banks, savings and loans, mutual savings banks, and credit unions. Some of these serve retail consumers only. Others, primarily banks, have large stables of corporate customers, in many cases preferring them to retail customers.

The label actually includes a lot more than the above list. If they thought about it a little, most of the public also would add consumer credit companies, brokerage firms, and investment companies (e.g., mutual funds) to the list. The more sophisticated individuals also would add insurance companies and the companies providing such services as factoring (buying accounts receivable at a discount).

For having such a spectacular diversity among its members, the industry demonstrates uniformity in much of its behavior. Basically all financial service companies make money because of a "yield spread," the difference in rates of return on their investments and the rates paid to their customers. Even such firms as investment funds, which return most of the yield income to the investors and make money on fee income, are sensitive to yield because of competitive requirements. High inflation has created a new world of high rates, but not uniform rates—the potential size of mistakes is larger than in the past. Also, the legislative and cultural barriers between the various services are coming down rapidly. The industry is undergoing tremendous upheaval. The cash value provision of life insurance policies is being forced to compete with money market funds. There is no consistent rate and yield structure across the financial services industry.

There also has occurred a coincident maturation of management, technology, and market penetration. The electronics revolution has arrived in the world of pinstripe suits. Funds can be transferred around the world in seconds. The gentlemen have given way to the tough operators. Saturated markets have a way of bringing out the competitive instincts in people. The trees are far from bare, but the ripe fruit is no longer hanging quite so close to the ground where the picking is easy. Banks and others are having to work for their profits.

The atmosphere of change is composed of two elements. The first element is the change in the services provided by financial entities. Competition and reduced opportunity for additional market penetration from the usual services have led to new services. Not new to the world, perhaps, but new to the institutions offering them. The savings and loans got their wish to offer checking accounts. They also lost their protection on interest rates paid to depositors and their legislated advantage over banks in such rates. Even the stockbrokers got into the act, offering money management accounts with withdrawal privileges that are checking accounts in every way but their actual name. The investment funds also changed their style by offering new products with current market yield and immediate withdrawal privileges—basically high-interest checking accounts, although they weren't allowed to call them that. By early 1983, the wheel had turned again—banks now are allowed to pay unrestricted rates on checking accounts. The turmoil caused by these events has been almost unbelievable until one realizes that an industry that had undergone no significant change since the 1930s was subjected almost overnight to a total restructuring.

Other examples of new services that go far beyond tradition also exist. Several savings and loans already have asked for legal permission to offer securities transaction services and investment advice. The life insurance industry is experiencing mass disaffection. Insurers are squeezed by making policy loans at low interest rates at the same time that they are unable to sell enough insurance because of the attractiveness of other investment opportunities.

Responding to change usually requires money. The well-heeled institutions have been best able to create and implement the strategy of new products. Merrill Lynch has gone far beyond being a brokerage firm. While spending tremendous amounts of money to add to their portfolio of services, they consistently have managed to be in the top three firms in earnings on Wall Street. On the banking side, Citicorp has expanded aggressively into almost every service and location permitted to banks. Bank of America, the other huge U.S. bank, in 1982 bought a brokerage firm. If you can't beat 'em, join 'em. Sometimes you don't have enough money of your own. Both Crocker and Marine Midland banks were acquired by foreign banks that pumped enough capital into them to keep them in the race.

So the strategy for the future involves new services. What else? Changes in the means of providing the services, such as the distribution system. Financial entities are integrating on a grand scale. Technical integration is one theme—banks, for example, are building electronic networks of teller machines. The credit card networks—Visa, for example—provide a starting point for the credit companies. Some of the bank networks are potent rivals, though. They already cover hundreds of banks in dozens of states. Organizational integration is another theme. Prudential Insurance merged with Bache, American Express with Shearson. Xerox bought Crum & Forster, an insurance company. Sears bought both Dean Witter Reynolds and Coldwell Banker (real estate) so that Allstate Insurance wouldn't be lonely at night. We are seeing the birth of a few financial giants that will blanket the U.S. with financial services of all types in deadly competition with each other.

The next turn of the strategy wheel will take the financial institutions beyond the creation and marketing of new services to more efficient operation and investment of funds, i.e., the internal operations to go with the market orientation. Only the ones that start making better investments will be able to afford to pay the high returns to customers on their new services. The insurance companies are already in this boat; other financial entities will be too, as their structure and markets settle down. The emphasis on technology will continue, abated only by rigorous financial analysis to ensure that the expenditures are justified. Improved cost control will be implemented, including better financial reporting systems by service line. Prices will be tied more closely to costs of services, through fees as well as interest rates. The companies will be required to go through cost reduction projects in the same way that manufacturing companies do. In some cases, cost objectives will be unachievable. This will lead to the last turn of the wheel—failure.

For cost or marketing reasons, certain services will not be profitable. Perhaps adequate differentiation from competitors' products will not have been achieved. Poor performing services will be dropped, taking some of the new financial giants out of certain businesses. Good management does not consist of preventing this from happening—some failure is inevitable in all companies. Good management consists of planning satisfactorily so that one can properly dispose of failures and move on to something else without adversely impacting the healthy parts of the business.

That summarizes some key points about financial services businesses in the future. New services. Competitive cost control. Keep these in mind as we go on to our next subject, which also involves money—spending it, that is.

The Leisure Industry—We Sell Fun

Selling fun is fun, i.e., profitable. The leisure industry has been on an upward course parallel with the rise in disposable income and the decline in the length of the work week. It's one of the few industries that is riding a trend resulting from the evolutionary pattern of an entire civilization—the pattern of decreasing work effort needed to obtain the essentials of life and a consequent freeing of time that has to be filled—sort of the opposite of Parkinson's Law. The industry pays for this rosy long-term prospect by being susceptible to cyclical behavior. When discretionary income drops, the leisure industry suffers, sometimes severely. For them, the question of business strategy is twofold: how to capitalize on good economic times and how to survive during downturns. Three recessions in the past fifteen years, plus such problems as high gasoline prices affecting specific leisure businesses, have left the industry very interested in strategies.

What is the leisure industry? Hotels, professional sports, gambling, resorts, golf courses, and so on. Are there businesses that are not clearly in this category or another? Yes—sports equipment—probably not a service industry. Movies—unquestionably entertainment, but is all entertainment the leisure industry? Not unless you want to classify book publishing and everything else supporting activities in non-work hours as leisure. For purposes of our discussion here, the leisure industry will be assumed to exclude sales of goods and to include only businesses that are reasonably discretionary in consumers' minds as opposed to those that are a normal component of living.

The leisure industry is so diverse that finding a company whose strategy typifies the industry can be difficult. However, Club Mediterranée (known familiarly as Club Med) may fit the bill if we concentrate on the common elements rather than the differences within the leisure industry. Club Med builds and operates "vacation villages" that basically offer short stays of one or two weeks in a package deal that includes lodging, food, social, and recreational activities. The atmosphere is summer camp for adults in glamorous spots like Majorca. There is one social organizer for every five or six guests. The company now has over a hundred villages and has moved into the top ten of the largest hotel chains in the world. What was the key to their international success when every other resort operator was competing for the same consumer dollars? They had something different, a fresh idea. Nobody else had tried the "camp" approach. Funny how so many success stories come back to that—not slicker advertising, but just a better idea.

What lies ahead for Club Med? Specifically, are they recession-proof? They have a couple things going for them. One is the geographical balance of the resort complexes so that a downturn in one part of the world would not be fatal. (Of course, no one is cushioned in a worldwide economic slump.) Another is the spreading of risk—many of the complexes are operated by Club Med but majority ownership lies in other hands. Are there some different sorts of dangers ahead? Possibly. Excessive expansion is probably the main danger, followed by excessive modification of the basic formula. Many companies simply are unable to accept natural limits to growth or the success of the status quo. By continually striving to grow beyond the natural market size or tinkering with success, they bring themselves to ruin. Club Med feels they are aware of the dangers.

Leisure—a true service industry—turns out to be responsive to a basic principle: product differentiation. Are the principles critical? Or is there room for companies that neglect the basics? Sometimes there is in the leisure industry. In good times, everybody wins—the high-cost operator as well as the low-cost operator, the me-too producer as well as the innovator. But in bad times the losers go under or just scrape along. If you want to win consistently, you have to learn and follow the basic principles. The failure to do so may not be as rapidly catastrophic as in dying industries like steel, but even in growth industries there are limits to acceptable incompetence.

Managing Professional Services

The leisure industry may be a growth industry, but the professional services business is living proof that not all service businesses are riding an upward trend. Consider a few of the major professions—medicine, law, accounting. The number of people in the professions and in the pipeline into them is increasing in some major metropolitan areas faster than the market is growing. This creates a unique set of problems for people who always have been able to sell their relatively specialized knowledge and skills at relatively high prices. In addition, there is a growing trend toward competition, in some cases focusing heavily on price.

Studying the professionals and their strategies and operational practices can be useful because the businesses are reasonably simple, without much of the fog that sometimes surrounds other industries. It's like being able to observe a clock mechanism with the case removed: Understanding how it works is a bit easier. The basic commodities are skill and knowledge. The best surgeons and lawyers and accountants can charge anything they want because their services are unique and valuable to their clients. At the other end of the spectrum are the lesser-skilled individuals offering the readily available services. The combination can be a double whammy—a mediocre lawyer can't charge much for a routine will. The basic audit of financial statements is well-understood and requires medium-level accounting skills, so base audits can be highly competitive and not very profitable. Every accounting firm strives mightily to differentiate its audits through industry expertise, skills of individuals assigned to clients, knowledge of client companies, or in other ways that appear to indicate a level of skill and knowledge that justifies high fees. The big law and accounting firms invest a lot of money into being a cut above the other firms. They are rewarded by the big companies or those with unique problems that need the little bit extra. The firms with less breadth and depth serve the companies with fewer technical needs, concentrating more on personal relationships and responsiveness than professional excellence. Everybody wins as long as he or she finds the right niche; the others are out in the cold.

The role of cost-effectiveness is as clear as the role of service differentiation. They are inversely proportional in importance. Cost-effectiveness improves earnings in a well-differentiated firm, but it's essential for survival in a firm without unique services or competing in generic service areas. The main costs are people. So you streamline procedures, use technology where you can, and work the underlings hard at low salaries. There are plenty of such firms that can't compete on skills; they compete on costs or they don't compete for very long.

It's all very straightforward, providing an excellent model. Let's keep in mind how simple it is while we discuss another service business that appears to have made life very difficult for itself.

The Airlines

Perhaps no other service industry has been as maligned as the airlines. They seem sometimes to have signed a collective suicide pact. We are not going to ignore the propensity for self-destruction that exists in the industry. In fact, we are going to review it one more time. Then, however, we are going to take a different direction and discuss the more positive aspects of being in the airline business if one applies fundamental management principles. Surprisingly enough, there are even a couple of examples of airlines that have done so.

The airlines are suckers for price-promotion tactics. Every imaginable way to offer low fares has been tried. Particularly interesting is the focus of the low fares. For twenty years the focus was the discretionary flyer who could choose when to fly and how long to stay at the destination. Therefore, low fares were offered only on alternate Tuesdays between the hours of 1:00 A.M. and 4:00 A.M., and not during holiday periods. Or the low fares excluded meal service. The airlines' savings from meals was peanuts; the trap was that only the true bargain hunter would accept the social stigma of sitting in the back of the plane with no meals. The non-discretionary (usually business) traveler, or the wealthy traveler was meant to be retained at full fare. In 1980, the marketing thinking changed abruptly on this matter. Western Airlines and eventually the others began to realize that flying frequent travelers many times at discount fares was much more profitable than flying the once-a-year vacationer at a discount. How to identify the frequent traveler? After the fact, of course, by awarding discounts after a certain number of flights or miles.

Do these ploys work? Not really, because they provide only temporary advantages before everybody else does the same thing. If you don't make a ton of money before the pack catches up, you haven't come out ahead. Very few of the airlines do, although their internal accounting systems often are geared to demonstrate success—everybody in the company has a vested interest in proving that discounting was the best course of action. The truth is shown in the financial statements: recent rates of return well under 10 percent, often negative, in a period of high inflation when 10 percent meant losing ground.

So what do you do to compete with other airlines' discount fares? If you have to match it, do. If you don't, don't. You decide based on your cost structure. If it's healthy, you can come out of the fray less scarred than the competition. If it's extremely healthy, you can let the rest of the gang beat themselves to death and eventually give up the discount battle without your ever entering. You can control your costs through a few basics, like planning. Planning passenger volumes and route structures so as to select the most cost-efficient airplanes and ground operations procedures. Airplane operating costs vary widely; the DC9-Super 80 is over 30 percent more fuel efficient than its predecessor. Taking delivery and financing the airplanes so as to minimize the company's debt structure. Airplanes can cost over $40 million each—the load to finance them is staggering. Maximizing fleet utilization. United Airlines was able to lay in plans to increase utilization by more than 20 percent in certain markets even before deregulation became the watchword of the day. Delta's hub-and-spoke system around Atlanta is famous.

And don't forget the people. They make the airline work. Most airlines lay off employees in hard times. Some have, in conjunction with this, asked other employees for wage concessions to be repaid in periods of higher profitability. That might be along the right lines. But compare it to this: Delta attempts never to lay off anybody, including pilots and flight attendants. That is almost unheard of in the industry, but it's been true for thirty years at Delta. What do the Delta employees think of this policy? In 1982 the employees, with their own money, bought a Boeing 767 for the company. Hard to believe, but true.

What is the bottom line? Can you make money in the airline business? Look at Figure 9–1. Quite a range for companies all basically in the same business. It appears to indicate that management can make quite a difference.

What lies ahead? For ,the successful operators, probably more of the same, with one twist. The airlines' strategists are getting serious about market segmentation and service differentation that can't be easily copied. We are going to see a real attempt to provide different on-ground and in-flight services. Scheduling, for example, cannot be copied easily because of the impact on utilization and operating costs, but it can be an advantage to travelers. For another example, SAS (Scandinavian Airlines System) improved punctuality, added on-ground customer service people, and went to a one-class (business class) rate structure in Europe. The three improvements resulted in much higher profits. The lesson is that companies providing meaningful differentiation will really fly the competitors into the ground.

Living and Dying by the Ratings

If the airline executives have a problem in wooing the public, think how broadcasting executives must feel. They live and die by the rating systems. If the public doesn't tune in, the ratings fall, the advertising rates fall commensurately and income falls. The industry is like a giant Rube Goldberg machine that takes in ratings at one end and spews out money—a little or a lot—at the other end.

Figure 9–1
Average Annual Airline Profits During the 1970s
(Millions of Dollars)

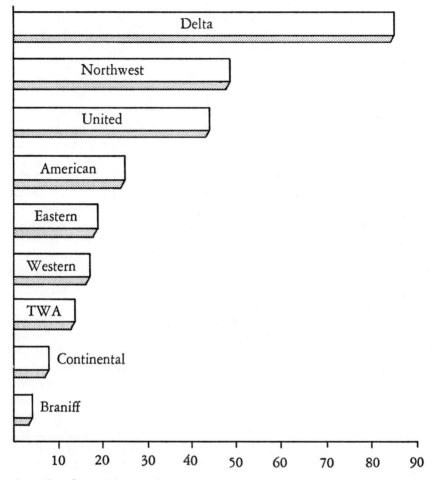

Source: Data from company earnings statements

Broadcasting takes many forms within the radio and television categories. Television includes all the various cable franchises. The organizational forms range from corporate giants—NBC, CBS, and ABC—to local educational television outlets. In one way or another they all are dependent on audiences. A large part of corporate strategies and operations is therefore directed to winning audiences. How is it accomplished?

The ultimate weapon is better shows, or programming. Juggling time slots may help, but it rarely makes a winner out of a loser. There are basically two approaches to programming, what we might call the Coca-Cola and Dr Pepper schools of thought. The Dr Pepper approach provides programming appealing to limited audiences—reruns, minor sports events, local programming, for example. Most of the television channels outside the major networks follow this approach. Radio stations that play only golden oldies are in the same category. The Coca-Cola approach goes for the mass audience. Who wins? In prime time regular television, the Coke approach wins—the network programming is just too powerful a draw. In radio, cable television, and non-prime time television operations, the opposite often has been true. Those appealing to mass markets have divided up the audience so often that each one's share is quite small, and the Dr Pepper approach comes out ahead. The conclusion—know your audience and the competition!

What about costs? In many ways, costs are not really important— the competition is over the service delivered to the customer. Operating costs determine precise margins but not the general magnitude of success. There have been some real breakthroughs in cost control, for example, through the use of sophisticated electronics, but broadcasting still is not a cost-control business.

Does strategy then consist of worrying about programming? Yes, in a broad sense, and no, in a narrow sense. The programming is becoming inextricably intertwined with the physical delivery system of the service—the cable, satellite, or whatever. The technological capabilities of the distribution system are changing all the rules of the game. Programming is very different for twenty-four channels instead of five and different further when the audience can reply through two-way transmission as do Columbus, Ohio, subscribers to Warner's QUBE System. The audience reached by the three major television networks has been dropping in size since 1980. The company with programming that best takes advantage of the technology will be a step ahead. Choosing an inappropriate distribution system or misusing it can be very costly. Rooftop reception from satellite or groundstation microwave transmission is coming to some areas of the country; when it does, it will make obsolete many of the cable installations. Obsolescence might, in fact, be the most important strategic danger facing equipment users in the broadcast industry.

In summary, a heavily customer-oriented industry survives by keeping customers happy. And most management efforts are devoted to that end, from planning through execution. Cost control is only the icing on the cake.

Regulated Service Industries

Let's cover one more example before recapping our knowledge of service industries. What if you're in a regulated industry? Leaving aside the fact that many industries are heavily regulated these days, we are talking about financial regulation to the nth degree. The kind of industry where the government tells you how to do your accounting and sets rates for you based on how much it thinks you should earn as a fair rate of return. Another term in common use is regulated monopoly. Natural gas companies. Electric power companies. Utility-type companies.

The management problems are different in these companies. Management consists of attempting to recreate in real life a financial model that was built for the rate-setting process. The financial models employ predicted levels of usage and forecasted costs to arrive at rates that theoretically would permit the level of return authorized by the regulations. Your objective as a manager is the same as in playing Blackjack or Twenty-One: to get as near as possible to the maximum return without going over. If you go over, you bust—the regulators lower your rates.

There is also the cost side of the equation. The rates are essentially cost based, so if you can justify the need for an expenditure you can get the rates to cover it, known as "putting it in the rate base." This naturally allows for some real game playing with the regulatory agencies, because the criteria for inclusion in the rate base may be based more on public social policy than on business logic. Nothing necessarily wrong with that, since the regulators have the entire public interest in mind, but interpretation of the public interest can lead to some disagreements.

Overall, the management picture that emerges is one of trying to hit a predetermined target, not only on total costs and revenues, but in specific areas. Regulators even get involved with acceptable levels of expenses for office supplies—that's no exaggeration! Your decision making is curtailed and what is left must conform to the regulators' expectations. The degrees of freedom to design your services and manage your costs is limited to the level with which the regulators, most of whom have never worked for a utility in a management position, agree. In this environment, the smart utilities tend to worry less about independent strategies and more about making themselves into effective instruments for determination and execution of public policy. It takes special skills and temperament to manage well in utilities. The people who want to buck the trend are better off in other industries. Not all disagreement is unhealthy, of course, but when utility executives find themselves disagreeing with the basic principles of the regulators, it may be time to move on. For all practical purposes, regulated monopolies aren't in the service business. They're extensions of the government and must be managed as such.

So, Are They Different?

We have left out some of the biggest service businesses, such as department stores, or rental vehicles. But we are seeing a pattern in our discussions. Customer orientation is important, especially when there are no goods involved with the service. The customer's interest lies with the service itself. Recognizing this is essential in industries where there is room for many competitors, such as leisure, or where quality is paramount, such as professional services, or where each element of the service is different from someone else's, such as in broadcasting (dry cleaning is dry cleaning, but no two television stars are the same). In addition, we have seen that efficient delivery of the service is important in some service industries, either because differentiation is not in itself adequate or because the customers don't distinguish between competitors as much as they could. Airlines and financial institutions experience this dilemma. Efficient delivery is, of course, an extra requirement, not a substitute for the customer orientation.

Through our analysis we perhaps also have changed some of the conventional wisdom regarding service industries, particularly the myth that they are simpler than a manufacturing company. Boeing has to design giant jetliners from scratch, build them, test them, and sell them—isn't that more complex than a service business? Likewise for a computer manufacturer. I offer a different thought. Hazarding oversimplification, I would say that service businesses are conceptually simple but operationally just as difficult. Running a far-flung network of savings and loan branches or a life insurance company competing for consumer dollars can be quite difficult, although the complexity of the principles involved may not rival the mechanical, electrical, and aerodynamic principles of designing and building a Boeing 767.

Another myth is the rapid responsiveness of service industries. They are conventionally regarded as being more flexible than a manufacturing company with investments in products and production equipment.

But not all service businesses are without the burdens of overhead and capital investment. Airline companies and hotel chains can't turn on a dime either, with their investments in facilities and equipment.

A third myth is the susceptibility to economic volatility. There are myths in favor of either side—that service businesses are more or less susceptible than goods industries. Certainly some industries, such as leisure, are susceptible. Others, not so much. Auto repair tends to do well in hard times, because people keep their cars longer. Conversely, automakers do not do well. In periods of economic stress, home entertainment industries tend to hold up while those involving expenses outside the home may suffer. The truth is: service industries are probably no more or less susceptible in general than goods industries. Looking at specific industries, we see some do well in hard times and some don't.

Do we conclude that service industries are different? In the context of this book, are the management skills required different? Let's recap the skills required. Understanding your markets and the competition. Knowing what you are selling. Understanding your strategy to be different, to communicate it through marketing, and to make money through cost management. And implementing your strategy.

Implementation—there's a difference. Service businesses are just plain different from product businesses. The product itself makes the difference. In a product business, you have people who design it, make it, stock it, move it, explain it, repair it, buy it, exchange it. The product is the focus. The people are the supporting actors.

In a service business, the lead roles are played by people. You can't get away from that. People produce and deliver the service. The customer deals with people as the primary focus, although more intensely in some service businesses than in others. In some service businesses, there is a pseudo-product, as in airline transportation, that approaches the existence of a real product. For others, there are goods to be sold by people. This just proves the world is a continuum, however, and that service industries vary among themselves.

So—you need to develop people skills in the service business. Interpersonal skills internal and external to the organization because people are the primary resource of the service business. Your product to the customer is the way he or she is treated and served. The friendliness, promptness, courtesy, knowledge, and general helpfulness of the people delivering your service. There is very little else to fall back on. Maybe the customer does not always see a human being, as when using an automatic teller machine, and maybe this will become more common.

But you can't substitute a product focus, as you can in the product industries. People will always be more important in service industries. You must place them in importance right up with service differentiation and management of costs. That's how service industries are different.

"Imagination is more important than knowledge."
—ALBERT EINSTEIN

Chapter 10

High Technology

What does the phrase "high technology" mean to you? Perhaps computers and other electronic products. The Apollo missions to the moon. Maybe modern microsurgery, the creation of wonder drugs or the advent of gene-splicing. Instead of the products, maybe a lifestyle comes to mind. Working in pleasant surroundings rather than a dingy factory. Or a mode of human interaction that relies less on traditional hierarchical, authoritarian relationships.

It's all these things, and more. High technology affects almost all of us, as consumers and as managers, although we might have mixed or negative feelings about the effects. Technological advances are more than only abstract concepts to most of the population. Most people have had their jobs and their private lives affected significantly, sometimes for the better and sometimes for worse. The dire predictions of technology leading to mass idleness have not come true. To the contrary, the Bureau of Labor Statistics of the federal government tells us that a net increase of millions of new jobs has come from computer technology alone.[1] The key word is "net"—there has been significant elimination of obsolete jobs, which has not been pleasant to the people suffering through the experience.

In the future, the impact of high technology will continue to spread through U.S. industry. Many people will get a crack at managing high-technology products or services. Therefore, it behooves us to spend some time here on the unique aspects of high-technology management.

What Is High Technology?

We have to define high technology in a different way from other industries. High-technology industries are product-driven in many

143

respects. Their lifeblood is new products. Therefore, a conventional definition that characterizes industries by the product is meaningless. There are broad areas of industry in which high-technology businesses flourish, but the same areas include many businesses that are not involved in high technology. We will be more successful if we define high-technology businesses by their characteristics. As we noted, they are product-driven. The product is not just the center of attention. The product has unique features that set it apart from other companies' products. Either it does new things or it does old things in new ways. The "high" in "high technology" means "new"—new technologies for accomplishing old objectives or, if it's new enough, never-before-considered objectives. In other words, high technology is a means of product differentiation.

In addition to the product dominance, what else is important? The new frontier aspect of the technology. Firms operate near the state of the art in science and engineering, not only in the final products, but in the intermediate products and the processes used in engineering and manufacturing. Consider the manufacturing of integrated circuits in which lasers trace intricate patterns of miniature electrical circuits. The limiting factor in making the circuits smaller and smaller is manufacturing limitations, such as the minimum line width that can be drawn by a laser. The process of making the high-technology product is itself high technology.

Another key aspect is the product orientation of the people in high-technology businesses. They typically are extremely interested in the product they are making and marketing, sometimes to the exclusion of other important business concerns. They also are likely to be less wedded to traditional ways of doing things. By osmosis, their pioneering and challenging natures that lead to technological success seep over into other parts of the business.

The newness of the products can be a marketing person's dream. Products can be wildly successful, at least for a short time. But the growth can severely strain the resources of the company.

Where is high technology found? All over the country, although there are pockets in such places as the Santa Clara Valley ("Silicon Valley") near San Jose and Route 128 near Boston. And in all sizes and types of companies. IBM is in the top ten of the largest companies (top five of non-oil companies) and still as nimble as a cat in electronics technology. Some very stodgy companies have high technology subsidiaries. Clearly there are differences in the way the technology is managed in the different sizes and types of companies. But there are more similarities than differences. What are the common elements of good management of high technology? Let's quickly review some major areas of high technology and then get into the management.

The Computer Revolution

We all have heard a lot about the computer revolution, but probably few of us have all the facts at our fingertips. We are vaguely aware that in the late 1940s the computer was invented and that progress has been made until today we have home computers, called microcomputers. Most of us don't comprehend the magnitude of the progress. Figures 10–1 and 10–2 illustrate the reductions in price and improvements in price/performance ratios over the last couple of decades (price/performance ratio is computer industry jargon that encompasses both the notions of lower price and increased performance; the price divided by relative performance gives a price/performance ratio). To appreciate the degree of improvement, consider automobiles getting 500 miles on a gallon of gas as comparable progress. That's technologically impossible, you say. Precisely so. The computer industry has been through four generations of technology to get where it is, whereas the internal combustion engine has not changed very much since Ford built the Model T.

Figure 10–2 illustrates that large computers used to be more efficient proportionally than small-to-mid-size computers ("Grosch's Law").

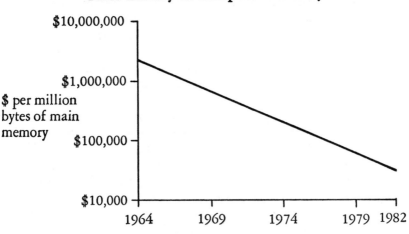

Figure 10–1
Price History of Computer Memory

Source: Data from manufacturers' price lists

Figure 10–2
Price-Performance History of Business Computers

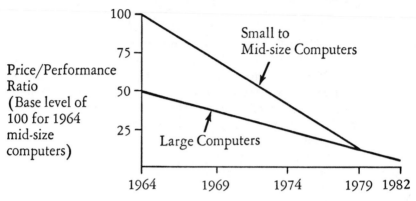

Source: Data from manufacturers' price lists

That situation changed about 1979 as the engineering of all sizes became more similar; economies of scale were no longer the rule. There are still computing tasks that simply cannot be done on smaller machines, but efficiency considerations no longer dictate using a large computer where possible. The new capability encouraged growth of "distributed data processing," whereby computers are placed throughout a company near their users, either independently or wired into a network of computers. This has been physically possible for a long time, but the smaller computers just couldn't do very much work. Concomitant decreases in physical size and improvements in ease of use have created a permanent place for the smaller machines. And smaller ones yet to come!

Computing technology is invading all kinds of companies, turning them into high-technology companies. Computer-aided design (CAD) and Computer-aided manufacturing (CAM) are changing the way engineers and production people do their jobs. CAD employs three-dimensional graphics on television-like screens to help engineers design parts and entire products, up to and including airplanes, (for example, the new Boeing 767). CAM provides computer control of production machinery and the control processes. The linkage of CAD and CAM—called CAD/CAM—can lead to the totally computerized factory. Talking and listening computers also are here—far from perfect, but good enough to be used already at such companies as Lockheed, in their Missiles and Space Division. Word processing terminals stopped being smart typewriters a few years ago: they are now full-fledged computers programmed to do word processing either alone or in conjunction with data processing. And they all can be linked in networks that communicate across the office or, as Hewlett-Packard does, in a giant worldwide network.

The competition is fierce in the industry, from the IBM giants to the Apple Computer upstarts. Tandy used their Radio Shack label to launch themselves into the computer industry and for a while dominated the desktop computer industry over such competitors as Apple. General Electric, who once failed miserably with computers, re-entered the business by acquiring Calma, one of the leading makers of CAD products. Other acquisitions include Motorola's $250-million purchase of Four-Phase, a minicomputer maker. There are integrated producers of hardware (equipment) and software (programs to run the computers). In addition, there are hundreds of companies producing one or the other, but not both. For most users of computers, software is the bottleneck, and dozens of new "software houses" that create the programs open their doors for business every few months.

And computers are only the tip of the iceberg in electronics!

The Rest of the Electronics Explosion

If automobiles were the U.S. industry of yesteryear, then electronics is the industry of the future. There are literally hundreds of new products appearing every year and thousands of companies making them. Let's tick off a few. The terminal industry is exploding with automatic cash dispensing machines and more sophisticated automatic teller machines (ATMs), as we discussed earlier in conjunction with financial services. Point-of-transaction terminals for retailers, including supermarkets, also are gaining acceptance rapidly. Are these devices really computers? Many have computing capabilities but labelling them all computers is constraining—like calling everything with an electric motor in it by the same name. Computing has come to be a normal function of many electronic devices. The French have developed a credit card-sized device with both memory and computing circuits to, they hope, supersede credit cards with magnetic stripes. Customer information and account balances could be stored on the card and updated when used in a terminal, possibly in a retail transaction. You could carry your entire bank account around in your pocket!

Nobody needs to be told about video games. One in every ten television owners has a video game attachment for the television set. The stand-alone games add to the volume of users. The makers of the game attachments aren't yet emulating King Gillette by giving them away, but the growth principle is the same. The game cassettes are the really big money makers. The application of sophisticated electronics to other toys is not as far along, but the day will came when toy soldiers respond to voice commands. Simple toys based on this principle already have been produced. In the way of adult entertainment, wall-size televisions aren't here yet but they're coming. As the manufacturers get serious about picture quality and cost, which are the remaining stumbling blocks, large-screen television sales will take off. It's the logical next step for an industry whose product—the television—is the focal point for many entertainment forms, including video games, cable television, and prerecorded movies. When Philo T. Farnsworth developed the first working television in 1927, he had no idea what he had sprung upon the world.

Speaking of cable television, did you know that more than a third of U.S. homes were wired for it by the end of 1982? That, in addition to television and movie channels, the cable systems were already being used for video shopping and video reception of stories from newspapers ("videotex"), as well as the two-way communication we mentioned before? Communications is big business. No better proof exists than the telephone industry. Dozens of companies grew up to challenge the Bell System during the 1970s, using their own satellite and ground transmission facilities. With the 1982 separation of AT&T into separate entities for local and long-distance communications, the competition will become even more fierce for the communication dollar. The rising cost of transportation, the increasing volume of information in our society, the decreasing cost of electronic alternatives to sending paper messages and documents—these contribute to the communications industry's success.

One way to put the various components of the electronics industry into perspective is to look at how electronic they are. That is, how many of the basic building blocks of electronics, integrated circuits, do they use? The answer is surprising in some ways and not in others. For instance, one survey showed that the communications industry of which we just spoke uses about 15 percent of the integrated circuit "chips" manufactured each year. About 30 percent goes to the computer industry. About 15 percent goes into industrial equipment and products, and a surprising 25 percent into consumer products, including video games. The auto makers take up about 10 percent for their computer-controlled carburetion and so on. The remaining 5 percent is spread around places like the government.[2] Certainly tells an interesting story about which parts of our society are going electronic.

Materials Science

Electronics are glamorous and highly visible. Their very nature is a sort of elegance of quiet operation and blinking lights. The science of materials is not very glamorous, yet it has been the source of some significant technological advances.

Metals have developed into the primary industrial materials, from basic iron and steel to exotic titanium. Most materials research is oriented toward either using metals better or finding alternative products. Fatigue and corrosion are two drawbacks to many metals. Researchers have figured out how to lower both through new ways of manufacturing metal parts, for example through making the metal into a powder first and then forming the parts. Another problem with metals: minute defects that affect performance. New casting methods have reduced these defects to almost zero. Who are these high-technology companies? Would you believe General Electric, one of our oldest "technology" companies, is one of them?

Airplanes are a prime user of lightweight, strong materials, an ideal place for non-metallic materials with adequate strength. Parts of a Boeing 747 are glass fibers. Graphite compounds are used in fighter planes. The engine pods on a DC9-Super 80 are largely non-metallic materials. Automobiles have lower stress requirements for body parts and are made with extensive use of glass fibers and plastic-like materials. The automakers have been successful at matching paint colors on metallic and non-metallic surfaces. You'd be surprised at how many of the exterior "sheet metal" parts on your car are not metal. Use of non-metallics in other parts of cars will come. Ford already is testing an engine made primarily of plastic parts.

Materials technology even extends into ceramics, ones that are not quite as brittle as the ashtrays in your house. Companies like Corning Glass are working on industrial applications for replacement of metals.

Clearly, materials are high technology, but not so controversial as one of the newest entries in the high-technology race.

Biotechnology

The recent stock market splashes of such companies as Genentech were the stuff of which headlines are made. The promise of modifying the genetic material in living organisms, the deoxyribonucleic acid (DNA), had seemed to be possible but remote science fiction ever since Watson and Crick deciphered the chemical structure of DNA (the famous double helix) in 1953. Science fiction turned to fact in 1973 when gene-splicing, the transplanting of genes from one organism into another, was successfully executed at Stanford University. Since then the basic process has been used to create new, albeit extremely simple, organisms. Commercial successes have been slight, limited to such examples as oil-eating bacteria for potential use after oil spills and similar events. Much of the money currently being made by firms like Genentech is coming from research contracts rather than from the fantastic new products that are expected sooner or later to revolutionize health care, agriculture, and other industries that deal in one way or other with living organisms. Genentech's first real product, synthetic insulin, received Food and Drug Administration (FDA) approval only in October 1982.

But the fantastic products will come someday. Fast-growing, hardy crops that are immune to the diseases that periodically ravage U.S. farmlands. New medicines painstakingly constructed to perform certain chemical functions inimical to bacteria or viruses. Optimum strains of livestock on U.S. farms. Some researchers think that biological computers may someday surpass the electronic variety. No one knows whether the industries spawned through biotechnology will ever rival the scope of the electronics industry. Probably not, but some segments of the population will be dramatically affected. The problems of high growth, financing, and entrepreneurial management will vex this industry as surely as they have caused fits in the electronics business. In addition, of course, the industry will have its own special problems, such as ownership of ideas. As opposed to electronics, many discoveries in biotechnology will be made with public funds or in quasi-public institutions like state universities. Who actually owns the rights to such discoveries? One thing is sure. The management successes will come to firms that do not relearn all the lessons of managing high technology businesses. They will pay attention to the experiences of others as recounted here and elsewhere.

Other High-Technology Industries

Obviously, high technology is pervasive in the United States. Are there other industries besides the ones we have mentioned? Certainly. Pharmaceuticals, for one. Not in the sense of genetic engineering, but using plain old traditional processes like fermentation. Other areas of medicine, including development of synthetic blood. The environment is pure high technology: operating on the frontiers of science, big bucks to be spent and made, product orientation, short product life spans before competition sets in, high risk and high reward.

So much for examples. We all now have a better feeling for what high technology is. Let's talk about managing it.

A Roadmap to Managing High Technology

Let's lay out what we are going to cover in the rest of this chapter. Basically we are interested in two things. One, which management techniques and processes are unique to high technology? There must be some to deal effectively with the product orientation, high growth potential, people characteristics, and the other common elements we have mentioned. Two, can we apply all or some of the fundamental principles that seemed to be effective in other industries? If so, how?

Before we begin, let's review some circumstances related to the kind of problems present in high-technology environments. These considerations will affect the importance and applicability of specific management practices. The first is the relative independence of the high technology entity and where it fits in the spectrum, from complete company independence on one end to being a small division in a large, stable corporation on the other end. As we have seen, high technology exists in all kinds of companies. The independence of the entity profoundly affects certain management needs, such as financing. The second consideration is a bit more subtle. It involves the distance of the company or entity from the product or process with the greatest degree of high or new technology: the closer you are, the more you are affected. In the electronics business, for example, the high-technology chip makers are very close to the problems. The companies that buy and use the chips are further away, and the people who buy and use the products containing chips are further yet. Each one may be involved in high technology, but the management problems differ in intensity and urgency and, consequently, the solutions also differ.

New Products

The importance of products in the world of commerce and industry forms a continuous spectrum, where high-technology firms lie at the end with high product importance. Also, the product differentiation is strongly unbalanced in favor of reality rather than customer perception. In other industries, reality and perception frequently are more in balance; in such industries as commodity health care and beauty products, the reality may actually give way to perception created through advertising, packaging and the like. Reality tends to be paramount in high technology. Since cost, the other major variable in addition to product differentiation, is also reality-based, high-technology companies have a need for truly differentiated products.

This requirement for distinctive products exists in an atmosphere that is not particularly conducive to product development. Product life cycles, i.e., the periods of time during which a product has a clear functional or cost advantage, are short. They range from a few months for simple electronic components or products (for example, some wrist watches) to a few years for sophisticated computer systems. But even a few years is an extremely short time to recoup an investment in products that sell for over a million dollars each! An introduction of a new product just turns the hourglass over and starts the sand flowing again while your competitors work on developing products to supersede yours. How can you prosper in this environment?

The key is a management approach that encourages and rewards product excellence, especially new products. The proper resources have to be committed. High-technology companies typically spend more than other companies on R&D activities. It is not unusual for R&D spending to exceed 10–12 percent of sales. That translates to one of every eight sales dollars invested in research for the future—an astounding percentage, when U.S. industry as a whole averages 2 percent of sales in R&D.[3] Cray Research, maker of super computers, averaged over $15,000 of R&D spending per employee in 1981. Also the proper climate has to be created. During the bad times for the semiconductor industry in 1981, Intel had an option of reducing its management force. It chose instead to use a "125 percent solution," asking its managers to keep their jobs and work 25 percent harder toward new product development. Doing the right thing during adverse business conditions characterizes the winners in high technology. In the midst of the same electronics industry slump, National Semiconductor maintained their 10 percent rate of R&D spending. If you don't develop products during bad times, there won't be anything to sell during the good times.

Strategizing in the Fast Lane

R&D emphasis is one element of corporate product strategy. But there is more to development of an effective product strategy than turning the scientists loose in the laboratory with piles of money. There have been some major strategic decisions made in the past few years. IBM entered the personal computer market in a big way. Texas Instruments decided to get out of the markets for digital watches and computer bubble memory. National Semiconductor also exited the bubble memory business. How do these firms make these decisions? What is involved in developing a corporate product strategy?

Perhaps the most important factor, and also the most unexpected, is a link between new products and the marketplace. Product differentiation or low cost is a useful feature in your product only if it makes your product more desirable to the customer. Similarly with new products—they must fulfill a need in the marketplace. Don't misunderstand: the need does not have to be specific such as a need for a calculator wrist watch with LED display, multiple time-zone capability, priced under $25. Truly new products seldom come out of efforts to design products that meet detailed specifications. But the basic needs of the marketplace must be understood, for example, the need to conserve energy. Products that run counter to the basic needs are likely at best to have a limited acceptance in the marketplace. Conversely, products that address currently unfulfilled needs are likely to be snapped up.

Obviously, since we are talking about new products, not spinoffs of existing ones, the idea of a marketing link in a product-driven industry is a little puzzling. How does one identify new products that are not based, or are only loosely based, on the past? Through vision and insight. That may be an unsatisfactory answer to you, but it is the answer. The founders of Atari had an idea that electronic games were a marketable product. The founders of Apple Computer thought their combination of multiple and easily executed functions for a low price opened up a whole new market. Both sets of founders were right. You can't turn on that kind of vision with a switch. But you can create an environment in which it will flourish. You can have management support of entrepreneurial thinking. And you can ensure that the ideas it produces have a solid foundation of marketability, which is to say that the marketplace really does have vacancies and that your product really will plug the holes. If this is not true—if you are making the equivalent of high-technology toothpaste when there are already a dozen brands on the shelves—you should be prepared for disappointment. The top companies know this. Several research studies, looking over technological successes and failures, also support this conclusion.[4]

One more thought along these lines. Be sure you know what you are selling and the dimensions of the marketplace needs that you are trying to fulfill. High-tech companies are selling products, but it's not quite that simple. The products come either with or without a host of other attributes such as reliability, ease of maintenance, company service, etc. IBM understands very well that they are selling all these things in addition to the steel boxes; not very many companies do as well.

Strategies have to be implemented. Products have to be designed, manufactured, and marketed. That brings us to the next point.

Operational Controls

The image of the eccentric, absent-minded scientist sometimes accompanies discussions of high technology. The unspoken idea is that product excellence carries the day. Or, mundane considerations like manufacturing efficiency are not important in high technology. Or even, low-cost products are that way because of brilliant design, not because of proper workbench design by the industrial engineers or efficient materials handling equipment. These ideas are downright dangerous. Good operational controls are a necessity in the fiercely competitive world of high technology. They offer a competitive edge. You can deliver your product on schedule when other companies can't. You can increase production rates or incorporate customer-requested design changes faster. Your reject rate from the customer's inspection process is lower. Even a low-cost product can offer you higher profit margins or a chance to undercut your competitors' prices if your costs are lower.

Good operational controls are the result of two steps. The first is the determination of the operational controls that are applicable to your specific goals of product differentiation or low cost. Objectives of low-cost production lead to such operational controls as sophisticated cost accounting systems, engineering controls to use common parts wherever possible, minimal inventory levels, stringent controls over scrap, and the like. These also are useful if your interest is product differentiation, but perhaps with different priorities. People can't do all things equally well at the same time, so it's important to understand how to prioritize one's efforts. To control product differentiation, one needs product-line accounting systems, engineering systems that can provide simulation and otherwise support engineers' creative abilities, production systems that maximize the flexibility of building multiple products simultaneously, and so on. Many companies naturally will have to balance the types of controls to conform to the relative weights they place on low cost and product differentiation.

The second step is figuring out what additional controls you will need if you are either wildly successful or wildly unsuccessful; if either event occurs, you should be able to deal with it without panicking. For example, if huge success will strain your production capacity, you should make contingency plans for obtaining in-house space or subcontracting, and then arrange for the necessary control systems. Success may require changing from a job shop to a continuous-flow production process; it may involve different equipment and their associated controls. On the other hand, if a lack of customer orders would drive you to the brink of bankruptcy, your budgeting system should be designed to report fixed and variable costs in some detail so that you can scale back costs rapidly if orders fail to materialize.

Consider Texas Instruments (TI) as an example of fully utilizing the benefits of operational controls. TI virtually has perfected low-cost, high-volume production of certain semiconductor products. By pricing the products on the basis of the low costs, TI achieves the sales and production volume required to attain the costs. A delicate balancing act, but they have pulled it off many times. IBM also has redoubled its efforts to improve operational controls. For example, they are pressing for both low-cost production, with extensive automation, and low-cost distribution, selling many of the new lower-priced products (e.g., personal computers) through distribution channels maintained by other companies such as retail stores.

Of course, there is more to the overall picture of operational controls than we have touched upon here. Our focus here has been on operational controls appropriate for high technology. In a later chapter we will consider the subject further.

Assembling and Coaching the Team

In a high-tech company, the managers and employees are not slaves pulling the oars under the direction of a tyrannical coxswain. Treating people as though they were slaves will lead to your own personal version of *Mutiny on the Bounty*. For all that he does well, Charles Sporck of National Semiconductor is a little autocratic and in one recent year caused the departure of his number two corporate officer, his financial vice-president, and his treasurer, for reasons of personal conflict (a charge agreed to by him). Such losses are difficult to bear.

Treating people well is important. What aspects are unique to high technology (as opposed to widely applicable principles that we will discuss in later chapters)? The key aspect is the support of creativity and independence. The environment is one of designing new products and bringing them to market. It is a natural "project" environment in which people can be given total responsibility for a product or project. Anything else, in fact, runs against the grain of the business. Part of National Semiconductor's problem was a highly centralized decision-making process for some business decisions that collided head-on with a decentralized product-oriented management structure in other parts of the business. Inconsistency is a way of life in most corporations, but there is a point beyond which it cannot be carried.

Naturally you need ways to manage the product teams that are established. The normal team schedules, budgets, responsibility assignments, activities and end products—all the elements of good project management. However, you are not managing a group of people pouring foundations for house construction. When clashes occur, you frequently have to back off from the strict controls and trust the people. If you can't do that to some degree, you probably have the wrong people. The people themselves may be ready to accept more responsibility. For instance, one aircraft manufacturer had considerably younger people working in the non-metallics area than the traditional metal-bending areas, because the non-metallic technology was so new. The shift supervisor in one area was a twenty-one-year-old woman, which was quite a departure from the older men who dominated most of the manufacturing floor. The company had "problems" with the younger people until they experimented with fewer stringent controls; at that point productivity picked up and soon exceeded the other areas of the plant.

As you can surmise, the product teams need some care and feeding; they won't prosper on their own. The single most important factor is top management support. Both research and experience have led to the same conclusion: The most successful product teams have the support of key top management individuals who can contribute to the team as well as share experience and wisdom and provide political support.[5]

Special Problems

Many activities require money: R&D, establishment or expansion of production capacity, advertising and other forms of marketing, inventories of raw materials, work-in-process, and finished goods, etc. There is a Catch-22 about money: You need it to be successful, but you can't get it without being successful. And that creates money problems at two points in your corporate life: when you are just starting out, and when you want to grow significantly. In the second instance, you may be able to generate sufficient funds from your company's earnings. But you may not be able to, and you certainly won't be able to do so when starting out. So you will need to get money from public or private investors, your parent company, or an independent company through a joint venture or acquisition. These methods all have one thing in common—you need to convince the source of money that you know what you are doing. That means detailed business plans with earnings and cash flow projections. That you ought to have anyway if you have planned in adequate detail. Therein lies a great truth: The planning required to obtain financing is not very different from the planning required to be successful; the absence of one usually indicates the absence of the other.

The second issue is size or the lack of it. What if you're a small start-up company? What are the keys to success? Fortunately, there is a lot of experience floating around. It turns out not to be so different than what you might expect after reading the first part of this chapter, but let's recap it, anyway. You need a good, marketable product—stress on both descriptors, good and marketable. You need adequate financing, supported by a solid business plan. You need an experienced management team covering the major areas of engineering, production, marketing, and finance. The absence of one of these factors is almost sure death for a small company—there is nothing else to fall back on. If you're successful, by the way, you will probably be acquired or go public—either for the founders to "cash out" or to obtain money for expansion. As I said, there is nothing magical about this profile of a small company. But it's the truth, carved out of the experiences of a lot of companies.[6]

External Competition

We are going to examine foreign competition in a broader context later, but it's worth a few words here to underscore the importance of the threat. The United States does not have a lock on high technology. The high technology elements of products such as automobiles are as advanced in German and Japanese cars as they are in U.S. cars. The automaking process is more advanced in other countries. Communications satellite launching, a very high-tech business, appears to most people to be a U.S.-dominated business, through NASA. Not so—the European Ariane rocket launching system has tentative bookings through a period of several years into the future. Computer-controlled steel rolling mills are also high technology, as are aircraft and missile components. Brazil is making and exporting all of these. Brazil—high technology? You bet!

And, of course, the Japanese. There is a perception that they only copy, rather than lead, in state-of-the-art electronics technology. That's bunk. Their market leadership in large segments of the office copier industry, facsimile transmission industry, and memory chip industry was not due solely to an ability to mimic others well. Their currently growing successes in fields as diverse as large computers, aircraft, and pharmaceuticals are due to technical innovation as much as anything else. Despite optimistic public statements, many high tech executives in the U.S. are privately concerned about the Japanese challenge. If *they* are, we all should be.

Fear of the Unknown

We understand a great deal about the things that make high technology different from other industries. We understand to a lesser degree the management approaches to achieve success. The lessons have all been learned through experience. Experiences that are yet to occur will yield lessons of which we are not now aware. This knowledge must temper our blind enthusiasm for management strategies that have worked in the past, but it should not deter us completely. There is a wealth of knowledge regarding high-technology management, to which this chapter has been devoted. By using it and concurrently keeping one's eyes and ears open for additional lessons, a high-technology manager should be able to improve his or her performance significantly. But remember—bold action is required more than perfection, or at least in a different mix than in other industries. Put another way, the high-technology clock seems to tick faster; time waits for no one and it waits even less patiently in high-technology businesses.

Facing Off Against the New Realities

"To most men experience is like the stern lights of a ship, which
illumine only the track it has passed."
—COLERIDGE

Chapter 11

Quality—The Hard Way and
the Easy Way

SO FAR we have been looking at various industries in different economic circumstances, attempting to illustrate some principles of successful management. We have noticed that the principles and their
application tended to vary by industry and economic conditions, but
that certain ideas were repeated, providing some degree of commonal-
ity. We now will discuss how to prepare for the changing world in
several key "functional" areas. We will discuss each area in general,
using specific industries for examples. The first key area is quality.

We have a product and service quality problem in this country.
Things really aren't made the way they used to be. The perception of
poor quality is so strong that it is sometimes difficult to separate it from
reality, and occasionally U.S. products are unfairly criticized. Overall,
however, the charge of inferior quality seems deserved. What are we
going to do about quality in this chapter? Basically we are going to de-
mysticize it and talk about the steps a company can take to improve
its quality. We are not going to reveal 'The Hidden Secret of Quality.'
There isn't any such thing. There are, instead, some management
actions that can be taken over time to gradually raise the quality of a
company's goods or services.

What Is Quality?

Dumb questions often lead to insights, so let's ask some of ourselves.
First of all, what is high quality? Quality is in the eye of the beholder,
but there must be a common theme. In a product sense, probably

workmanship; reliability; suitability for its intended function; ease of use, maintenance, and repair are all good indicators. For services, promptness; courtesy; mistake-free delivery of the service; a pleasant environment; and assistance in resolving problems all come to mind. You may have specific concerns that you can add to this list, such as efficient use of natural resources where appropriate.

Next question—why should we be interested in high quality? After all, there's a body of evidence that many U.S. businesspeople thought that high quality wasn't necessary. Were they right? Or did they just make decisions that looked good at the time but turned out to be wrong? We all do that, and the only real crime lies in not admitting a mistake when it becomes obvious you've made one.

High quality basically has to do with selling your product. If you can be convinced of that, the battle is half over. Quality may occasionally be an issue of short-term viability of the product. If all the competition is delivering products and services at a high quality level, then your low-quality entry in the marketplace at the same price simply will not last any longer than it takes the customers to find out that you don't measure up. Frozen food products and fast-food outlets seem to be particularly susceptible to this problem.

Longer-term problems are more the norm, however. Either the spread in quality between one company's product and another's is not of significant proportion, or other variables, such as price differentials or inexact matches in product specifications, tend to confuse the issue. In this case it often is possible to rationalize a low-quality product's demise as a natural result of market saturation or consumer boredom with old products. Only over a long period of time with several declining products, in the face of competitors' success, does company management begin to look in the mirror for the source of their difficulties. U.S. management has been forced to do this often over the last decade, reaching unpleasant conclusions. That's the bad news. The good news is that further analysis is not necessary. The secret is out. Low quality is not acceptable. Not another nickel of market research funds nor another five minutes of corporate experience is necessary. Time to stop analyzing and to start doing something.

But where does price fit into the quality picture? Don't customers wish to pay as little as possible for a product and won't unnecessary quality add unacceptably to the price? The current evidence suggests two things. One—quality doesn't usually cost much more. We'll come back to this thought. Two, when it does cost, more people are choosing to pay for the quality. They're not arbitrarily accepting higher prices, but choosing products and services with the best "true value," the quality per dollar spent. They won't pay for frills, but they will pay for quality. The evidence consists both of the obvious behavior patterns in the marketplace and of research surveys conducted among U.S. customers.[1] Sociologists and economists can debate the reasons for this: higher standards of living, increased disposable income, high expectations, etc. The reasons would be interesting to know, I suppose, but worrying about them is like worrying about the reasons why a dam broke when the water is hurtling past you. Whether they are buying a car or a computer, taking a vacation, having their film developed, or sitting in a restaurant, the customers are sending a clear message: quality counts.

Where Quality?

Let's say that we accept the hypothesis that quality is important. The next question is, where is it important? Which products and services demand higher quality? The conventional wisdom points to two kinds of products or services requiring higher quality: all premium-priced products and services; and lower-priced ones encountering stiff competition from higher-quality offerings from other companies. Absolute high quality is not demanded anywhere; merely staying ahead of the competition is enough.

What can we say about the conventional wisdom? Let's take the premium end of the market. Cadillac is an interesting example of what happens when relative quality is substituted for absolute quality. Cadillacs and their other U.S. counterparts are of higher quality than lower-priced American cars. But Mercedes blew their doors off several years ago by introducing different standards of quality. The luxury car market has actually increased in the U.S., but Mercedes, BMW, Porsche, and similar cars have a bigger share of it, in part because of quality. Imported beers and wines have had much the same impact in their industries. Giving up the price-insensitive premium end of a market to imports is truly one of the great *faux pas* of U.S. corporations.

The low-to-medium price segments of the market traditionally have been viewed as segments where quality can be lower because the prices are lower. The conventional wisdom says that quality improvements should be a reactive response, i.e., when the competition's quality reaches levels that begin to hurt you, then you increase your quality. The devastating results of this practice are all around us. It fails for two reasons. One is obvious: the inherent drawbacks in the reactive approach. The competition has stolen some of your customers before you take action, and it is unlikely that all of them will ever return to the fold. Over time you will lose a few points of market share here, a few there, and pretty soon your market penetration will be far too low. The other reason is an outgrowth of improvements in technology and management skills, often in other countries. Many foreign companies and some U.S. companies have discovered that quality is not necessarily an additive cost. (Within a product range, of course; a Rolls-Royce always will cost more than a Chevrolet.) Even when it is and selling prices are maintained, the sales volume increases may more than offset the increased costs. U.S. companies are accustomed to thinking of quality costs in terms of additional inspection stations, inspection labor, rework and scrap costs. However, if quality is built in through the better design and delivery of services and products, the additional costs may be close to zero. This is important, because requirements for higher quality have moved down the market ladder to the low end. It is difficult these days to think of a product or service where below-par performance or merchandise is acceptable. Twenty years ago, this was not true, and many discount stores were founded to sell poor quality items at low cost. The world has changed.

Automobiles and the Quality Problem

Here we are again, back in Detroit. I'm sure the automakers are tired of being picked on, but they are an excellent example of an industry facing many of the challenges that we are discussing. They are a major industry beset by government regulation, foreign competition, and changing customer desires. To date the response of their management has been largely defensive, grudgingly modifying their product offerings to copy foreign successes, while still fervently proclaiming the unfairness of the regulatory burden and the cost advantage of certain foreign automakers, primarily the Japanese. Facing the reality that they are going to have to do things quite differently in a big way has not been their strong suit. The quality issue illustrates this.

Ford has a top-level quality assurance manager who has been quoted saying such things as the company will never ship a defective car. Such hyperbole doesn't help when it is so far from reality as to be laughable. Ford's Escort and Lynx were touted as the new generation of Ford cars to meet the demands of the '80s. Yet by mid-1981, the cars already had been recalled eight times to correct design and manufacturing defects. In 1983, Ford said they're proud of the quality of the Ranger truck built in Louisville. Yet over 25 percent of Ranger owners reported problems in the first four months—that's something to be proud of?

The situation is no better at the other U.S. companies. After initially ballyhooing the quality of the X-cars (Chevrolet Citation, et al.) General Motors was forced to admit that the quality was not up to their expectations. As we noted in an earlier chapter, Chrysler has had quality problems with the Omni/Horizon. In fact, their problems started before customers even took delivery: The first recalls took place on dealer lots only two days after the cars were introduced to the public. All this comes on top of a history of quality problems in the 1970s. The Chevrolet Vega became known for its engine and rust problems, and Chrysler's Aspen/Volare models racked up one of the highest rates of recall. Ford's experiences with Pinto fires and automatic transmissions mysteriously shifting from park to reverse have been well-publicized. And these problems show up later in the public's attitudes. In one survey, ninety percent of owners of such foreign cars as Hondas said they would buy another one; the comparable figure for the Escort/Lynx and X-cars was 70 percent.[2] Even the professional public shares the perception—a survey of U.S. automotive experts and engineers revealed that these people thought Japanese cars had higher quality.[3]

What or who is responsible for the poor quality record of U.S. auto manufacturers? The most important factor is the attitude of all layers of management. The concern for quality is simply several notches below the concerns for cost, meeting production schedules, and sales promotions. The notion that quality is related to these other things has not penetrated. Attitude by itself can't make a poor car. But it translates into ineffective quality control during manufacturing. It is not possible to detail all the deficiencies here, but let's consider a few. During final assembly, the car line moves at a set speed while workers perform predetermined tasks. Inspecting after every task would be very costly so it isn't done. Workers normally can't stop the line if they make a mistake, so unless you believe in infallibility, defective cars are going to be built. The same principle holds after the car has been completely assembled. It's hard to believe, but a thorough inspection is not performed on each car. The U.S. automakers have so neglected quality control that only a few things are checked on each completed car, a product for which a consumer pays an average of $10,000. Part of the rationale for this is potential transit damage, so the dealers are expected to make the final inspection and correct defects. Right. If you believe that, I'd love to get you into a poker game.

Rather than spend any more time discussing poor quality control, let's do the opposite. Let's see how the Japanese get high quality and how we can improve the quality in this country.

Facts and Myths About the Japanese Approach

Much has been said and written about the success of the Japanese approach to quality. Before we can discuss its possible adaptation to the United States, we need to understand what it is. Let's review the highlights, from the policy levels down to the procedural aspects.

At the policy-level, high quality is recognized as good business. The Japanese consider long-term and short-term whereas U.S. managers think only short-term. The Japanese are interested in building a significant market share over the long haul, knowing that their operational controls will keep costs at a level that will provide adequate earnings. Rather than focusing directly on the bottom line, they focus on the process for getting there. Their U.S. counterparts tend to attempt to influence the bottom line directly in each fiscal quarter. Building in quality is clearly a long-term consideration, so U.S. managers are inclined to miss it. We also can see that high quality to the Japanese is not an isolated goal on which to focus. It is a natural byproduct of the objectives of long-term success in the marketplace. The emphasis on quality, therefore, is not something that can be questioned. Questioning it would be tantamount to questioning the long-term approach. The implicit acceptance of high quality goals is one of the great strengths of the Japanese system.

The organizational effects of the quality emphasis reflect the fact that quality is part of the culture. Everybody in the organization believes in quality and is trained to design or build a high quality product or to deliver a high-quality service. The long-term nature of Japanese employment complements the long-term philosophy of company management. Again, the high quality is a byproduct. As an employee, if you are in the race for the long-term and not planning to change companies, it just makes sense for you to do a quality job—it's good for your self-satisfaction and the customer's happiness. Competition for promotions among Japanese management is virtually nonexistent because the culture doesn't work that way, so managers likewise have no incentives to cut corners. They may be in their jobs for a long time, so they had better make sure the customers are satisfied.

How does the quality emphasis actually get translated into action? What do people actually do differently? Everything. Let's start with the front end. Product or service design. Designed for reliability, ease of use, maintenance. Services designed for error-free delivery. The KISS principle—Keep It Simple, Stupid. Facilities design, process layout—

conveyors, storage, traffic patterns. Production equipment. All chosen for their contribution toward making a quality product or delivering a quality service.

People, from workers through management, are involved in design of procedures, equipment, etc., even when their primary responsibility is to use the equipment or procedures rather than to design them. The famous Japanese consensus-building process operates here. It is natural for them to involve concerned people with any issue rather than stick to the letter of the organization chart. The team approach occasionally spills over into the formal organization, as with the formation of quality control (QC) circles. QC circles are small groups of workers (up to about ten) that meet to discuss anything that comes to mind regarding quality improvement. In some firms over half the workers belong to QC circles. Incidentally, the term quality is used very broadly to encompass cost reduction and almost anything else that involves product improvement.

The entire company is geared to accept only high quality. The attitude extends to their suppliers. Companies do not accept low quality from their suppliers. But they do more than inspect incoming goods and reject unsatisfactory items. They and the suppliers work together on defining the quality goals and the means to achieve them. Clearly each company has different responsibilities, but teamwork is essential— the whole is greater than the sum of the parts. Contrast this to the U.S. system where the goal of suppliers often is to maximize the defect rate in their products while still retaining the customer.

At the other end of the process, quality is pursued even after the product or service has been delivered to the customer, to ensure that customer satisfaction is maintained at a high level. Problems are brought to the attention of the designers at the head of the chain, and corrections are made. This is somewhat easier in Japan than in the U.S., because the Japanese tend to have less fragmentation of responsibilities among several companies. The U.S. system of different companies for design, delivery, and after-sales service exists in Japan, but not as extensively; for example, the manufacturer will service the company's products to a greater degree than in the United States.

The concern for quality implies sophisticated measurement systems. Such systems do indeed exist in Japanese companies. They are based on statistical methods to identify and categorize defects, establish causes, and plan corrective action. A word of caution here. The statistical approach of Japanese companies frequently has been misinterpreted by U.S. executives. In Japan, statistical methods are used because they are efficient; there is no need to conduct comprehensive studies when statistical methods will yield the same results. Statistics also are good for identifying trends and determining severity of problems. When corrective action has been instituted, statistics are valid means for determining quickly if the results of the corrective action are satisfactory. In the U.S., the focus of statistical methods is frequently very different. A U.S. company establishes acceptable defect rates for its suppliers, for example, 1 percent, and for its products, say 2 percent. Statistics are used to ensure that reject rates fall within these ranges and to pinpoint problems when they do not. Many U.S. executives believe that the Japanese approach to statistics is the same, only better executed. Not true. The Japanese are driving towards zero reject rates by using statistical tools. U.S. companies have been very slow to realize that the Japanese consider "zero defects" to be a major competitive advantage, in that it allows their customers to maintain less inventory, provide fewer buffers in scheduling, have a smaller inspection staff, etc. In the electronics industry, for example, the low Japanese reject rate on chips and other electronic components is starting to give the U.S. makers fits. Hewlett-Packard publicly announced in 1980 that their Japanese suppliers made better chips and that U.S. firms had better shape up.

There is another side to the measurement system—management reporting of operating results. U.S. management reporting systems still tend to be short-term oriented and to exclude quality measurements. It is very easy to justify cutting quality control budgets when the only effects reported are positive effects on short-term earnings. The Japanese have not fallen into this trap. Their measurement systems focus on long-term success and the action required to attain it.

A New Approach for the U.S.

Let's consider the most simplistic solution to the U.S. quality problem—transplant the Japanese approach to the United States. After all, there is nothing wrong with it. It's common sense in many respects. People familiar with U.S. companies known for quality work—Boeing, IBM, or McDonald's—might not detect any major differences between the ways they have achieved their quality levels and the Japanese approach that we have just described. Can we educate U.S. managers and workers in Japanese methods and achieve their results? Can we do it quickly enough? The Japanese took about thirty years to reach their current level of excellence. We clearly do not have that much time, although we probably aren't starting from quite the low point that they were.

There isn't a snap answer to the question of whether we can implement the Japanese approach. There are many critical differences between the two countries, but whether the culture is an integral part of the approach or merely an implementation advantage to the Japanese is far from clear. Let's examine each of the key elements of the Japanese approach and see how well it would work in the U.S., or, in different words, how it would have to be implemented in U.S. companies.

Top Management—White Hats or Black Hats?

I think we have concluded that U.S. top management, by and large, is not sufficiently supportive of efforts towards improving quality. Window dressing is popular, such as GM's top-level Quality Assurance position, but reality has not kept pace. What has to be done to get top management back into the ball game?

Two kinds of steps can be taken—policy and procedural. But somebody needs to kick them off, somebody at the highest levels of the corporation, probably either the chairman of the board or the CEO. In rare instances, the chief operating officer or an executive vice-president may be appropriate, but not any lower in the organization. The person has to have the respect of the entire organization and has to be taken seriously. In addition, he or she has to have the clout to make the procedural changes after making the policy-level commitment to higher quality.

The primary procedural changes that top management can make are in the reward system. From engineering through after-sales service, the people in the company have to see their compensation affected by their contribution to quality. Top management is not responsible for detailed design of reward systems, but they can establish the general outline. It might include when to rely on cash compensation and when on awards or other forms of personal recognition; or how much to reward direct personal effort and how much to reward individuals for the overall improvement in quality, so as to encourage teamwork. The circumstances in individual companies will determine the exact shape of the reward system, but all possible types of rewards should be considered.

Now for a more subtle point. It's difficult to have reward systems that are at odds with the management reporting system. The reports measure performance, and presumably it would be a good idea to have the reward system be consistent with the results. That means changing the short-term mentality. This would mean a momentous change for most corporations, but it has to be done. Short-term results still can be measured, of course, but they have to complement longer-range considerations. Most middle and lower management will probably welcome the change. Top management really will feel the heat, however, because the change will be in conflict with the rest of the U.S. business environment, including the investment community. Privately-held companies that can follow their own course have a big advantage in this kind of situation. The publicly-traded companies will be at the mercy of the public that supports long-term thinking conceptually but backs off fast when short-term earnings are affected. This is when top management earns their pay.

One possible counter attack for top management is to publicly adopt a strategy of quality, i.e., make it part of public pronouncements about the company or its products. Nothing overt—just a subtle message. Cross pens and pencils carry lifetime guarantees. That kind of strategy tends to carry some weight in bad times, because people know that the high quality probably precludes actual threats to the company's survival. It won't work forever, but it will keep the wolves away from the door for a while.

Which Side Are the Workers On?

Moving from management to the workers, we encounter the question of the day: Which side are they on? You can find people who believe that U.S. workers are still the best in the world. You can also find those who believe that the U.S. worker is the best ally the Japanese have in their fight for dominance.

Let's see if we can take a position in the middle. Let's also deal with the workers as a whole, rather than as individuals, since that viewpoint encompasses the organizational dynamics found in a work force. Taken as a whole, there can be little doubt that the U.S. work force is no longer the best in the world, if you measure the work force not only by real output per worker at equivalent quality levels, but also include flexibility and support for the company's future actions. The Japanese and perhaps some others are ahead of us. But we are not as bad as we are sometimes made out to be. Many Japanese executives (not all) who are managing workers in this country will comment privately that U.S. workers are lazy, unreliable, unconcerned about quality, and looking out only for themselves. This picture is also an exaggerated distortion of reality.

A cultural revolution is taking place in the United States. The independence that workers have acquired as consumers has spilled over into their lives in the work force. People have individual identities. We have never had such a homogeneous culture as the Japanese, so we have had less distance to go toward individual independence among workers. In addition, admiration of Wild West rugged individualism is still pervasive in our culture. We always have admired individuals who take on the establishment and win. Our surprise should not be that the work force is not a totally supportive group as are the Japanese, but that we ever thought it could be.

What then can be done? Are we giving up the notion of workers contributing to quality improvements? Of course not. But we are saying that the cultural issues are important. It's the other side of the same coin. The Japanese side is the side on which quality easily can be built into everything because their culture is supportive. Our side is the side on which the culture is not directly supportive and each issue has to be addressed as part of effective management of human resources. Not changing the culture—I don't think that's possible. But working with it to satisfy the objectives of the corporation and the individuals. In this sense, quality is no different from any other management objective. Achieving management objectives within the current worker culture is a subject we will return to in a later chapter.

Detailed Planning and Execution

We reviewed the Japanese propensity for addressing quality at all levels of planning and execution, involving many groups of people besides those responsible for the specific activities on the organization chart. Why are U.S. companies different in this regard? Do we lack the tools for planning for quality? Or the education, the know-how? The expertise to improve production processes? Are we using the wrong tools?

I don't believe so. I think we have all the tools to do the job, probably better tools than most other countries if you consider our advanced computer systems for design assistance and other advances. We don't have the top management support, but let's assume we can get that. What else is needed? A more fluid organization. For example, in Japan the engineers are constantly involved with the workers. In the U.S., such involvement would be interpreted as an admission of engineering error or inadequate engineering documentation. We need different functional units in the company to work together better. How will they find time? That's the other problem with U.S. planning and execution—never enough time to do it right, but always time to do it over. Many U.S. managers get an emotional kick out of crisis management. The Japanese are the opposite—careful planning, involving more people, building the consensus. They can move fast when they have to, but in this matter I'm afraid they come out ahead. We need more emphasis on our people crossing organizational boundaries and taking the time to do it.

Another thought. Japanese plants are staffed with veterans because of the "lifetime" employment. Ours aren't. Therefore, even though we have the knowledge and tools, we will have to use them differently. We will have to create formal systems whereas the Japanese rely on people's memories. This really happens. For example, the Japanese build quality into the production processes by veteran workers and engineers sitting down together; the resulting written process instructions are poor by our standards, but both individuals know what has to be done. If a U.S. company didn't document the production process thoroughly, it would have to start over in six months when the engineer or worker transferred to a different job or resigned.

By the way, what makes us think that the culture isn't the paramount concern in planning and execution? Why do we believe that better procedures can make a difference for us? Let's take two examples. Matsushita bought a U.S. Motorola television plant, kept the U.S. workers, changed the quality procedures, and reduced reject rates by more than 95 percent. In other words, the new reject rates were less than 5 percent of the previous reject rates. Sharp Corporation moved into Memphis after RCA had closed a television plant because of labor and quality problems. Sharp's television and microwave oven plant, with American workers and managers, has had no labor problems in its four years of operation and produces at quality and productivity levels comparable to Sharp's Japanese plants. The prosecution rests.

Quality Control Circles

QC circles pose an interesting dilemma to many U.S. companies, particularly the unionized ones. They have spent over a century divvying up the responsibilities of managing and doing, defining clearly management's role of managing and planning and the workers' role of execution. Now the proponents of QC circles come along and suggest that workers ought to have a say in how their jobs are performed. And not for humanitarian reasons, which could be dismissed, but for economic reasons: The plant will work better. How should management react?

It probably depends on the company. Those that are ready to take the step probably should. Where it won't work, don't force it. It may well be that you need to put QC circles on your agenda of objectives to tackle with better human resource management instead of as independent objectives.

If you decide to proceed with QC circles, keep a few things in mind. They have to be an integral part of the functioning of your company, not an add-on. Allow time for them to meet; don't expect people to meet after hours or to continue to accomplish the same degree of other work as before, at least until they've been meeting for a while. Don't expect immediate, tangible results, for example, 10 percent cost reduction—you can't predict beforehand what improvements are possible in any one area or which problems the circles will target. Minimize management involvement; you're trying to get the workers' input, not to intimidate them. And don't expect instant success. The Japanese started QC circles in the early 1960s and it took several years to add significantly to their product quality. Even then, QC circles are not a panacea. They are only one element in a comprehensive quality improvement program.

Dealing Outside the Company

As we discussed, in Japan it is customary for companies to have within their sphere of influence both suppliers' quality and the aftersale experiences of customers. This is so uncommon in the United States, especially supplier relations, that one is tempted to dismiss this approach as one for which the U.S. is not quite ready or properly structured. However, let me share a provocative thought with you—some of the best-managed U.S. companies employ the approach. Boeing feels no compunction about getting deeply involved in the operations of their suppliers and subcontractors, sending entire teams in to help them when necessary. Boeing also demonstrates other characteristics of the Japanese interest in quality. The results: the best mechanical safety record among the major aircraft builders. *And* the top quality ranking in a 1983 survey of U.S. industries—the best ranking of all companies in all industries.[4]

Does this change our overall conclusion? It modifies it. If you think you're ready to take on supplier relations, go ahead. The advantages of success make the effort worthwhile. What about the aftersales aspect? If your company doesn't get involved directly with the final customer after your sale, you can't change that. But you can conduct surveys and analyses to determine how your product or service is holding up in the field. You can help your customers in quality matters. Boeing maintains extensive relationships with all its airline customers on maintenance and repair procedures, operating procedures, and so forth. You can be a source of assistance when there is any problem with your product. Boeing provides investigative capabilities whenever there is a crash or other problem with one of its aircraft, regardless of whether there is any suspicion of equipment malfunction. That's a concern for quality (and customer service).

Of course, when you control the relationship with the end customer, you can do even more. The airlines have standards for everything from on-board supplies of reading materials to allowable time for a reservation call to go unanswered. Not surprisingly, there is a correlation between effective performance to the standards and customer perceptions of quality. American and United try very hard to perform in a high-quality manner, and they usually rank near the top of customer preference surveys. These airlines are living proof that quality is important in making money. If you refer to Figure 9–1 in Chapter 9, you'll see that United and American have both been top money makers over the last ten years. The fact that they aren't the first two most profitable airlines simply means that other things in addition to quality are also important.

The Role of Statistics

Statistics are a universal language. The Japanese do not have a monopoly on their application. In fact, the quantitative orientation of the education of many U.S. managers is a real benefit. Usually, U.S. managers are accused of being overly numbers-oriented, a charge that certainly isn't appropriate for the world of statistics! The role of statistics in U.S. business should change, however. Statistics should no longer be used to assist in producing goods and services at the minimum acceptable level of quality. They must be used, as they are by the Japanese, to identify defects and their causes, to progress toward a zero defect rate or as close as practicable. Statistics are equally applicable in product and service businesses. Citibank, for example, identified and eliminated several types of check processing errors through statistical methods.

As with any other information, statistics are useless if nobody sees them. They must be circulated to three groups of people—top management (for the critical statistics), the people responsible for the errors, and the management responsible for error correction. Arranging numbers in a readable format is almost an art form, especially so with statistics. Charts and other graphic presentation devices usually are helpful. In many companies, highlighting statistics of both good and bad quality performance in "war rooms" has proven effective. Workers and managers know that their efforts are being taken seriously when their contributions are displayed publicly on the walls of the rooms in the form of trend charts, for example. This management tool originated in its present form in the aerospace industry and today is used by dozens of companies.

To conclude, statistics are one of the more potent weapons in the U.S. manager's arsenal because the technical knowledge already exists in the organization or can be acquired easily. All that is needed is to focus the weapon differently from before and the competition will at least have a fight on their hands.

Why the Hard Way Is the Easy Way

Quality is important. There is no magic answer, and gimmicks are not the answer. Following the gimmick path is appealing, but definitely qualifies as the Hard Way referred to in the title of this chapter. The Easy Way is only easy conceptually (or, because it works, as compared to the Hard Way). It involves fundamental changes in the attitude of the people in the company and then a lot of hard work. Its only redeeming feature is that it will be effective. Maybe for your company you have to take that on faith, but if you look around, as we have, you can see plenty of examples. Perhaps one more would be useful. Somehow in this crazy world we live in, it seems appropriate that Disney World In Florida should be well-managed. They have virtually a monopoly, a famous name to trade on and fantastic word-of-mouth advertising. Wouldn't it be easy to make a few bucks more by skimping on quality? For a year or two, possibly. Then the whole enterprise would start to slide downhill. The management knows this without a lot of tangible evidence to tell them so, and they maintain a high level of quality service, year after year. So, the next time you think of Mickey Mouse, remember that he's more than a cartoon character. He's a long-lived symbol of quality in a nation that has been losing the quality war.

"So many men, so many opinions."
—TERENCE

Chapter 12

What the Customers Want

THERE ARE several faces on our magic prism that allows us to look into the future. We have had a glimpse of what is likely to happen in many industries. Along the way, we also have taken a peek at the trends for products and services. In so doing, we have seen some of the workings of the marketplace. But we have not seen how the various industries, products, and services interact and compete in the marketplace. We have had, in effect, a pile of pieces to a giant jigsaw puzzle and we have been analyzing the pieces separately. It is time to look at the marketplace from a top-down perspective to see how the pieces fit together. In many cases, we will learn nothing profound—at least three sides of each piece of sky in the puzzle will match with other pieces of sky. But in a few cases, a piece of sky will end up touching a piece of land or water, and then we shall learn something.

We shall see that certain industries, products, and services do not stand alone in the world. Their success and, in some instances, their viability are affected by other players in unfamiliar companies with unfamiliar competitive offerings. Examples abound. The steel beverage can makers forgot to consider aluminum makers as competitors. Pinball machine makers didn't catch on to the electronic game bandwagon. Movie theaters didn't look upon home television as competition.

We have one little problem in putting together our puzzle. The pieces are made of some kind of cosmic silly putty. Their sizes and shapes keep changing, although they still all slide together into an integrated whole. We have to figure out how the components of the marketplace are changing as well as analyze how the various industries, products, and services can be positioned. It's like having to choose your weapons at the same time you're trying to draw a bead on a moving target. It won't be easy. And it will be a frustrating experience, since we can't possibly be correct in all assessments about the future. Let's begin, as the King of Hearts suggested, at the beginning—the structure of the marketplace. Then we'll focus directly on the customers. Finally, assisted by examples, we'll see how management in the future can position products and services to take advantage of the new marketing realities.

Who's Buying What?

"The marketplace" is too big to get our arms around. We need to break it into manageable pieces, along lines that will permit us to consider traditional industry segmentation where appropriate but that will not constrain us where it is not appropriate. Perhaps the most basic cut that we can make is between high-growth and low-growth markets.

Although it's not perfect, a distinction between industrial and consumer markets can also be useful. For a start, then, let's look at the potential high-growth industrial markets. What are they? For one, information handling, which includes the current labels of data processing, word processing, document reproduction, graphics, library services. This is a perfect example of a market served poorly by the current industries, products, and services that don't consider the common elements of the labels and the integrated needs of the customers. In the future, they will undergo fundamental transformations to be better aligned with the markets. Throw in communications requirements and you've really got a mishmash. Data, voice, and image communications over the same lines. And it's increasingly clear that publishing companies will be competing for many of the same dollars being sought by the electronic communications firms.

Electronics are high technology. Will other high-technology industries fare as well? In general, probably so. Whether for Jay Forrester's long wave reasons or simply for being on the frontier in an era of change, the high-tech companies will be in the right place at the right time.

The market for alternatives to oil and natural gas is also an expanding one, with the competitors often unable to recognize one another. Architects are in competition with companies building more efficient electric motors. Conservers in competition with prospectors. Passive solar engineers in competition with photovoltaic solar engineers. The marketplace demands alternatives to oil and it always gets its way.

Money will, as usual, attract a crowd. As the legislative, judicial, geographical, and technological barriers continue to fall, the people who provide money, handle it, and move it around are going to be doing some fast scrambling. Money is the fuel of all business enterprises. In expansionary times, there is always room for someone who can provide the fuel at lower prices, deliver it more quickly, transport it more efficiently, etc. The present chaos in the financial services industry is only the beginning.

Capital goods—primarily productive equipment of all sorts—are going to find a receptive market. As we discussed earlier, even service industries need tangible articles to work on or with. The high-technology industries will certainly need capital goods. And, frankly, the basic veteran industries will need them too—not across the board, but in selected places. You can call it wishful thinking or you can call it the only course of action for rational people, but we have to assume that some companies in the veteran industries will improve their productive capabilities.

And here's a story with many possible endings—government spending. The government is like the professional gambler in the penny-a-point card game. It has a lot of money to throw around and it influences the pot in every hand it plays. The political winds at any given time determine whether the government is betting more on aerospace and defense or on social programs, but somebody will benefit regardless.

Let's take a crack at the high-growth consumer market. What are the characteristics of the marketplace? Independence. High standard of living. More than adequate disposable income. Diversity. Somewhat accustomed to a paternal government. Restless, with a low boredom threshold. What do these things presage for consumer-oriented companies? Specialization, for one. A continuation and acceleration of the trend towards retail goods and services geared to needs of specific small groups of people and, where possible, individual consumers.

For another, things suitable for a lifestyle where one's job is less important. Things to do with the extra time and money—self-improvement, entertainment, etc. Nike's running shoes moved them to $700 million in sales in ten years. Possibly more direct interaction among people, direct trading or bartering of new skills. At the same time, in an odd twist of events, more emphasis on a safety net of services to cope with major problems such as catastrophic illness.

New toys—games or rock stars—with short life spans. More consumer electronics. Things that make life easy, which in turn creates more demand for them—and so on and so on.

In addition, there will be some crossover from the industrial marketplace. High technology affects everyone. Consumers have many of the same needs as commercial customers. Alternatives to oil and improved ways to manage finances, to name two. Clearly, the ways to satisfy the demand may be very different, but the basic objectives are the same.

Let's now turn over the rock and see what unpleasant things are under it. What are some low-growth markets? First, however, let's differentiate between industry growth expectations and possibilities of success for a particular company. We demonstrated, in reviewing such industries as steel, that there is always room for the well-managed company to be successful. What then is the advantage of catering to a high-growth market? The chances of success are greater. Also, the upper limits of success are higher. The upside potential is greater for home computers than for steel, no matter how you slice it.

Having said that, let's go back to our chore of identifying the future losers, the low-growth markets. As before, let's start with the industrial marketplace. The primary candidates for slow growth are the basic industries that have been unable to meet foreign competition or competition from other domestic industries meeting customers' functional needs with different products. Metals, rubber, chemicals, vehicles, perhaps transportation. Although I truly believe that many of these industries will be equal to the challenge of improving their management, my expectations do not include all companies in all veteran industries, or even a majority. Many of them will face slow growth. In the strictest sense, slow growth due to strong competition is not a market phenomenon, but the reality of it impels us to consider it here. If we also look at pure market considerations, we see that several basic industries will encounter difficulty. Metals industries, for example, will have to fight with plastics, composites, and other non-metallic materials.

While focusing on the veteran industries, we must not lose sight of their suppliers, who may be suffering the most. They often do not have the financial resources or breadth of product lines to survive prolonged hard times. Small tool-and-die makers will go out of business long before a billion-dollar conglomerate will. And, speaking of going out of business, some companies can't: regulated monopolies. Yet the traditional gas and electric utilities are being squeezed by being on the wrong end of the energy business. They are too big and too locked into existing arrangements to move swiftly toward alternative energy sources. This part of the energy business will not be fun for a while.

What else? It's hard to think of a great number of other industries that are in permanent trouble. Are we saying that there are fewer low-growth markets than high-growth markets? Or have we just chosen more examples for one than the other? The examples do fit a pattern, but I think the pattern is valid. If we anticipate that, barring transient recessions, the world economy is going to continue to expand, then we will have the major national economies like the U.S. skewed toward growth. The natural processes of technological evolution and competition will kill off some industries, so the picture is not 100 percent rosy. Overall, however, it is fair to say that industrial markets will grow more than decline.

Is the same true for consumer markets? In a global sense—yes. Worldwide there are going to be more consumers with a lot of unsatisfied needs. But the link between the global economy and the United States economy will not be as strong for consumer goods and services. There will be entire markets that exist only outside the United States. Most U.S. corporations will not have the inclination, talent, or resources to tap these markets, but will choose instead markets in which the U.S. consumer can participate in some way. This decision will subject them to certain low-growth characteristics of the U.S. market. For instance, the U.S. total population is not growing very fast, so population-oriented mass markets will not grow fast. On the other hand, specific subgroups, such as working women or the middle-aged group which will grow rapidly in the 1980s, will be important to marketers. And, as we have noted, specialty markets will be strong. The antithesis of specialty markets is not only mass markets, but also traditional markets. Values change. For example, automobiles, and even boats in many parts of the country, are not as important as symbols of economic status, personal stature, or whatever as they once were.

Is the world as simple as high-growth and low-growth markets? Of course not. There are markets with such extremes in growth that the long-term trends are not relevant except for the strongest competitors. Construction, for example. Such companies as Bechtel will always do well, since they are well-capitalized and operating worldwide. Others will go up and down like yoyos. Transportation is another confused market, primarily because of its history of government interference. So, the picture is not black and white. But the growth characteristics of markets can't be neglected. They must be conbined with other information about markets and a company's capabilities to develop a marketing strategy. What other information? Let's focus on the customers in the marketplace and see what else we can learn.

Customer Idiosyncracies

Consumer and industrial markets are changing, with new market segments being created and boundaries shifting between old segments.

Are the individual buyers—consumers and commercial customers—also changing? We have seen hints of changes in behavior patterns and discussed them regarding specific industries. Is there evidence of changes in customer expectations that transcend industries, goods and services, perhaps even the distinction between consumer and commercial markets? I believe that such evidence exists. Let's consider a few points.

We have touched on some examples of consumer independence. Corporate acquisition of goods and services has reached a similar stage where corporations expect to be treated individually. You see it in contract negotiations. You see it in companies spending $100,000 to develop a custom accounts receivable computer program when they could have bought a "canned" package for $10,000. With a canned package, they would have had to modify their accounting procedures a little bit. Maybe the corporation is experiencing an identity crisis in parallel to the personal searches for identity. Whatever the reason, it's arrived. The need for personalized goods and services. The better banks always have dealt with their best customers individually. You now see a broader move towards personalization and also extension to customers other than the blue-chip corporations. I have sat in bank planning meetings in recent years where the topic was personalized account analysis systems for every corporate customer! Think about it for a while. What's important to you as a consumer and in your corporate job? Is it obtaining the plain vanilla goods or services that everybody else gets? Or are you beyond that? Do you need special treatment so that you can be personally more satisfied or be more competitive with your customers? Maybe a little of both. But you'll probably come to share my conclusion that personalized service is an idea that is here to stay.

As we discussed in the previous chapter, higher expectations for quality are also pervasive in our changed world. However, I think their genesis was different from the matter of personalization. Personalization is a very complex phenomenon, the result as much of cultural factors and the stage of civilization as to the ability of business to provide personalized service. Quality concerns, on the other hand, arose largely out of a proven capability of foreign companies to deliver higher quality goods and services. A combination of technology and managerial skills that has blown away the lower-quality companies. In some cases quality costs more, and here some issues of cultural maturity come into play. How? Both consumers and commercial customers have progressed beyond economic survival as a goal. They are able to think beyond putting bread on the table for today and tomorrow. When you begin thinking beyond tomorrow, the costs of quality become apparent. They are really savings because you won't need to go to the well as often. Of course, as a test of this hypothesis, if you are actually making an economic decision, then price competition should still be an issue. There should be at least a qualitative correlation between higher quality and higher prices, as opposed to quality possessing its own intrinsic value. This frequently has happened. Many goods and services have a price-quality relationship. The starting point in the relationship, the base quality level, is higher than ever before, however. In other cases, the poor quality merchandise and services have simply been superseded, because often good quality items cost no more to produce than the poor quality ones. People understand these facts, perhaps mainly subconsciously, and quality has become a force in the marketplace.

What are some other examples of customer changes? Let's talk about a narrow topic—brand loyalty. Is it greater or less than it once was? Both. Surveys and marketplace evidence indicate that the overall incidence of brand loyalty has been declining recently.[1] This is consistent with our perception of increased customer awareness that looks behind brand names. (By the way, although the term "brand loyalty" is used mostly in conjunction with consumer products, we are using it here to include commercial customers. Brand loyalty always has been highly important to business customers; if they find a reliable source for a product or service, they are likely to stick with it rather than try something else on a whim or for a temporary price reduction.)

But, at the same time, something else has been happening. Some companies have been reported in independent surveys to have loyalty ratings that were the highest in their corporate histories.[2] What we are seeing is a breakdown in the general incidence of brand loyalty, but an increase in earned or deserved loyalty. Customers leave poorly-performing companies faster and stick longer with those that perform well. You can also observe it for yourself. The consumers who leave General Motors for Nissan or Mercedes don't keep hopping around forever. They find a brand they like and stay with it as long as the company meets their needs. Is there a name for this phenomenon? The Era of the Smart Customer? I'm not sure I'm ready to go that far, but the trend is in that direction.

A Fresh Look at Markets and Customers

Let's stop briefly to try to synthesize our ideas on markets and customers. The basic tenet of our approach is to look at marketplaces and customers almost independently of your company and industry. Not completely, of course. That would be foolish and a waste of time. You can be the judge of how best to isolate your specific situation from the marketplace and the customers. Develop a profile of marketplace needs that is not extrapolated from the products and services that you offer, but instead is derived from a fresh look at the markets and customers you could potentially serve. Cast the net as wide as possible in defining the potential buyers. Identify *their* needs, not what the company would like to sell to them. Many of their needs are not under their conscious control, but are caused by things like cultural changes—don't forget those aspects. Look at them the way we have in this chapter. As you start to understand them and generate the profile, bring it into your corporate sphere by identifying the products and services you are capable of delivering to meet the needs. Think big, but think realistically. This step will lead you right into a product and service strategy.

The next step will be the conversion of the strategy into tactical and operational plans. These have several characteristics, of which two of the most important are the management control systems and the shorter time frames. The "systems" include the organization, methods, etc., by which you are going to carry out and control the implementation of the strategy. The real-world considerations of getting things done will shape your actual course of action. As will the time frames. Short-term realities will influence your day-to-day actions. However, the overall effect will be similar to the way a rainstorm affects your personal life. You work around it, but it doesn't change your long-term outlook, if you know what your goals are and have a strategy to get there.

Consider a basic industry like chemicals or glass making. Don't think about the product sales trends or how other markets might be able to use the products or what changes to make to product offerings to make them more competitive or to open new markets. (You need to do these things, but not as part of this kind of planning.) Start at the other end—what will the world need in the future? We previously discussed myriad options for these industries, but not this option. It's not difficult to get started. Glass is used to construct objects. Chemicals aren't—they are used in processes or as end products that make chemical reactions happen. So even by taking a broad view there is a natural structure to the planning. We are not going to be able in these pages to construct a product strategy to get the glass industry back to where it was when glass was the major substance used to make containers. But you can see how the market-customer orientation works. Try marrying the idea of constructing objects with some of the high-growth industries that we mentioned earlier. You'll come up with some surprising possibilities for glass. For two that have already paid off, consider glass fibers for insulation (the energy conservation market) and optical glass fibers for communications, replacing metal lines.

The mathematical or other quantitative techniques for doing the planning are not very important. It's vital that you like and understand the one you choose, but all techniques are tools and most aren't new. What's new in the planning process is the judgment, creativity, and wisdom that we are suggesting here. Matrices, decision trees, or whatever you prefer—use the tool to support the planning process, not the other way around. And, as a reminder, don't forget that the market-customer planning does not work any better in a vacuum than do the other kinds. You have to balance them, because you will learn something different from each one. If you rely too much on any one approach, you are likely to overlook something.

It is worthwhile examining a few of the high-growth markets that we identified earlier and see how the planning has worked. Where's the danger? In taking the answers too seriously. We are not looking for how Company X became successful. We are trying to learn some lessons from Company X that would apply to your company. Bearing that in mind, let's begin with ourselves—consumers.

Consumer Products—The Gold and the Dross

"Consumer products" covers a multitude of products that range from marketplace disasters to immense successes. Major companies in the consumer products field have rates of return on equity ranging from over 30 percent down to zero and below. There is generally a good correlation between financial success and an ability to meet consumer needs that can even be seen by one untrained in business planning.

Did we say that quality was important to consumers? And independence? What would happen to an apparel maker who combined quality with an image of independence and ruggedness in clothing? They'd probably go right to the top, which is what Levi Strauss did with a return on equity over twice their industry average. Blue jeans have been the right image in clothing: three out of the top five most profitable apparel makers have a big stake in jeans (the other two are Wrangler and Lee jeans). If you buy Levi's you know they aren't inexpensive. But a lot of folks think they're worth the price. On the other hand, the company has not done as well with other merchandise. Their few forays into high fashion have failed, and their expansion into product lines like basic shoes have not been as profitable as the tried-and-true jeans.

And, while the company was expanding beyond jeans, the jeans market was becoming more competitive because of designer jeans and generic imitations of Levi's. Levi's returns on equity started falling. What is the lesson here? Simply that Levi Strauss probably ought to focus more on their first market—jeans—and less on other areas. They've been caught up in the expansion myth of U.S. business—that expansion is always good—and they've paid the price.

What is the restless consumer interested in? Convenience foods. Frying chicken is too much trouble, so you can buy frozen fried chicken. Can't bake a pie? Same thing. Don't feel like cutting up frankfurters into a can of beans? Buy a can of beans with cut-up franks already in it. Many people in this country have no idea what fresh vegetables taste like. We're raising a generation of children who have no idea that peas come in pods or that green beans don't grow naturally with diagonal cuts at each end. If the meat substitutes can ever be made to taste something like meat, maybe the same thing will happen with them.

Are the companies that manufacture convenience foods doing well? Some are, and some aren't. The national brands with quality images are doing fine—the Green Giant has several million close friends. Doing fine when they stick to the areas where their image is strong enough to support good prices, that is. The Giant and others have taken some nasty spills when they tried to compete in markets where the image wasn't strong enough or with inferior products that didn't fit the image. The "generics" also are doing well, appealing to the customers who think that beans are beans are beans. But food processors as a whole are playing in a game with a fixed number of pieces— people are only going to eat so much food, and additional market share for one company is going to come out of someone else's hide. The people who sell home convenience foods are facing a lot of competition for the convenience dollar from fast-food outlets and restaurants. The market as a whole will grow well, but maybe the subsegments will grow at different rates than the total.

At one time Campbell's soup was the king of the convenience foods. They had over 80 percent of the canned soup market. They had Swanson TV dinners. Then they found out what it was like to fail to keep up with changing consumer lifestyles and spending habits. At one end of the market they were hit by lower-priced store brand soups. At the other end of the market, consumers were able to eat out more and to turn to alternatives that were more upscale than soup or TV dinners. The middle segment of the market was loyal, which in conjunction with profits from the company's expansion efforts (e.g., the Pepperidge Farm acquisition) enabled Campbell to stay in the middle of the pack in terms of earnings. A far cry from the company's glory days, however. What was their response? A repositioning of soup as a healthful food. Consumers are clearly on a health kick, and Campbell decided to take advantage of it. "Soup is good food" became their advertising slogan. They also created a department of consumer services to act as a liaison with consumers, including communicating consumer needs to the company. They don't intend to miss the boat again.

Retailers—The Quick and the Dead

Is retailing a good business? Depends a lot on what market you're after and who you are. Drugstore chains average almost 20 percent rates of return on equity without much dispersion around the average, i.e., there are no big winners and no big losers. Fast-food chains look almost as good on average, but there are a lot of companies doing poorly and a few eye-popping successes like McDonald's. Jewelry stores, furniture stores, shoe stores, book stores (the specialty retailers) are also a mixed bag with average rates of return comparable to U.S. industry as a whole, but with some real success stories (Radio Shack–Tandy at over 40 percent returns) and some spectacular failures.

What is happening with the full-line merchandisers, the opposite of the speciality retailers? The department stores and the discount chains. The rates of return are, surprisingly, very similar for both groups. Returns for both run about 25 percent below the average for all U.S. industry, whether you measure return on equity or total capital.[3] There would appear to be a lesson in this fact.

The lesson goes back to our discussion of new traits of consumers. Besides one-stop shopping, the full-line merchandisers no longer offer anything unique. Specific consumer desires for quality, fashion, selection, price, etc., are being met by specialty retailers who are focusing on their customers' needs rather than trying to satisfy everyone and, in the attempt, satisfying nobody. Does this mean the end is near for the full-line merchandiser?

It's difficult to say. Discount operators like W. T. Grant and Korvettes were once huge chains, and now they're gone. Many department stores have been absorbed into one of the large department store chains like Allied or Federated (known better by their member-store names, like Bullock's, Burdines, Bloomingdale's, and Rich's). Others just lumber along with rates of return that are not competitive for the investors' dollars. Sears, with their financial services, and others are pushing aggressively into other industries because they feel the market for full-line merchandisers may never return.

Sound pretty discouraging? Then consider this—a few large chains are earning up to twice as much as the average for all the full-line merchandisers. Some are earning up to 50 percent higher rates of return than the average for specialty retailers. Evidently the obituary of the general retailer is a bit premature. There are some companies that have found ways to get consumers into their stores. Let's look at two such ways.

One way is price attractiveness. Not necessarily low prices—attractive prices. Figure 12–1 illustrates the attractiveness to consumers of various price-quality relationships. Retailers traditionally have stayed in the shaded areas. For instance, the traditional discounters provided low quality at low prices. If their price levels exceeded their quality levels

Figure 12–1
Attractiveness of Price-Quality Relationships to Consumers

QUALITY

		High	Medium	Low
PRICE	High	2	1	0
	Medium	3	2	1
	Low	3+	3	2

3—Very attractive
2—Average attractiveness
1—Not attractive
0—No market at all

for very long, they went out of business. In the last ten years, some discounters have moved out of the shaded areas in the other direction—providing quality levels higher than the prices. These gilt-edged discounters have been quite successful, expanding at incredible rates and earning good profits for themselves or their parent companies. Their names are familiar to nearly everyone—Mervyn's, Target, Richway, Gold Circle. These stores certainly are not all alike in the merchandise they stock and the customers they seek. But they do all have in common a basic market positioning philosophy of giving the consumer good value for the dollar.

Another road to success in general retailing is to stay in the shaded area, preferably at the high end, but do it as well or better than the specialty retailers. Macy's, led by the contingent of stores in California, has done this about as well as it can be done. One successful technique is the store-within-a-store. Using this approach, departments in a store are literally walled off from other departments and have their own decor just as though they were specialty shops. It works. Attention to customers is also crucial to successfully combating specialty retailers. When the big retailers can combine the personal touch with the big-store professionalism, they have a winning combination.

So, concern for the customers' real and perceived needs apparently does pay off. Let's raise our sights a little bit and look at the consumer market abroad to see if the principle travels well.

Satisfying the Foreign Customer

There are a lot of people in the rest of the world. Too many of them live in conditions of poverty. However, a great number also live in conditions of relative affluence. Since U.S. business is supposedly the greatest consumer marketing machine ever to be developed, it would seem logical that its manufacturers ought to get their share of the international consumer's mark or yen or whatever. How have we been doing?

The record is unclear. There have been some very successful industries and companies. Textile producers are a good example. Our textile mills are turning out high-quality, reasonably-priced basic textile products, e.g. bed sheets that compete well with both European and Asian products. We have over 25 percent of the market for certain goods in some countries.[4] However, we are not strong in apparel or goods that are likely to be dependent on national or local tastes. And therein lies a tale of arrogant marketing.

To put it bluntly, many U.S. companies expect foreign consumers to buy what we have to sell. They use marketing techniques developed for the United States and then wonder why their products don't sell well abroad. (Of the forty-nine 1982 international advertising film awards, U.S. ads garnered only one award.) Or they accuse foreign nations of erecting non-tariff barriers to U.S. competition. We don't build minicars for foreign markets. But the foreign automakers conform to our market. We don't attempt to learn foreign consumers' tastes in food. It probably strikes many of us as a poor risk to market something as oriented to local culture as food. Yet Nestlé is a foreign company and does well in Japan and the U.S. We generally don't market clothes designed with different physiques in mind to Oriental countries, but they turn out hundreds of thousands of articles of clothing to fit American consumers.

Can it be different? Yes. Levi Strauss holds down the high-priced end of the Japanese jeans market with pants made to conform to local styles and fitting customs. Coke's universal appeal gives it over half the carbonated beverage market. Procter & Gamble adopted Japanese-style packaging and advertising and has been able to acquire profitable market shares for several of its products there, including half of the disposable diaper market. And if you can succeed in the Japanese market, you can succeed anywhere! It can be a humbling experience to realize that U.S. tastes don't rule the world. But the rest of the world has known that for some time, and it's up to us now to try to catch up.

As with the consumer market, the overseas industrial market is enormous. How are we faring? The situation is analogous to the consumer market. Where we can use U.S. expertise or products that already exist, we do well. Boeing dominates the world aircraft market, and U.S. computers are the most formidable competitors in the field. Where we don't have ready-made products or services, we don't do as well. The construction industry is an example of both phenomena. Bechtel and Fluor are U.S. companies that have competed for and won some of the largest international construction contracts ever let—for hotels, airports, refineries, you name it. Yet in comparison to the number of such projects that have been done in this country, we aren't doing well internationally. The country that has had the greatest number of large construction projects in the world did not maintain the capability and market it to less-developed countries. The same is true in other areas outside construction. We built the best telephone system in the world, but government policies and lack of private initiative have given us only one major company—ITT—capable of competing in world markets. If the wave of the future is electronics, we're in trouble. Even our own companies, like Hewlett-Packard, admit some of Japan's electronic products are better. As the globe continues to shrink, we had better improve our skills if we want to keep or expand our share of its customers.

Putting it All to Work

One of Lewis Carroll's characters said, "Everything's got a moral if only you can find it." What is our moral from the foregoing discussions? Simply that we have a handle now on how to go about differentiating our products and services through their characteristics or cost. As corporate managers, we don't have to rely on conjecture regarding what will sell or what won't. We don't have to build on our current product or service base as our only hope for the future. Instead, we understand some of the key factors in the consumer and commercial marketplaces that interest us. We understand some of the motivations of our customers. We have seen how to establish a planning process to identify market and customer requirements, and we have seen the results of doing so for the companies that invested the time and effort.

The results are impressive. Product differentiation can become a reality and be effective because the differentiated products satisfy differentiated needs. The role of low costs (and low prices) can be established to complement the differentiation and meet the price needs of customers. Successful market penetration and differentiation from the competition lead to good earnings, which enable you to stay in business and start the process all over again. That's what success looks like.

"Veni, vidi, vici."—"I came, I saw, I conquered."
—CAESAR

Chapter 13

Winning the International Battle

INTERNATIONAL TRADE is big business. Hundreds of billions of dollars annually flow between corporate coffers in different countries, because every nation has an imbalance between supply and demand. The establishment of commerce between nations allows for correction of the imbalances. Naturally, national governments and business leaders are not always in favor of the corrections as they would be made by a free-market system. Tariffs, quotas, and similar import/export policies are adopted to optimize the influence of one's own industries on the external world. As such, the international trade system is hardly a free-trade system.

All countries, ours included, would like to use the system to increase export successes and reduce the number of import successes. Can the U.S. do it? If we don't do it, we will continue to see our industries crippled by foreign competition. All of us will get great bargains on everything we buy, but the only ones of us that have jobs will work for importers. Is it possible for us to reverse the trend? I think it is. My faith in the ability of U.S. managers is what led me to this book. In it we have explored and will continue to explore methods for improving our management, sometimes based on detailed analyses of foreign management methods. Specific issues like quality have been examined in depth. It also seems appropriate to look at the big picture of foreign competition. Like looking at an aerial map instead of walking in the forest. We will learn something different by looking at the overall environment in which specific management actions take place. Let's start by briefly chronicling the events that led us into the patch of imported quicksand.

A Historical Perspective

For all practical purposes we are dealing with a post-World War II phenomenon. The period following the end of the war was a watershed for the industrial nations. They either had to rebuild their economies or they had to turn them 180 degrees from wartime to peacetime production. The Marshall Plan and other programs fostered a degree of cooperation between nations. Leaving aside the question of whether U.S. economic aid simply rearmed our enemies with different weapons, the aid programs did create an environment of international cooperation in which international trade began to flourish. Export markets are marvelous devices for achieving sales volumes that can support increased work forces in countries trying to find places for unemployed soldiers. Then the sales volumes create stability and efficiencies that lead to lower costs and increased competition in the export markets. Since you are trying to rebuild your country, nobody really minds if you erect barriers to imports. Eventually the protectionism will start to work against you, but then you can get together with a few of your neighbors and set up a community of countries that has freer internal trade than it allows with countries outside the community (for example, the Common Market). Let the government help where it can through tax incentives, export rebates, or any other supportive policy. Above all, get the populace behind you. Create a climate in which the national interest is perceived as benefitting from economic health. Create an us-against-them atmosphere; that's not hard if you were the losers in the war. When you're done with all these things, what have you got? The formula for post-war economic recovery!

Did it work in all countries? No—there were a few exceptions. For one, Great Britain. They were a winner in the war, not a loser, and so had no reason to change. They went back to business as usual, resuming their drive towards socialism. The class structure and resulting strife were perpetuated. And they were (initially) shut out of the Common Market by their continental friends. Except in times of war, the British seem to have a hard time pulling together for the national good. On the losing side, the Italians had a mixed record. Their social problems have been a serious factor. Overall, however, the warring nations recovered nicely. Most of them, winners and losers, realized that a new day had dawned.

None recovered more nicely, as we now know, than the Japanese. If you had to pick one factor as the most important out of the several that we listed, you might pick national determination as the key to recovery. The Japanese have it. It is unquestionably their greatest advantage, the ability to act for everyone's good. It is expressed in many ways. Some, such as company loyalty, may seem to be counter to the national interest. That's only because we are accustomed to a system in which loyalties are carried to the extremes of creating conflict. The Japanese are culturally incapable of letting the loyalties conflict in such a way as to do harm to the overall good. Instead, the loyalties are of a hierarchical nature in which each has its place and its time for application. In addition, the Japanese are no less industrious than other people, so when they set out to learn and implement good management practices, they were able to do so. In many cases, as we have seen, they were able to improve on U.S. methods or to practice what we merely preach, such as long-term thinking. They do very well at defining a corporation's long-term goals, the strategies to attain them, and the nitty-gritty systems and operations procedures to implement the strategies. The relative homogeneity of the culture (compared to ours) has allowed their corporations to assimilate new management methods perhaps more rapidly than could be achieved in the United States. The glue holding it all together is the corporate team-building philosophy of the Japanese culminating in a cohesive yet individually-supportive corporate organization.

The reward to Japanese companies for doing all these things well has been record penetration of export markets. We have already talked about autos and other examples. Let's broaden our scope and review some other elements of their success.

Japan Rides the Crest

The Japanese are riding the crest of a big wave. We are all familiar with the consumer goods like autos, televisions, and other home appliances that they have produced for the U.S. market. Some other products are less well-known but equally ominous. They are like the part of a wave that is below the surface of the water—it can't be seen but it is as powerful as the surface wave that makes all the noise and spray. For instance, many parts of cars that carry U.S. labels, like GM's Chevette, are actually made in Japan.

U.S. industry used to rely on U.S. manufacturers for valves. Now Standard Oil of California uses Japanese valves in their refineries. Jones & Laughlin, one of the big U.S. steelmakers, has installed Japanese equipment in its steel mills. Why have these events occurred? Same old story—price and quality. And the story is starting to be heard in executive suites of the U.S.'s hottest industries, such as electronics. Memory chips are the television sets of this generation of U.S. executives. There are many types and sizes of these chips, which provide the memories for computers, electronic games, and other devices that store information. There are both standard and custom-designed chips. The Japanese elected to focus on popular standard chips of certain designs, where success could lead to large production runs and high market share for a product that is highly visible in the marketplace. They succeeded in becoming the largest producers of the most popular standard memory chips. Japanese chips are used by virtually all U.S. computer makers that buy from external sources. Although they are a long way from dominating the semiconductor industry, the Japanese have made an impressive entrance. We are indeed in trouble if they can give us a hard time in one of our most promising industries.

To comprehend Japanese industry's firepower, let's look at some of their victims other than the United States. It would be very misleading if we were to conclude that the U.S. is the sole 'beneficiary' of Japanese excellence. Consider this statistic—Japan exports over $15 billion more to Europe than it imports from Europe.[1] The list of successful Japanese consumer products in Europe sounds depressingly like the list from the U.S. Autos, wrist watches, cameras, televisions. We are not talking about small markets. Per capita imports in Europe are higher than in the U.S. A surprising statistic, given our standard of living, but a true one. The market penetration of Japanese products naturally is not precisely the same from country to country, but we find a familiar pattern. Penetration ranges from 10 to 20 percent of automobile markets to over 90 percent for some consumer electronic items.[2] And, as in the U.S., industrial markets are not immune. Japanese steelmakers are selling successfully in Europe. The Japanese also are selling industrial equipment, for example, machine tools, both conventional and computer-controlled. I could go on and on, but you get the idea. The Japanese are blanketing the world with their products.

We have built a convincing factual case for Japanese superiority in areas such as quality. The management methods of the Japanese appear to be designed to achieve marketplace success, and the actual results appear to confirm the validity of the methods. But there is another test that we can apply—the opinions of business peers. The best all-star teams in sports are selected by the athletes themselves, not by the fans. What would happen if we polled U.S. executives regarding their Japanese competition? Well, it's been done, and the all-star team is primarily Japanese. U.S. executives believe that Japan overall is a more formidable competitor than the United States. They believe the Japanese have a clear lead in cost and quality matters. They believe that the U.S. is holding its own in the area of marketing. A rather remarkable picture of a non-competitive U.S. economy.[3] The only positive aspect of it is that evidently U.S. management are willing to admit that the Japanese are doing something right. You could be cynical about it and observe that it's difficult not to admit the other team's superiority when you're being ground into the dust, but the fact remains that it's a step in the right direction. Without the admission that one has something to learn, a book like this would not have much impact.

Other Players in the Game

The Japanese are clearly the primary international industrial force to be reckoned with. But it would be unfair to leave an impression that Japan is our only concern. Earlier we talked about Japanese valve makers infiltrating U.S. industry. European valve makers are also making inroads. Steelmakers have imported technology and equipment from Japan, but also from West Germany. In consumer goods, we have already mentioned Mercedes. Leica cameras from West Germany and Swiss watches are other products that continue to do well in U.S. markets, although their market share has been decreased by Japanese competition.

The so-called Third World, outside the mainstream of world industrialization for so long, also has acquired a share of the action. South America, led by Brazil with its $25+ billion of exports, is becoming a force in world markets. Asian countries besides Japan have begun to cash in on some of their inherent advantages, many of them similar to Japan's. The effect of oil wealth in the Middle East is beginning to be felt in production as well as in consumption. We shall spend more time discussing the future roles of countries in these areas. Right now, however, let's finish our discussion of the primary foreign competition, the Japanese and Europeans.

Establishing a Beachhead in the U.S.

Foreign companies, in varying degrees, have been landing invasion forces on U.S. soil and enlisting U.S. citizens in their war against U.S.-owned businesses. We are not referring here to passive investments, namely purchasing minority interests in U.S. companies so as to collect dividends and share in stock appreciation. We are referring to establishment of U.S.-based operations by foreign corporations or purchases of controlling interests in U.S. companies followed by imposition of foreign management practices. The impact of such moves is good in many ways. Adding a plant or service operation in a city or reviving an ailing company frequently increases employment and generates funds for the area. There are also some negative effects. The foreign owners may repatriate the earnings rather than spend them in the U.S. Both short-term and long-term declines in the morale of U.S. employees and others affiliated with the company may occur. It is seldom easy to measure the net gain or loss from the presence of the foreign company.

Retailers have perhaps the most experience for us to look at. Consider the following list of U.S. retailers. Ohrbach's. Marshall Field. Gimbels. Saks Fifth Avenue. A&P. Grand Union. Fedmart. Korvettes. Winns. F.A.O. Schwarz. All purchased by British and European companies since 1962. All success stories? Hardly. Korvettes went out of business. A&P is a question mark. Several others are marginally profitable. Some others are outstanding successes. Perhaps the most honest evaluation of the foreigners is that they maintained status quo or improved the position of almost every company they bought. Korvettes and A&P were in big trouble before they were acquired. All in all, therefore, not a bad record. The foreigners seemed to have done whatever was necessary to prosper. They brought money or management talent, or both, to their acquisitions. Also, the negative effects have been minimal. The foreigners have not "milked" the U.S. companies. And their presence as foreigners certainly has not been an issue. Most people probably wouldn't even guess that the companies were foreign-owned.

The invasion has been successful. Not only are the Japanese dominating many consumer and industrial markets, but other countries are also eating our lunch. How are they doing it? Here's a quote from the chief executive of a leading foreign firm, describing his viewpoint on managing an acquired business. "Ten years is not too long when you are going into a new business." The typical long-term Japanese approach? Hardly—the speaker was the head of British BAT Industries, owner of Saks, Gimbels, and other U.S. retailers. We are surrounded on all sides by long-term thinkers. Perhaps U.S. managers should consider changing their approach.

Of course, things don't always go smoothly for the foreign companies. Putting down roots in the United States has been a slower process for foreign manufacturers than for retailers. They have been concerned that their competitive advantages, such as quality and cost, could not be preserved in U.S. manufacturing plants. Volkswagen initially couldn't attain acceptable quality levels in its Pennsylvania plant. Quality has since improved, but not to that of German-made cars. Cost is also a problem. The company originally negotiated a wage pact lower than that of the Detroit automakers, with planned movements over time toward parity. The wage increases, and high fixed costs, have put a cost squeeze on the Germans that they would prefer not to have encountered. Slumping sales haven't helped.

What about the Japanese? They have been reluctant to manufacture cars or trucks in the U.S. Many of them are truly convinced that the U.S. culture is not conducive to efficient, quality manufacturing. The culture issue is very real—at management levels as well as at worker levels. Japanese electronics companies have had U.S. manufacturing operations for a number of years. The U.S. executives who were the heads of Sony's and Pioneer's U.S. operations each left after a few years, convinced that Japanese and U.S. cultures were so different that working together was very difficult. Some students of management would say that the Europeans have been working with us longer, and that the Japanese will eventually catch on. Others would say that the Japanese do not want to catch on, that they see no reason to emulate the Europeans who are faring no better against the Japanese in world markets than we are. Looking at the facts, the Japanese have invested in U.S. manufacturing operations in a way that would indicate something less than unbridled enthusiasm. I think we can expect the attitude to continue. However, the results may change as the Japanese feel more threatened by U.S. government action and decide that U.S. manufacturing is a better alternative than strict quotas or high tariffs. The U.S. government is not as much a friend to its industries as other governments are to theirs, but when the stakes are big enough it can act.

The Government as Ally

The role of the U.S. government regarding U.S. industry is close to adversarial, for the reasons we outlined back at the beginning of this book. Being a government "of the people, by the people, and for the people," it was only natural to constrain business whenever people's interests were threatened, actually or potentially. As the dominant economic power in the world, the U.S. had no need to protect its industries from those of other nations. An exception was an attempt to limit foreign price competition to "fair" competition, i.e., pricing at low levels only if such prices could be supported by low production costs. A few tariffs and quotas were enacted, but nowhere near what existed in other countries. The executive branch of the government often faced conflicting responsibilities in enforcing pro-U.S. business laws while attempting to carry out foreign policy that was heavily weighted toward preserving the friendship of trading partners. The foreign policy concerns frequently took precedence.

Things have been different in other countries. The Japanese developed a very strong system of cooperation between business and government, coordinated by the now famous government Ministry Of International Trade and Industry (MITI). MITI and other government agencies have been able to set import/export policies, control the flow of research funds, and in general support the industries that were deemed to be in the national interest. For example, in early 1982, the government awarded over $40 million of research funds to computer companies. Cooperation between business entities was not thwarted by the web of antitrust laws and regulations that exists in the U.S. The system has not always worked perfectly—MITI and the Japanese auto industry fought for years, instead of cooperating the way it is usually assumed that they did. But it's worked better than other systems, because it is founded on the national determination that we mentioned earlier. When cooperation is recognized as being in one's self-interest, then all that is needed is the mechanism. If, on the other hand, the attitude is not present, then no mechanism will work.

Several European countries also determined that a strong government role in industry was desirable. The subsequent developments have been very different from the Japanese model. The most direct form of government influence, of course, is government ownership of industry. It is not generally realized how pervasive government ownership is in Europe. For example, take the following list of industries: autos, steel, airlines, railroads, gas and electric utilities, telephones. Of these six industries, four or more are owned at least 50 percent by each nation in Europe. Governments also have significant positions in electronics, chemicals, and aerospace companies. There is no clear trend; the French socialist victory was a political phenomenon, not part of a European trend. But there is no effort underway to remove the government as boss.

On top of the government ownership, the European nations have generally piled the same sorts of economic disincentives that are used everywhere. Quotas. Tariffs. Foreign exchange controls. Investment limitations on foreign companies. They have also made it harder for companies to change their minds after they are established in the country, with tough laws on layoffs, plant closings, and worker benefits.

Other countries outside Europe and Japan have not followed a single pattern. Canada, especially in recent years, has been extremely nationalistic, but has not shown much interest in socialism. Conversely, Brazil has put many of its industries into the hands of the government. The only common thread among other countries is a degree of government ownership higher than in either the United States or Japan.

There is a dangerous myth that the government ownership approach does not work. First of all, it clearly works in achieving short-term goals of maintaining national employment, increasing the export/import ratio, and protecting industries that need to improve their competitiveness. The government can do all this by diverting business their way, providing financial support and generally propping the companies up beyond what they could do for themselves in a competitive environment. But the myth says that sooner or later the governments have to pay the piper for their violation of the natural law of surival of the fittest. The myth is usually accompanied by the example of Great Britain. But what if many British companies just didn't do it right? Is that a possibility? Renault is owned by the French government, is one of the largest automakers in the world, and at times has been more profitable than U.S. automakers. ELF Aquitane is a profitable $17-billion chemical company that is majority-owned by the French government. (Both Renault and ELF were state-owned before Mitterand took over.) DSM, the huge Netherlands-owned chemical company, has frequently been profitable. So it's possible to be state-owned and profitable in some tough industries. Does this mean I am advocating socialism? No. In fact, there are many more unprofitable government companies than profitable ones. Studies have shown that private enterprise is still more efficient economically. But it does mean that government-owned enterprises can be tough competitors. The existence of the unprofitable companies proves another point—the time to pay the piper can be delayed indefinitely if you wish

What is the message for the United States? We are wasting a lot of government and industry's resources on internal bickering rather than on effectively combatting foreign competition. Every so often there are encouraging signs like tax law changes to encourage R&D, capital investment, or something else. But overall we still seem to be mired in the philosophy that government's role is to be at best neutral and at worst parental towards business. This will no longer be satisfactory. Just as business has some new responsibilities that it must not continue to shirk, so government must turn over a new leaf. Many U.S. industries and companies are fighting for their lives, or soon will be, against foreign competitors who are doing nothing illegal under U.S. law but are simply helped rather than hurt by their governments. The margin of victory in this war will be slim. U.S. companies will need every skill they can muster to produce quality products and do the other things we have discussed. But they must also receive a quid pro quo from the government for accepting their new responsibilities. Transplanting the Japanese, German, or other solutions into the U.S. will not work. We need to develop our own approach, as other nations did. Something on the order of the Japanese model, supporting private companies, will be more appropriate than the British model.

For one thing, the structure of our approach will need to emphasize cooperation with government, not coercion through legislation. Second, it will have to encourage cooperation among business people that now is largely prohibited through antitrust and similar laws. Finally, it will have to ensure that the inevitable inequities in the world are shared by nations that engage in commerce with each other, i.e., we cannot continue to go on with other nations taking advantage of us in trade relationships. Both overt and subtle import barriers exist to a greater degree in other countries than in the U.S. For example, Japan has erected a number of unfair barriers against the U.S. tobacco industry, from high tariffs to harassment of Japanese retailers selling American cigarettes. Although political action is beyond the scope of this book, business people have to continue to press for elimination of the additional barriers. If we can take this three-point policy and translate it into action, we'll have something. It won't win the war for us, but it will give us some armament.

A Global Balancing Act

One of the things that each nation is fighting for is the opportunity for its industries to succeed where they are capable of doing so. Except for national security or public relations considerations, no nation is interested in indefinitely subsidizing industries that cannot stand on their own feet. Since nations do different things well, it is possible to conceive of a sort of balancing act whereby nations could utilize their skills in producing a portion of a good or service, the remainder of which would be produced in another country or countries.

The classic division is between capital and labor, considering both the costs and availability of each. The U.S. electronics industry has availed itself of cheap labor in other countries for more than two decades. The capital-intensive process of producing the heart of the integrated circuit devices was carried on in the U.S. while the labor intensive "assembly" process of attaching the wire leads was done in Asian countries. Wiring harnesses, lengths of current-carrying wire cut to measure and bundled together for ease of handling, are used in everything from automobiles to computers; they are often assembled outside the U.S. for cost reasons. Almost all video game production is outside the United States. We are not alone in this practice. Even the Japanese are using unskilled labor in other areas of the world, such as South America. A variation on this theme is the use of labor from other countries when the low-skilled labor in one's own country simply is not available. Many European countries are in this situation, which they deal with by importing the workers into their factories, for example, from Turkey.

Another way to share responsibility between countries is by functional activity, such as by engineering versus production. Countries with moderately skilled work forces can sometimes perform all of the production functions at lower costs than the workers in the product's host country. The host country can be responsible for product design, marketing, and field service for the worldwide market. This approach allows the sharing to take place with countries that have other production resources in addition to a pool of low-skilled labor. It eases the political tensions that sometimes accompany a rich country's use of the low-skilled labor of a poor country. Otherwise, the benefits to the poor country can be lost behind the rhetoric of "exploitation."

Political considerations are often a key factor in another way. Countries can help each other by jointly expanding the market for a product and sharing responsibility for its production. The aerospace companies have been leaders in this approach. Production of the F16 fighter is shared by many of the countries that will buy it for their defense forces. Boeing has spread production of some components of the 757 around to countries whose airlines will buy the airplane. Sometimes countries act in creative ways to get their share. Lockheed won an airplane order over Boeing because the British government provided attractive financing for the Lockheed airplane that used Rolls-Royce engines made in England. Countries also can be mutually supportive by filling each other's economic needs on a planned basis rather than through ad hoc "free market" action. Japan and Australia have formalized their trading relationships with things like cultural exchange programs. Australia provides many natural resources, such as iron ore and natural gas, that keep Japanese industry going. The countries realized it was in their best interests to work more as partners than as adversaries in a free enterprise system.

What lies ahead? A lot more economic cooperation. It will not replace international competition, but it will supplement it. U.S. managers understand using low-cost foreign labor, but are not yet very skilled at other forms of international cooperation. They are going to have to become much better at it. The alternative is further loss of market share to foreign competitors.

As the World Turns

The world economic landscape looks like a mine field. Picking our way through it in the next few years is going to be a real challenge with all the things that we have working against us. However, there are two rays of hope to help us find our way. One is the skills of U.S. business people. We wouldn't have made it to where we are if we didn't have talented people in our corporations. The second is the way other societies of the world are changing. Our society will continue to experience changes, some favorable to business and some unfavorable. The changes in other countries are likely to affect their business communities in a relatively more negative fashion. This is far from certain, but it would make life easier for us.

Japan is a major economic threat. Yet Japanese government and business in the years ahead will be under pressures more severe than anything they have known. The hostility of the rest of the world to Japanese exports is likely to increase. The Japanese will have to walk a tightrope between voluntary limitations on exports and imposed quotas. They are going to have to allow more imports into their own country. They will be put in the same position that we were in terms of labor cost competitiveness on many of their products. Numerous poorer countries now have the Japanese example to emulate. Japan will need to duplicate its successes with televisions and autos with higher-technology goods. As we have seen, they are hardly failing at this, but it is like any other new frontier—the problems are unique and must be tackled one at a time. In addition, they are rapidly moving towards a standard of living for their citizens that will squeeze business between demands for a more luxurious lifestyle, requiring advanced products and more imports, and higher wages that will reduce competitiveness of Japanese products.

In fact, the lifestyle issue may become Japan's single biggest problem. Bearing in mind the differences between U.S. and Japanese culture, it is still no exaggeration to say that they are facing an upheaval in their society of no less a relative magnitude than the one that hit the U.S. Many Japanese executives have described to me their concern over the attitudes of the young people in Japan. The concerns are right out of the 1960s in the U.S.: me-first attitudes; lack of respect for elders; lack of loyalty to family, country, company; materialism. Women are entering the labor force in greater numbers. Lifetime employment is coming under attack as outmoded and inefficient. Gentlemanly ways of doing business are giving way to more rough-and-tumble tactics. It is dangerous to see too many parallels between the societies of U.S. and

Japan. But the signs of significant social friction are unmistakable. They will slow the progress of the Japanese economic machine.

The other developed countries also have problems. Different problems for each, but all of them severe. Great Britain's problems border on economic survival. France is attempting to make socialism work. West Germany is trying to regain its luster. In recent years, both labor cost increases and inflation have been more severe in Europe than in the U.S. Our problems don't look as insurmountable when we look at what other nations are facing.

The rest of the world does not have an easy time of it. South America's rampant inflation is well known. Brazil and Mexico have not managed their foreign debt well at all. Africa has political problems that dwarf similar problems in other nations. Even the nouveau riche—the oil countries—have problems, many of which center around the clash between Western and traditional religious values. Their social problems may make the U.S.'s and Japan's look like minor domestic disagreements.

So the future doesn't look all dark for the United States. One more thing remains for our consideration—the countries that will be additions to the world economic game in the future.

The New Players

As soap operas periodically introduce new characters to spice up the action, so does the world economy. The new players fall into two camps—the ones entering competition for the first time, and the ones graduating to new positions in the game.

The ones entering the game for the first time tend to do so when their productive capacity has developed to the point that it can fill a void created by another country moving on to greener pastures. The lessons of low cost and product differentiation have not been lost on such countries as South Korea, Hong Kong, Singapore, and Taiwan. They are already into steel, electronics, garments, and shipbuilding, to name a few industries. South Korea is the largest maker of black-and-white televisions. China is turning into a closet capitalist to utilize its work force of several hundred million people. These nations will be tough competitors. Not only do they have many of the characteristics that made Japan successful, they have others in addition. The Japanese, for example, sometimes rely too much on cooperation with business associates while Chinese achieve more with an adversarial approach.

The additions to the world economy are not confined to Asia. South America will continue to develop if the countries can get over their recent economic mismanagement and political troubles. Mexico, with its oil wealth, was making a serious run at international competition until the petroleum market fell out. And the Arabs are emerging too, although in a slightly different way. They are already a world economic force, and they have chosen to expand into new areas. Not only into production of goods, but into management of their other great resource besides oil: money. They have assets to deploy of over $500 billion. They are beginning to manage their own money rather than relying on other countries' institutions. They own impressive, although minority, parts of many U.S. banks, Eastern Airlines, Texaco, and Exxon. Kuwait owns Santa Fe International, a billion-dollar petroleum company. The oil connection is no accident—they want more control over the refining and distribution aspects of the business, as well as additional leverage in exploration outside the Middle East. In 1983, Kuwait bought Gulf Oil's refinery and gas stations in Belgium, Luxembourg, and the Netherlands. The Arabs also are building a banking system to rival the money centers of the world. It will be a full-service system for corporate customers, competing with New York, London, Paris, and other banking capitals. It is tied in, of course, with the governments of the oil countries involved, so it will have no internal problems to worry about. It will be a potent force for Arab influence and control. Don't underestimate the Mideast oil countries. Their influence is less than it once was, because of plummeting oil prices during the recession, spurred efforts toward conservation, additional oil exploration, and use of alternative energy sources. They might never be as dominant again as they were in the mid-1970s. However, reduced influence or not, social problems or not, they may be the ones to watch in the future. They may rival Japan or the other up-and-coming new industrial nations. U.S. business people will have to manage better or be content to suffer against more competition than ever before.

What Does the Reconnaissance Show?

We have completed our reconnaissance of the world and constructed our aerial map. It shows a rather menacing terrain, not at all like the flat plain that we are used to traversing. A lot of twisting trails, jagged outcroppings of rock, and sheer cliffs to scale. In other areas, dense jungle inhabited by any number of unpleasant creatures. And numerous hiding places for our enemies to wait in ambush. Not the sort of environment in which you'd like to try to make your way while burdened with all the other problems we have discussed.

But the situation is not hopeless. All the enemies lying in wait for us are also after each other. Many countries would rather fight among themselves than with the U.S. Our size and strength do count for some-thing. We still have deep pockets, the resources to be a formidable warrior.

Best of all, the weaponry is not all in our opponents' hands. We may lack a few weapons such as strong government support, but we have others such as the raw talent of our management and workers. This talent can be combined with experience and lessons from our com-petitors on things like long-term thinking, effective marketing, high quality, low cost, and product differentiation. The victory is far from assured, but the same is true for the competition. As long as we do our best and don't become overconfident, there is a good chance that our heads will not be among those on pikes when the battles are over.

Chapter 14

Designing Corporate Strategies for the New World

CORPORATE STRATEGY is important. Why? Answering that question involves figuring out what strategy is. Webster says it is "the art of devising or employing plans towards a goal." That's not very helpful since it's so broad. It could cover everything from how to stage the annual Christmas party, to a decade-long program of corporate acquisitions. So we need to do better. In previous chapters we have discussed many management decisions that probably would fall under the umbrella of corporate strategy. But we haven't yet defined strategy; in this chapter we are going to do so. We will amplify some previously discussed ideas and discuss the approach and timing of others. We also will introduce some new concepts. By building on what we've done before, we will finish with a better idea of how to look at the corporation strategically.

What Is Strategy?

Most business people think of strategy as setting and achieving the major long-range goals of the company. Tactics and operations have to do with shorter time frames and lesser goals. Academicians tend to have very precise definitions of corporate strategy determination or strategic planning. The definitions may be useful to them in their classrooms or research work, but for practical applications add only a dose of complexity.

The key element of strategy is the importance of the elements being considered. Importance to corporate viability and to meeting its responsibilities for profitability, social contribution, etc. Decisions or plans that significantly affect important things in the company are strategic in nature. A decision to promote an individual can be as strategic as a five-year product plan. The time frame isn't necessarily important. As with all definitions, this one suffers in certain applications. But it has the advantage of cutting through all the nonsense that frequently accompanies a discussion on strategy. In this chapter, then, we are going to talk about planning for things that are important to the corporation or, more precisely, things that will be important in the future. That will be our notion of corporate strategy.

Theory is not much good without a test in the real world. Therefore, we are going to discuss management techniques that have been tested. They have not been widely implemented, so their description here should be valuable to many business managers. These managers' futures should be brighter because of the success of the few who have applied the ideas. At least that's my hope; it also explains the quotation I selected for this chapter.

What Do You Want to Be When You Grow Up?

Most of us have always had goals in our personal lives. Maybe the earliest goal was to be a doctor, followed in our teens by more dashing occupations such as professional athletics, acting, or international espionage. As we grew up we became aware of the less romantic occupations of engineering, the law, accounting, public service, and so on. Maybe we chose one of them. Or perhaps raising a family or doing volunteer work was more satisfying. The timing and the permanence of the goals are as different among all of us as the goals themselves. For some of us the goals are twenty-year goals; for others, five years. Some of us change goals frequently, not whimsically but as a result of experience or different values that we develop. Others of us hold to the same goals for a lifetime.

Establishment of goals helps us to plan our day-to-day and month-to-month activities. Some of us are more interested than others in linking everything we do to the goals, but the linkage is there in some fashion for everyone. If it's not, you won't achieve the goals, unless you're very lucky. In fact, it's almost impossible to plan one's life without knowing where one is trying to go. It would be like planning a cross-country driving trip on the basis of getting to the nearest cities without knowing what the final destination was.

Yet many corporations have no idea what their final destinations are. They live for quarterly earnings increases and annual earnings increases. There is nothing wrong with making money, but a steady stream of earnings increases is not likely to be always consistent with investments required to attain long-term goals. And since there is a finite amount of time in the day, the time has to be allocated properly, and time spent on short-term activities is time not available for long-term thinking. Even the best football teams have to spend time developing a game plan rather than working solely on perfecting specific offensive and defensive skills.

Wait, you may say. Some very successful people have money as their main personal goal. True. But they also focus on a specific vehicle for acquiring the money—real estate investments, for instance. Their real goal is to be good at real estate investments, because that will make money for them. Simply making money is a far too unfocused goal.

Our personal goals encompass more than simply the labels 'corporation president,' 'real estate millionaire,' or whatever. They imply a way of living, a culture, a set of values that are important to us. Corporate goals should be as complete. They should establish a corporate culture and way of thinking that permeates the entire organization. In their book on Japanese management, Pascale and Athos refer to the Japanese "superordinate goals," the "overarching purposes to which an organization and its members dedicate themselves." Is this yet another lesson to be learned from the Japanese? Not really. In the mid-1960s, Marvin Bower, managing director of McKinsey & Company, in his book *The Will to Manage,* recommended that companies establish objectives in terms of "what we are trying to do" or "the kind of business we want to have" instead of in terms of profits. He recommended that the objectives "define how the organization will serve people." The Japanese may have supplemented this idea or implemented it more successfully, but the concept is not foreign to U.S. business.

What to Be Good At

Let's assume you agree that corporate goals would be nice to have. What should they be? And how should they be formulated and communicated? Let's take the second question first. Corporate mission statements seem to be in vogue at the moment. They are succinct statements of corporate objectives with sometimes a hint of strategies. If they are your cup of tea, that's fine. However, I've seen many corporate management groups become more concerned with the precise wording than with the content. If you're worried about whether your statement has the right tone for the annual report, you're on the wrong track. If your executives are fighting over specific words, then you actually have disagreement over the concepts. Carefully considered ideas can be expressed simply, in terms that almost anyone can read and interpret as they were meant. Besides, corporate strategies aren't necessarily for the consumption of the general public, but more for the informed members of such public who have a need or a right to know. Winning a slogan popularity contest is not the objective.

Back to the first question—the goals themselves. They should describe your ways of fulfilling the main areas of responsibility of the modern corporation—legal, social, and product/service delivery. Working backwards, you must have a corporate identity based on your products, services, and customers you serve. You must fight the temptation to be vague in order to leave your options open in the future. Vagueness will only create confusion. You always can change your mind in the future, so long as you don't do it every year. If you're in the home appliance business, don't call yourself a "consumer products" company unless you plan to start marketing toothpaste. If you sell 80 percent of your products in the U.S. and 10 percent each in Canada and Mexico, you're a North American company. Don't call yourself a worldwide competitor unless you plan to expand into a number of other markets. Mislabeling your company will give a lot of people, including your own employees, the wrong message and they will behave in counter-productive ways. You need to think through your product/service objectives, based on the needs of the marketplace. Maybe you foresee continued economic cycles and want to protect yourself. Borg-Warner has gone from a strategy of pure manufacturing to a goal of 50 percent manufacturing and 50 percent service businesses such as security services (they bought Burns International Security Service in 1981). Your objectives should include not only which products and services, but levels of reliability, safety, quality, etc. Then distill the key elements, remove the inconsistencies, and fill in the weak spots. When you're done, you'll have something that's more than the sum of the parts. You'll have tied together your product and service objectives so you can develop new products and services that fit and discard ones that don't. Determining the key elements and focusing on them will automatically remove the possibility of having to redo the objectives tomorrow.

What will the result look like? Maybe an emphasis on popular-priced home electronics with high reliability. Not home entertainment—too broad unless you're planning to go into the poker chip business. Actually, "home electronics" is too vague. I use it here only to show that it is more specific than a similar sounding thing. You would need to be more specific—maybe home computing. Depends on your company—home computers would be more appropriate for Commodore than for Atari, whose product line is broader.

Legal responsibilities are at the other end of the spectrum in terms of definition. The laws applicable to a corporation do not have to be developed or invented, as do product/service strategies. Although they may be complex and open to varying interpretations, the statutes exist. Corporate goals should include compliance with the law. The objectives should be stated in terms of the laws that generally are likely to affect your corporation, such as those regarding political contributions, antitrust, fair advertising, pollution control, etc. In the area of legal responsibilities the corporate culture and internalization of the objectives come into play. As we discussed in the beginning of the book, many U.S. corporations have been guilty of serious lawbreaking. I doubt that any of them included lawbreaking in their public corporate objectives, but somehow their management groups privately perceived it would be tolerated. This practice has to stop. Also, compliance must be with the spirit of the law, not just the letter of it. Many executives would cry "foul" at this statement, but I say that such compliance requires no more than good business judgment of the kind being exercised continually by these same executives on other matters.

Besides, the judgment required to make the correct legal decisions is only a fraction of that required to meet the corporation's social responsibilities, which we know cannot be avoided. The basic objective is to be a good corporate citizen in the community, the nation, and the world. That means different things to different corporations. Being concerned about the impact on employment of closing an operation. Or of changing the operation into one that requires different skills. Taking part in national debates on economic policy, as General Electric has for years. As we have seen, business leaders can no longer hide from public view. They will either seek the limelight or be sought out by the harsh glare of a spotlight wielded by people who are not likely to be friends. So, construct your social objectives soundly and carefully. Go beyond pompous statements about accepting social responsibility, and decide what that means for your company and communicate it clearly. Only then will you have a well-rounded set of corporate objectives.

Getting to Be Good . . . And Staying There

Setting a goal isn't useful if you don't try to attain it and continue trying for as long as it is an appropriate goal. How do you go about getting to be good at what you want to be good at? Is it the same as being successful at delivering a quality product or service? Or is it different when we're dealing with the corporate goals that transcend specific products and services?

It's a little of both. Take the question of organization. Earlier we reviewed some different forms of organization and new management jobs that are necessary in many corporations. We have now also discussed the specifics of developing and implementing product and service strategies. How do we put these things together? Two steps. One step is to recognize that organization structure and jobs are dependent upon your specific company goals. You can't select a form of organization, such as matrix management, let alone determine the functional and program/product positions, until you know what your goals and supporting strategies are. The rule is to conceptualize and strategize before you organize. The second step is to link up what you want to be good at with people who are good at those things. Put the right people in the jobs. In recent years U.S. business has been seeking its top executives mostly from the ranks of the financial and legal professions and less from the engineering, production, and marketing people who design and deliver the products and services. Sometimes it has been useful (Irving Shapiro at DuPont, for example), but it has been carried to extremes. In contrast, the Japanese have consistently ensured that many of their top people have product and service backgrounds. There are some signs of change in the U.S.—technical backgrounds are increasingly prevalent in the chemical industry. But more must be done.

What can happen if you have the right organization but don't put qualified people in the jobs? A popular U.S. tactic in recent years has been to appoint a financial person as the chief operating officer, with the intent of providing a financial perspective on operating decisions. More often than not, the result is that operating decisions are turned into accounting decisions. The accounting and controllership functions in a company are intended to provide a check-and-balance system. As prime movers, such executives often are ill-equipped, and poor decisions usually are the result. The same problem occurs if we ask unqualified people to assume posts that deal with corporate social responsibilities. A clear linkage between goals, jobs, and people must be maintained.

Beyond the organization and people there are the inanimate resources that the corporation relies upon—the systems, procedures, equipment, facilities, processes. These have to support the corporate goals. What does that mean? It is obvious that you need the ability to produce and deliver your differentiated goods or service at the price you desire. What else can we mean? Once again we mean the concerns that are bigger than specific goods or services. Or the specific legal and social problems of this year. It means making decisions on the basis of the entire set of corporate goals and your total corporate approach to competing in the marketplace. For example, an international company has to decide whether to build an integrated worldwide logistics, manufacturing, and marketing network or to set up many smaller, independent manufacturing-marketing-distribution networks for specific countries. This is a strategic decision.

Suppose you want to allow for future products, not yet designed, that fit your corporate goals. To do this you may elect to use only production processes that are capable of expansion. Such thinking could lead you to a corporate policy favoring subcontracting over in-house facilities even though the in-house facilities appear to offer lower cost. In-house facilities actually may cost more when the costs of changing to produce new products are considered. Another name for this kind of thinking is "flexibility," but I prefer not to use it because of the implication of reaction rather than planning. One must always react well, of course, but one should also plan where possible. *Planning* the corporation's capability to satisfy its goals will provide the *flexibility* to produce specific goods and services as required.

And of course you will need new goods and services to fill market needs and better the competition's offerings. Some of these will be modifications of existing products and services. The corporation can be geared up to develop them if the corporate goals supporting new products have been established. Some other products and services will be totally new. In fact, surveys indicate that new products may be more important to company earnings than ever before.[1] To be developed properly they need both a customer-market orientation and a solid foundation in technology or another kind of differentiation. In other words, you need a product or service that truly is different and you need someone who wants to buy it. How do you find such an animal? Answer: You create the conditions in your company under which new products or services that meet corporate goals will be invented by your employees. You fund basic research that is consistent with the overall goals, regardless of whether it is related to current products. Let your production engineers tinker with their equipment in hopes of developing another Ivory soap (invented when too much air was accidentally added to a soap mixture, producing a cake of soap that floated). Let your customer service representatives brainstorm ideas with the customers. Let your marketing people play with wild concepts and spend money on surveys of "dumb" ideas. The only constraint is to keep the actions consistent with the corporate goals. Are many companies doing these things? Frankly, no. Good ones do. High-tech companies. Highly profitable companies long known for new product expertise, like 3M (Minnesota Mining and Manufacturing). Also Polaroid, which exemplifies both the spirit of new products and the reality of problems in trying to bring them to market profitably (as with the company's instant movies).

Internal or External Expansion?

Let's play devil's advocate and say that you don't believe in goal-setting or planning. Maybe you're in the whole fruit and bottled fruit juice business, selling your brand to supermarkets across the country. Only you don't see yourself as being in the fruit or juice business, because you deal with only one kind of fruit. You think you're in the market for X kind of fruit. You have a lock on that market with your well-known brand and plan to go on forever coining money from it. Since you don't know what business you're in, you don't realize that you have the production, marketing, and distribution capability to successfully compete in other fruit markets. The problem with going on the way you are is that you're vulnerable. Suppose your one product fell out of favor with the public. Or the government declared that a chemical sprayed on it during its growing season caused cancer. You'd be in big trouble.

Sound farfetched? It happened in 1959 to Ocean Spray cranberries. Just before Thanksgiving the government made the cancer announcement. Perfect timing. The year 1959 was not a very profitable one for Ocean Spray. But their management saw the error of their ways. Use of the chemical was discontinued, of course, but they realized that they had a bigger problem that would take longer to solve. They could have added other whole fruits to the product line, but that would have required different handling equipment. So they attacked the problem head-on by adding more juices to the line. The juices would blend well with company operations, require basically the same skills the company had, and benefit from the Ocean Spray brand name. The now-famous Cranapple was born from this strategy. Non-cranberry juices such as grapefruit were also added through acquisition of a grapefruit growers cooperative. The goals were achieved—Ocean Spray is now well-diversified under the overall umbrella of packaged juices. Financial rewards? More than two decades of an average annual sales growth rate, compounded, of over 12 percent. All in all, one of the better tales that can be told.

Ocean Spray developed a whole new strategy for itself. Then the company reached its goals through inside and outside expansion, e.g., acquisitions. What about acquisitions? They're controversial. When should you buy another company? Generally speaking, the last few years have been good times to acquire companies. The stock market continually moves, of course, but recently the average (over hundreds of companies) company's stock has been selling at only slightly over half to two-thirds of its asset-replacement values. If you could use the assets of such a company, it's clearly a lot cheaper to buy the company than to build your own assets or acquire them piecemeal on the open market. A word of caution: If you are in the market for a new car, don't buy a pickup truck because you're offered a good deal. Sounds like common sense, but many companies have made acquisitions first, then tried to build strategies around them. It usually doesn't work. RCA bought Banquet Foods in 1970, suffered problems for ten years, and sold it in 1980 to ConAgra, an agribusiness company, for less than half of RCA's purchase price. Under ConAgra management, who understand food, Banquet is doing well.

A Corporate Report Card

Today's corporation is in a curious kind of war. Sometimes the enemy is other corporations, and sometimes it is inactivity or doing the wrong thing in meeting its obligations to society. Battle lines are not clearly drawn, nor is it always clear when battles begin and end. The overall progress of the war is virtually impossible to determine with our current battlefield reporting systems. We get body counts—e.g., earnings statements—but these always reflect short-term performance and neglect corporate responsibilities that cannot be reduced to dollars and cents. We are fighting hard, but a lot of our effort may be misdirected or redundant. We need a new measurement system, a new report card for business.

There's much to measure. Progress towards corporate objectives. Success of product and service strategies. Progress on multi-year programs. Cost and utilization of resources, including people. Performance against social objectives and legal responsibilities, measured some way other than through judicial action. Things that don't fit within the framework of monthly, quarterly, and annual debit-and-credit accounting systems. Things where costs and benefits are not confined to the corporation but affect society, e.g., employment practices.

Business management generally is receptive to the idea for a new yardstick. Executives from environments as diverse as banking (Continental Illinois Corporation), consumer food products (Beatrice Foods), and oil (Royal Dutch Shell) have gone public with statements supporting changes in systems for evaluating corporations and their management. However, a recognition by individuals of the need for improvements is about as far as we have come. There is a consensus neither on what has to be measured nor on how to measure it. There is a wide variety of ideas for standards or criteria for measurement. And, since these issues have not been settled, we are a long way from uniform formats for corporations to use. Perhaps most discouraging is the lack of a mechanism to address these concerns. The accountants have the Financial Accounting Standards Board (FASB) to coordinate the development of accounting and financial reporting guidelines. The SEC is also involved in accounting and reporting issues. So are several other groups with their own interests. Many people feel the accounting profession suffers from too much guidance. On the other hand, the issue of overall corporate management and reporting is an orphan, neglected by all but a few individuals. Let's get the ball rolling by exploring a few ideas for improved measurement systems.

Financial people have a report called Sources and Uses of Funds, showing where a corporation's money came from over a certain time period and what it was used for. It is a summary report where sources of funds are depreciation, operations, debt, equity sales, and other large categories. Uses are dividends, asset purchases, and so on. The result is a nice snapshot of financial activities. The principle could be carried to a lower level of detail and also extended beyond dollars. Product line profitability statements are a particular variation of this. In addition, entire markets and strategies could be analyzed this way. The point is to see where corporate effort is going and where the resources for the effort are coming from. The potential for use in nonfinancial areas is very exciting. Suppose, for example, that you identified the activities of your people, i.e., the "uses" of your human resources, and the origin of their efforts, the "sources," by company department, employment source, other activities deferred, cost of the people, etc. You could really see where people were concentrating their efforts and where the efforts were coming from, including their direct costs and opportunity costs. The principle could be applied to machinery, facilities, or anything else. It could be used to isolate and monitor corporate efforts to satisfy social and legal obligations. It would be a powerful tool.

Beyond Accounting Systems

Concentrating on the unique aspects of what you are trying to measure is another way to go beyond conventional accounting systems. Traditional systems have been oversold and poorly used. In their usual form they can deal only with events (transactions) that can be crammed into a predetermined structure (chart of accounts) and regurgitated in summary form at short regular intervals (as financial statements). Most businesses don't fit this model. You need to identify the unique objectives, responsibilities, activities, schedules, and end products of your company's strategic and tactical plans. Then you can measure the actual progress against the planned progress. The key element is the end products—that which is going to be accomplished by the people who are assigned responsibility in the plans. The end products should be well-defined and, where possible, expressed in quantitative terms. Human nature being what it is, this will cause you some problems—people don't like to be pinned down. What can you do? Make sure the people are in agreement with their end products and schedules. Sounds obvious, but a lot of plans are imposed from the top down rather than worked out with the people who have to implement them.

Another problem: Many plans don't lend themselves to spewing out end products or achieving quantitative objectives at frequent intervals. What can you do if the end products aren't due for eighteen or twenty-four months or longer? The more complicated a strategy, the longer it may take to see results. Do you simply wait out the eighteen or twenty-four months? Sometimes you have to. But that's risky. You would like to have some way of knowing in the interim whether you are making adequate progress. Solution: Establish intermediate milestones. This is more difficult than you think, partially because you know it's a good idea and have already done it in the places where it could be done easily. Now you have to do it where it's not so easy. But if you understand where the effort is going, the milestones can be established. As a last resort, milestones can be written documentation by independent experts that things are proceeding smoothly. Beware of informal progress reviews. Beware also of reviews where the formality seems to overwhelm the information being presented. But insist on serious evidence of progress.

And don't fall for the trick of accounting progress. Reports of accounting progress sound something like this: "We're two months into our six-month project; we've spent a third of the budget; it looks like we're on schedule." Or maybe they're considerably more flowery, but the idea is the same—you've spent the amount of resources that's proportional to the calendar time you've spent on the project, so you must be on schedule, right? Wrong! Have you actually accomplished anything? Or suppose you have generated all the necessary end products. Have you expended the right amount of resources? Under the earned standards concept, every activity in a plan has a budgeted or standard amount of resource expenditure—money, labor hours, equipment usage. When the activity is concluded, the standards are "earned." The actual expenditures are also collected, and the two can be compared at any time. The earned standards are a dynamic project budget that is independent of the calendar. As we've all experienced, your time-phased project budget that was established at the start of the project will become progressively more useless as the project proceeds and activities are completed earlier or later than scheduled even though overall (say on a critical-path basis) you're on schedule. Your only way to measure resource consumption is through Earned Standards comparisons to actual expenditures.

Resource consumption should also be evaluated another way. We are accustomed to thinking of return on investment for dollar expenditures on income-producing projects. What can we do about all the other kinds of projects and all the other kinds of expenditures? We need to start thinking about our return on resources for all corporate activities. If we are trying to create jobs in a community, how well are we doing for the resources expended? If we are making safer products, how much safer are they becoming for how much resource expenditure? In service businesses, how many fewer errors for how many resources? Some companies have attempted things like this, but usually in a negative manner to illustrate the cost of social programs. It's time to expand the effort and turn it around to be a positive kind of report. Like any other business activity, if we know how much return we're getting for our resources, we can dive into the details and figure out how to do better. We have a long way to go on improving our efficiency in achieving results other than quarterly financial success, and we'll get there a lot sooner if we start properly evaluating the use of all our resources.

The Creation of Management Systems

Thinking strategically is more than figuring out the important things to do. It is also defining the "report cards" that we have just talked about. And it is determining how to create them and the other critical management systems for the corporation. A corporation cannot be run well by the seat of the pants. It needs systems for accomplishing its goals. Evaluating the performance of the corporation and its management. Designing products and services under management's guidance. Taking and filling customer orders. Maintaining optimal inventory levels. Cash management. Producing payroll checks. Et cetera. Various levels of management are involved with these systems. Not all the systems are of strategic importance. The corporation could endure many of them operating at less than perfection. But some of them are critical, so the process for creating them must be effective.

This means that the strategists in the corporation must be involved with the systems. Who are the strategists? The individuals, regardless of title, who make important contributions to the corporation's goals and plans for achieving them. Remember—our broad and pragmatic view of strategy will sweep up a diverse group of people in the corporation. Perhaps not a larger group than at present, but we will drop out a lot of people who don't really contribute much and replace them with others who do. Senior management is clearly part of the group. The chairman, CEO, president, chief operating officer. Which brings us to an interesting dilemma.

A lot of the important information in today's corporation is massaged by a computer at some point. The CEO may never see computer reports, but most of the information he or she gets has spent some time in computer files. Computerized information processing requires computerized systems, so most of the systems that we are discussing are probably going to be at least partially computerized. As prices of information processing continue to fall, the situation is going to get worse for the people who don't understand computerized systems, i.e., most senior management and many members of other levels of management. How can we resolve this dilemma?

For one thing, the corporation can obtain good people for its computer or information systems operation. Whether you need one part-time programmer for your microcomputer or a thousand people for your worldwide computer network, you need good people. They need to be paid well and placed at the level in the organization that corresponds to their importance. A sign of the times is that in most corporations the computer people report to the CEO or another executive with broad responsibilities, such as an executive vice-president, instead of to a functional vice-president.[2] That has come about in the last few years. You also need to treat computer people like human beings working in your corporation, not like technical freaks. They have to have budgets, plans, reporting systems, and other management tools that lesser mortals have. And they have to use them effectively or be out on their ears. You also have to define their role. Are they technicians or business problem-solvers, or both? Do they help managers in other functions with their problems or do they just design the technical parts of the system that the other managers define?

The key phrase in the last sentence is "help other managers." Regardless of the role of the computer people, at best they will help the rest of the corporation. The CEO and other managers must have primary responsibility for determining their systems needs and designing the systems. This sounds more difficult than it is. Every system has a few essential components, illustrated in Figure 14–1. A system gathers or uses information to do something, after which the performance is measured and additional information generated as necessary to improve the performance of the system. Information might be anything from detailed data to key indicators—inventory turns, sales per employee, etc. There are dozens of system design tools to assist managers in designing systems with these components. They are available from other companies, computer vendors, consultants, and universities. Some system components are stronger in certain kinds of systems than in others, and not all components of every system require computerization. If managers stick to the basic concepts and use system design tools in conjunction with their knowledge of their business areas, they will be able to design effective systems. Is anyone doing this? Yes–Ben Heineman, chairman of Northwest Industries, designs many of his own information systems. Other executives are beginning to get the message. In a 1983 survey of CEOs, almost 20 percent said they personally used computers or computer terminals at work or at home.[3] However,

Figure 14–1
Essential System Components

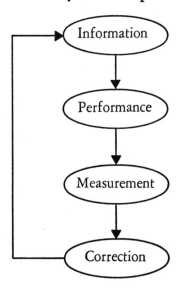

a sizeable portion of the remaining 80 percent will have to change their ways before we can say that computer literacy has arrived in the executive suite. When this happens, corporations will be better able to implement corporate strategies effectively, which is why we say that the process of systems design and development is itself a strategic consideration.

Life in the Trenches

Well, we are now pretty far along in our war against ineffective management. We know who the enemy is. We know what fronts we are fighting on. We know how to develop global war plans and how to translate these into plans for specific battles. We have set up a chain of command and a communications system. We know how to determine how many airplanes, tanks, and other competitive weapons that we need and how to deploy them. We even know how to measure whether we are winning or losing a battle without waiting for the retreat signal from the other side or our side. Are we ready to push the button and start the war? Not quite. We've missed one thing. The soldiers in the field. The workers in the corporation and the field commanders who do double duty as management and as soldiers. Human resources are the most important resources we have. Nothing else works without them. We cannot have meaningful corporate strategies without strategies for the people. We cannot implement anything without the people. And that means we have to manage them properly.

Managing the Human Element

"Education makes a people easy to lead, but difficult to drive."
—LORD BROUGHAM

Chapter 15

Culture Shock

U.S. BUSINESS has mixed emotions about people. As consumers, people are courted by companies trying to sell them goods and services. Individual tastes are catered to. You can have a hamburger or a car made exactly the way you want it. Millions of dollars are spent annually on market research to figure out what people really want and/or need. The result has been the creation of an almost unbelievable level of consumer expectations, as we have seen. Price, quality, selection—you name it, and the consumer wants it. Not because of an insatiable appetite for material goodies, but because of conditioning that the expectations will be fulfilled. The impact of this conditioning on the product/service design, production, and marketing efforts of U.S. corporations has been profound.

But what happens when the consumer goes to work in the morning? Is he or she treated like an individual? Does the corporation attempt to understand the employee portion of the psyche as well as it understands the consumer side of it? Not likely. We are much further along in the development of our ability to maximize consumer spending on particular goods and services than we are in our ability to manage people to maximize their contributions to their jobs. This has to change.

In our discussions of product and service planning, we said that understanding the marketplace and the customers was crucial. Let's take the same approach here—let's really try to understand the workers in the U.S. We have all heard of "worker dissatisfaction" and "changing lifestyles." However, few of us really have the facts on these phenomena. In this chapter we are going to explore the facts underlying the changing work force. We will see that the facts lead to some inev-

223

itable conclusions about management in the future. Then in the subsequent chapters we will see how specifically to modify jobs and improve our people management skills in accordance with the conclusions.

What Is Culture Shock?

Culture shock is a term used to describe the reaction of a person who is placed into a vastly different culture than the one he or she is accustomed to. The reaction also can occur when elements of the different culture are brought forcefully into the person's life rather than physically moving the person to the new culture. Disorientation, confusion, fear, mental paralysis, denial, and hostility are possible symptoms. Passionate embracing of some parts of the new culture and total rejection of other parts may occur. The overall characteristic of persons suffering from culture shock is an inability to assimilate all that is going on and to behave rationally.

A kind of culture shock is affecting many people in the United States. Things are very different from the way they were in the 1940s, '50s, '60s, or '70s. Many of the things that have changed were and are very important to us. The long arms of the news media have made us aware of many changes that in previous years we would have blissfully ignored. Our knowledge of these changes is usually superficial, often producing feelings of unease and discomfort regarding all the potentially significant things going on of which we are poorly informed. In addition, there are still big differences in the way we are treated as consumers and the way we are treated as workers. Most of us are both consumers and workers in the U.S. economy and we'd like not to be shocked whenever we step from one role to the other.

There are other aspects of cultural shock, of course, besides the consumer-worker role mismatch. Having defined culture shock, let's examine some of the other contributing factors to it.

Changing Demographics

Demographics, as the statistical study of populations, is concerned with the size and other characteristics of entire populations and population subgroups. Statistical studies of the U.S. population are important to business decisions because for the first time in many years some big changes are taking place.

Consider the sizes of the various age groups in the U.S. Clearly the number of people in each age group, or the percentage increases or decreases over time, are important pieces of information. Many products, such as baby food, are aimed at population segments according to age. The number of retired people receiving Social Security payments has a strong influence on the work force since Social Security is actually funded out of current contributions, not the contributions made by the retired people. People in the work force develop more skills and maturity as they grow older, qualifying them for different kinds of jobs. It's important to know how the number of people in various age groups relates to the number of jobs available.

The post-World War II baby boom is an important part of the demographic changes that started affecting the U.S. in the 1970s. You've noticed, for example, that schools have been closing in your community recently because enrollments are no longer adequate to keep them open. But there is more to the story. For the first time in this century several separate age groups of the population are undergoing large upswings and downswings in size over short periods of time. (See Figure 15–1.) This phenomenon affects most managers and managers-to-be.

Management Ranks

People who elect to move into the ranks of corporate management typically begin to do so in their mid- to late twenties through promotions into supervisory or junior management positions. They move steadily upward during the next twenty years. As they approach their late forties, the ones who are going to enter senior management usually start to assume significant amounts of responsibility. Although it's impossible to describe an "average" career path for executives, that probably comes close. Does it appear to be consistent with the demographic data?

Candidly, it's not. That career path is a legacy of the 1950s, '60s, and '70s when the population subgroup from which junior and middle management were drawn was a reasonable size. This age group—mid-20's to mid-40's—has grown so large, and is still growing (20 percent more during the 1980s), that there simply aren't enough management jobs for the people of the right age. The same problem will affect the senior management group—mid-40's to early-60's—in the 1990s. The senior manager problem requires some planning, but the problem is not so acute in the near future as it is for lower to middle-level managers.

What can be done? The answer is inevitable. For part of it, let's look at the very young end of the work force. The people in their late teens and early to mid-twenties. What is going to happen to this group,

Figure 15-1
Relative Sizes of Age Groups in the U.S.

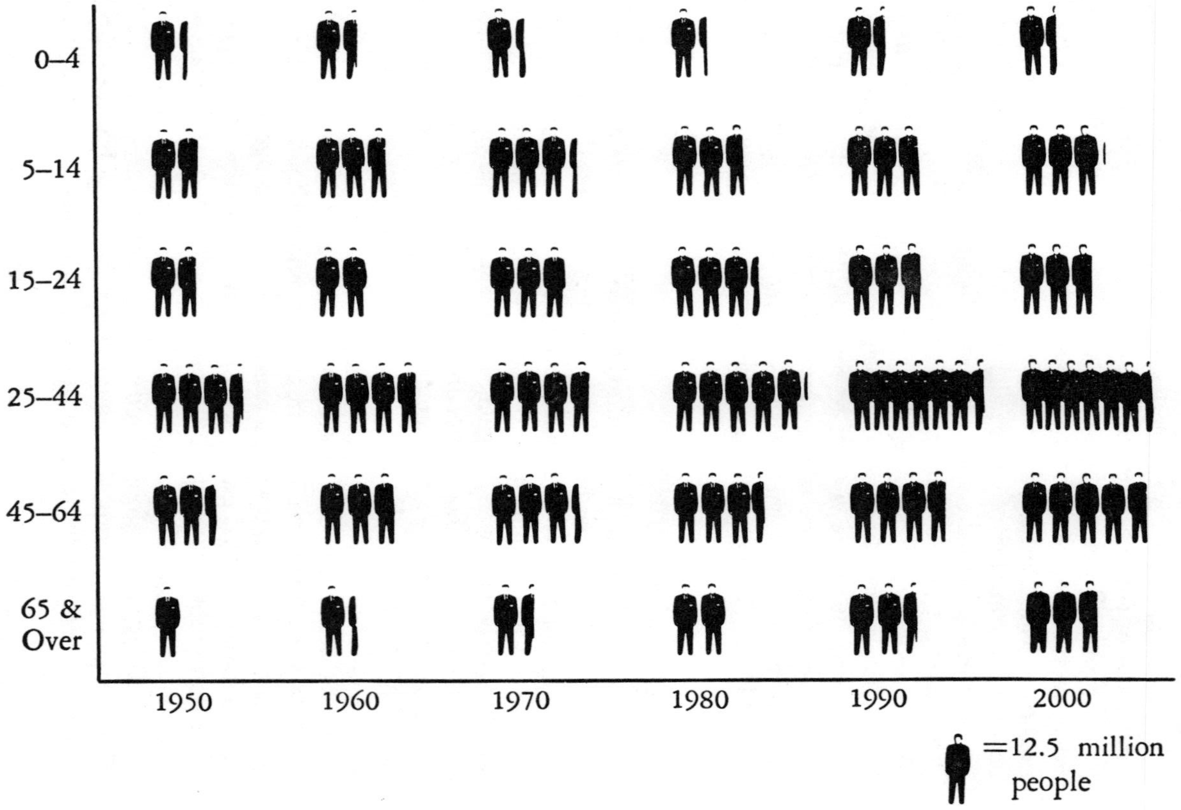

	1950	1960	1970	1980	1990	2000
0–4						
5–14						
15–24						
25–44						
45–64						
65 & Over						

= 12.5 million people

Source: Data from Bureau of the Census

which traditionally holds down the lower-paying jobs that are commensurate with their skill and experience levels? This group is going to shrink by 15 percent during the 1980s and early 1990s and turn up again after 1995. In the next decade there won't be enough of them to go around. The group slightly older than them—growing by 20 percent in the same period—will have to backfill into the lower-level jobs. Not a pleasant prospect for people whose parents, at that age and with the same talent, held management posts.

Another part of the answer is more acceptable: redefinition of success in U.S. business. Success is now equated with a management title. Most U.S. corporations have many more layers of management than their Japanese equivalents. We need to reemphasize the importance of the doer in our corporations. A person can be successful and respected without being a manager or an administrator. Many of our professions operate this way. A surgeon's career path doesn't necessarily include running the hospital. The surgeon or lawyer can reap respect and financial rewards while exercising the professional skills. We have to implant the same attitude in our corporate work force and back it up with the required recognition and compensation. This will also make life easier for the people who would have elected not to go into management. Better jobs will be a benefit to everybody.

More Demographics

Ready for some more statistics? Over half of U.S. families are two-paycheck families—both husband and wife have jobs.[1] On the other end of the spectrum, one quarter of U.S. "households" (a Census term) have only one person.[2] Conclusion? A lot more people than ever before are working or trying to. Where should the emphasis be placed—on working, or on trying to find work? The relatively high unemployment rates would lead you to believe that people aren't able to find work. On the contrary, since the mid-1960s the amount of employment (number of employed people) has grown faster than any period since the end of World War II. U.S. employment has grown at a rate over double the rate of population increase.[3] We have higher unemployment mainly because more people are looking for jobs than in the past.

This is not to suggest that the job seekers are not serious about their searches or that the unemployment rate is artificially inflated. Certainly there must be some reduced incentive to find jobs among people who already have one paycheck in their families or who are currently receiving government assistance. But my point is exactly the opposite. We have to assume that these people—married women, for example—are quite serious about being in the work force. This point is not yet well accepted, but it's true. And the people are competing, by and large, in the same population categories as everyone else. Ergo, there is no chance that our demographic employment problem will go away. It may well get worse as more people in the 25–44 age bracket, the expanding population in the future, decide to look for jobs. We will definitely need some solutions to the problem other than wishful thinking or continuing to report that white, married, adult male unemployment is relatively low as if that statistic meant anything any more.

Where the People Are

The nation's twenty-five largest metropolitan areas are spread out over the country, from New York to Miami, and San Diego to Seattle, with Minneapolis and Houston in the center. During the decade of the 1970s seventeen of them experienced population increases, and eight had decreases in population. The eight: New York, Philadelphia, Detroit, Boston, Pittsburgh, St. Louis, Newark, and Cleveland. Some of the seventeen: Los Angeles, San Francisco, Dallas, Houston, Atlanta, Denver, Seattle, Tampa. The pattern is clear.[4] The employment picture is the same—shrinking in the Midwest and Northeast, increasing elsewhere, with the greatest increases in the Southwest and Southeast.

So far, so good. It appears that more jobs are being created and filled in the parts of the country with increasing populations. That's the way things are supposed to work. Only it's not quite that simple. The economic center of gravity of the U.S. is shifting away from the traditional industrial strongholds. The jobs that are going South and West are not the heavy industrial jobs that are being lost in the Midwest and Northeast. They're more in light manufacturing, high technology, energy, and service industries. And the people are different. During the 1970s many more people under 35 years of age than over moved to the fast-growing areas of the country.[5] We are creating separate economic entities in different parts of the country. It's easy to exaggerate the importance of this, of course. The various sections of the country have always been different. But previously we had more uniform economic growth across the nation and we had roughly the same population distributions in each major area of the country. Now we must face the prospect of parts of the country having the industries of the future with younger, better-educated workers and other parts of the country having the opposite. This scenario is no longer fiction—it's happening today. And we are not prepared to deal with it. Managers in the U.S. Northeast and Midwest still think of themselves as being in the industrial heartland of the country, experiencing a temporary setback.

New Lifestyles

New lifestyles—an explosive issue. They're great when you have a unique product to sell to people with different lifestyles, when you're pushing products or services that cater to the lifestyles. On the other hand, new lifestyles are a contributing factor to the decay of Western civilization when your workers appear to be afflicted with them. Who do you think is buying your products and services? You can't have your cake and eat it, too.

Different lifestyles are a major source of culture shock. You don't understand my lifestyle and I don't understand yours. Since we each tend to be comfortable with friends who share our lifestyles, we don't spend enough time together to develop any mutual respect. In our business lives, we have to be together, but we don't have to get along. Unless we're smart, that is. Then we'll get to know each other better. Or, more to the point, managers will try to understand the lifestyles of the people they have to manage, all the way up to the chairman of the board.

What are people doing with their money—spending it or saving it? The answer to this question can tell us a lot about the psychological makeup of U.S. citizens. Figure 15–2 shows a sharp decline in the rate

Figure 15–2
U.S. Personal Savings as Percent of Disposable Income

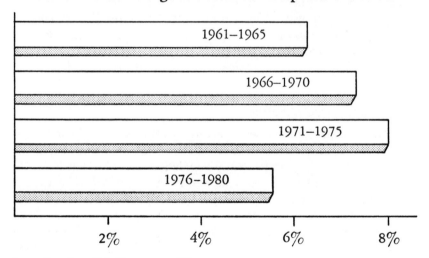

Source: Data from U.S. Department of Commerce

of personal savings. Economists are not in agreement (naturally) on the cause of this decline. Generally speaking, however, the reasons given tend to focus on high inflation, lack of government policies to stimulate savings, and keeping-up-with-the-Joneses pressures on families. Undoubtedly these factors all influence the savings rate. But I think we're being remiss if we do not consider the possibility of fundamental changes in personal values.

People in the United States always have saved less of their income than people of many other industrial nations. The Japanese save almost 20 percent; the Germans and French, about 15 percent.[6] Savings imply caution and frugality, building a nest egg for the future. This country wasn't built that way. It was built by aggressive individuals who used their money to create something more than a balance in a savings account. This frontier spirit, although diminished a great deal by the passage of time, still survives in the U.S. People tend to do things with their money rather than save it. Not necessarily blowing it on hedonistic pursuits, but purchasing goods and services that will improve their lives now and possibly also improve future earnings power. I submit that the recent decline in the savings rate is primarily an extension of this phenomenon. People are living their lives more fully. Again, not necessarily only seeking pleasure, but trying to make the most of their lives, which requires spending money. And I think this will continue. Recent legislation has provided excellent financial rewards for increased savings using such instruments as Individual Retirement Accounts (IRAs). As a result, we are starting to see the statistical savings rate begin to creep upward. This kind of increase, however, represents taking an offer you can't refuse, not a return to frugality. It certainly would not be comparable to past times when the savings incentives were supposed to be personal in nature rather than created artificially by tax laws.

More Self-Actualization

There is additional evidence of this concern for one's life in the here and now all around us. Consider the renewed interest in health and physical fitness. It spans the entire population. Part of it may be faddish in nature, but it's too widespread and too broad-based to be a fad for everybody. And it doesn't have the other characteristics of a fad. It's not easy to get in shape, eat right, etc., and most fads are easy. Fitness has to be pursued regularly, not on again and off again when the whim strikes, as with a fad. And it's demonstrably good for you, whereas most fads have attractions other than being good for you. We can conclude that many more people than in the past are genuinely interested in their physical condition right now.

Another example? Adult education. In 1970, adults comprised a little over 20 percent of college enrollments. By 1980, the figure was close to 40 percent—almost a doubling.[7] Some of the students are working in degree programs. Others are taking single courses to bolster their education to do better in their current jobs or to find better jobs. Still others are taking courses in the arts or other areas of personal interest. Regardless of the reason, people are improving their mental fitness as well as their physical fitness.

Surely, you say, there must be some surveys that are more scientific than my handful of examples. Yes, there are. A majority of people say the following things are important to them: a better life now as well as in the future; leisure and recreation time; good health; financial and professional success in their jobs; low indebtedness.[8] Doesn't sound like a Puritan speaking, but it doesn't sound like a hedonist either. It's a profile of a person with a well-balanced life. Maybe that's what the new lifestyles are all about.

Or what they are about for most people. There is a dark side of the moon, too. The culture shock of the new lifestyles is very hard for some people to accept, but acceptance is made a bit easier by the generally honest nature of the new lifestyles. People are not trying to take advantage of other people. Unfortunately, there are always a few people who overstep the boundaries, who carry self-indulgence to the point of hurting other people. It would do us no good to pretend that such people don't exist or that they aren't more prevalent among the population subgroups that are more attuned to new lifestyles, i.e., younger people. If you'd like a real-life example of trends in dishonesty, go into a store that caters to people in their late teens or early twenties and use a credit card to purchase something. You'll be amazed at the extent of the credit verification procedures compared to what you're used to in the high-class stores. We are mentioning the bad apples here because many of them have jobs; some of them may work for you. You're going to have to deal with the ugly side of the new lifestyles as well as the side that is more understandable. And, speaking of things that may require some effort to understand, let's ask ourselves one of the questions that seems to be on the tip of many executives' tongues.

Where Did the Work Ethic Go?

This question is usually accompanied by various emotions that indicate distress on the part of the person asking the question. Anger, outrage, anguish—all are common emotions. The implication seems to be that the question may well rank in importance with whether there is a Supreme Being. I think the answer is self-evident. Let's see why this is true.

First let's define the problem. There are various descriptions of the vanishing act that the work ethic has supposedly performed. Like any good detective, we need a description of what actually took place. One witness says that the problem is that people don't seem as committed to their jobs as they used to be. That they spend less time at their jobs. Well, that's easy to deal with. It's true. The new lifestyles have seen to that. After all, you have to find the time somewhere for physical fitness or other outside interests, and there are only 24 hours in the day. This is not to say that everybody goes home when quitting time comes, any more than it's fair to say that everybody has the same job and other interests in the same proportions. It is fair to recognize that something has to give for people that have adopted the new lifestyles, and that something is often the hours given to the job. Not the job itself—only the hours devoted to it. Let's make that distinction clear. Many people who are putting in less time on their jobs are no less interested in performing well than they were before. As we've just noted, the surveys show that. They just don't want to be chained to their desks. There are other people, naturally, for whom the job has become fairly unimportant compared to other interests. It's a big world and the people don't fit into pigeonholes very easily.

There are some other dimensions to the work ethic problem. One is the increase in the number of people who are dropping out of the labor force to do other things that they can afford to do because of savings, retirement and benefits programs, or government assistance. The number of women who are dropping out is difficult to decipher because the statistics are mixed up with the tremendous increase in the number of women who are looking for work. The picture is clearer for men: the percentage of men of normal working age who are not in the labor force has doubled since the mid-1960s. It's climbed from only 3 percent to 6 percent, but it's still an important trend.[9] And that doesn't count early retirees. Despite the clamor for elimination of mandatory retirement ages, the statistical evidence indicates that early retirement would not be affected.[10] A change in the law would allow those who wished to work longer to do so, but there is no evidence that it would be an incentive for the early retirees to change their minds. So something dfferent is going on. Many people are less interested in working.

Others want to work only on their terms. Available jobs go begging because they pay only minimum wage or are considered low-status jobs such as warehouse or janitorial work. Nationwide, there are hundreds of thousands of low-skilled jobs available for the asking. Even high-unemployment areas like Detroit have them. Reasons for the lack of interest in such jobs clearly include high unemployment benefits. They also include a natural unwillingness to lower one's sights from $15 an hour jobs working for the automakers. But there is also an element of people being more selective about the kinds of jobs they want. And where they want to work. Even with the willingness of many younger people to relocate, there is a serious imbalance in this country between where the jobs are and where the workers are. The middle-aged workers who would appear to be most in need of jobs to support families, make mortgage payments, etc., are the most reluctant to move. They have social and cultural ties to their communities and they want to remain there. In the 1930s, 300,000 to 400,000 farmers migrated out of the "dust bowl" in the Plains states because they could no longer make a living there. Here we are now, fifty years later, with many times that number of people being unable to find work in their local areas. Yet how many are moving to places where they have better opportunities to find work? The values of the workers of the 1980s are different than those of the farmers of the 1930s.

Me, Myself, and I

"All for one, and one for all"—the slogan of the Three Musketeers. Unfortunately, the modern worker isn't quite as much a team player. Most executives not only would not dispute this conclusion, but would also question the team spirit of many of their managers. People seem to be out for themselves. They feel the corporation does not have a sense of fair play, that good performance is likely to go unrewarded, that their destiny in the corporation is not really tied to their contribution. Why do they feel this way? It's a complicated issue.

Put yourself in the shoes of a worker at Chrysler or another of the Detroit automakers. Or International Harvester, which has been on the brink of bankruptcy for a couple of years. You're a reasonably competent worker as are most of your buddies, but you've been laid off because of the sales slump. You probably ought to be able to look in the mirror and tell yourself that you were being paid too much compared to the Japanese, then pack your family and belongings and move to Houston to find another job. That is difficult for many people. They instead come to the conclusion that they've been done in by the company, the union, and society in general. And they don't show much company loyalty when they're recalled. Or when they find another job in a different company at lower pay or in a different area of the country.

The jobs held by the "typical" worker, whoever that is, often aren't very exciting. Let's not bother with the question of whether people get what they deserve by reason of education, interpersonal skills, and so on. Whatever the reasons, they have the jobs that they have. Their consumer conditioning spills over into the workplace, and they expect more from their jobs. Only a small minority develops feelings of hostility that translate into sabotage or even substandard performance. Most workers are doing what they perceive to be an adequate job. However, they also feel that there is more to life than their jobs and that nobody but themselves is going to get the "more" for them. Management researchers from universities and other think tanks have tested these conclusions by taking workers' jobs incognito and developing their own impressions as well as talking to workers outside the format of a formal survey. Their results: A lot of the jobs are dull; some workers are treated unfairly by management; many, if not most, workers have a right to feel that life must hold more than their jobs.[11]

Psychologists also have substantiated the feelings. Job "burnout" is a term gaining increasing popularity. The term encompasses frustration, enervation, and other symptoms of disenchantment with one's job. Burnout leads to serious job performance problems and it only affects a minority of people. But the incidence of it is on the rise among both workers and managers, providing additional evidence that work is not all it's cracked up to be.

For indications of how extensive job frustration actually is, we have to turn once again to the survey takers. The statistics are truly frightening. One survey revealed that about two-thirds of the work force are not motivated by their jobs.[12] Individuals range from those who are doing an adequate job by just going through the motions to those who are doing as little as they can and still get by. Surveys aren't perfect, of course. But they do appear to confirm what we already know.

People need outlets for their energies besides their jobs; they are convinced that the corporation isn't going to be the focal point of their lives.

Other Work Force Realities

The data on worker attitudes are pretty solid. We can be sure that people today don't have many of the traditional attitudes. We are far less certain of why this is. Job design is undoubtedly part of the reason. We'll get into some solutions in the next chapter. Let's review a few other facts that may help to explain why people are less trustful of their corporate bosses and more interested in looking out for themselves.

Unfair discrimination is one fact. Against minorities such as blacks. The situation, though not resolved, is a bit better than it used to be. Almost all large companies and many smaller ones have no-nonsense policies supporting affirmative action and discouraging racial discrimination. Most have bulky procedures manuals to ensure fair treatment of minorities. But the formal systems cannot eliminate prejudices overnight or even over the three decades that we've been trying since the *Brown vs. Board of Education* Supreme Court decision. It takes several generations to resolve a problem like this and we've only given it one so far. Racism still exists to an unacceptable degree in many areas of U.S. life including the business world. The victims of it are understandably not entirely loyal to their corporations.

Nor are women to be blamed if they are dissatisfied with their progress. As in the case with minorities, direct comparisons with white males' compensation is tricky because of the hidden effect of past discrimination that has placed women in lower-skilled, lower-paying jobs. However, some interesting data does exist. The average pay of women in all jobs has remained at approximately the same fraction of the average pay of men, around 60–65 percent, for about the last forty years.[13] Four decades. The figure is a troubling statistic if we have been led to believe that women moved into higher-paying jobs during the 1960s and 1970s. Twenty years or even ten years is enough time to have promoted women into middle- or upper-management jobs.

Another problem is that women in executive slots earn less than their male counterparts. They also have far fewer of the corporate perquisites than men have. We are not talking about ceremonial positions, such as the corporate secretary, earning less than a financial vice-president. We are talking about vice-presidential jobs in the same function in comparable companies or jobs of equal management responsibility in the same company. Women generally earn 10–20 percent less than men.[14] There is some opinion that this is changing, that women at lower-management levels have finally achieved parity. However, a recent Stanford University study found a $4,000 differential among new MBAs three years after graduation. But compensation parity is only one measurement. Acceptance by the organization and achievement of other intangibles are still out of reach for many women. Prejudices from the past die hard. The prejudices against women may even be more pervasive than against minorities. It varies by company, industry, geography, etc., but overall it seems that neither women nor minorities have the inside track in their struggle for equality.

Older workers have been the victims of corporate staffing decisions based on considerations of age rather than capabilities. The 1967 Age

Discrimination in Employment Act made such practices illegal. Unfortunately, many corporations have not wholeheartedly embraced the concept of equal treatment for workers of all ages. Workers have had to go to court against companies such as Chrysler, Eastern Airlines, Heublein, and Textron. It doesn't matter who was right or wrong in particular cases (although workers did prevail judicially in the four cases mentioned); the point is that the workers felt they had to take matters into their own hands.

As they are doing increasingly in other employment-related issues. Looming on the horizon is the potential outlawing of the ancient "at will" employment doctrine. This doctrine says that, except for contractual obligations, employees serve at the pleasure of the employer and can be let go at any time for any reason. The reasons have been narrowed down so as not to include religious, racial, sexual, or age discrimination. The principle is still generally in force, modified by the conditions under which it cannot be exercised. However, a few lower court decisions in worker lawsuits, for example in Michigan, have upheld employees' rights not to be discharged arbitrarily. In the rest of this decade we are likely to see both more court decisions and legislation dealing with this issue. Once again, workers have succeeded by acting on their own.

Let's consider the world at large that the worker has to live in. What has he or she been faced with for the last ten years? High inflation. Struggling to make ends meet. Housing costs that would be laughable if they hadn't crushed so many dreams. At the same time, whenever workers open a newspaper or listen to the evening news, their noses are rubbed in the fact that people who look out for themselves are doing all right. Congress votes themselves expense account increases while restricting Internal Revenue Service audits of them. Professional athletes strike. Dave Winfield signs a $10 million-dollar contract. The average salary for starting players at all nine positions in major league baseball is over $100,000. And the average worker is supposed to feel that the world is fair?

Well, enough of this. Our little potpourri of facts I hope has demonstrated that workers have gone beyond unquestioning acceptance of their dictated roles in the corporation. Let's put this conclusion together with others we've reached and see where we come out.

Switching, Not Fighting

The composition of the work force is changing in terms of age groups. Rooted as it is in cycles of births and deaths, there is nothing we can do to influence it. We are going to have to live with the changes.

Lifestyles have also changed. But they are an integral part of the culture we live in. Few people would seriously suggest that it would be possible to make significant changes in the lifestyles of tens of millions of people, especially when the lifestyles are fine in some respects (consuming) while they bother the traditionalists among us in other respects (working). And the individual people in the work force? Their new attitudes are consistent with their personal experiences, the new lifestyles, and the overall work force changes. The tide of worker change is upon U.S. management. It's time to stop fighting it. We must instead harness the energy of the tide and put it to good use. We've had our dash of culture shock and had a chance to express our feelings—pro or con—to our friends and business associates. Now we must put the emotions behind us and get on with the tasks of changing the jobs in our corporations and managing our people better. Let's go on to the next chapter—changing the jobs.

"The fates lead the willing—and drag the unwilling."
—SENECA

Chapter 16

Linking Jobs to People

SO PEOPLE are changing. You, me, everyone. In the midst of all this change, we still have to go on working for a living. Our management methods have to cope with the changes in the corporation's employees, the overall work force, and the attitudes and cultures of both. We have not only to maintain the performance level of workers at their jobs, but to improve it in many cases if our companies and our country are to remain competitive.

The objects of our attention—the jobs—are moving targets. Changes in the jobs are imposed by external forces other than culture changes, for example, development of industrial robots. The result is an equation with multiple variables for us to solve. Looking at human resource management only in terms of workers and their culture would lead us to answers applicable to yesterday's jobs, not the jobs of today and the future. This approach has been responsible for some of the misguided suggestions for improvements in human resource management.

We are going to look instead at the whole picture—the jobs and the people doing them. Our understanding of both will enable us to formulate a human resource strategy that considers both. It will also help us incorporate the flexibility to modify jobs as well as people-management techniques.

The Jobs Circle

A new way of thinking about the problem is required to accomplish the objectives. We need to break the problem into its components and

238

illustrate the interaction between the components. Figure 16–1 presents one such way to look at the situation.

Three elements influence the jobs of the future, as shown in the circle. One is the products and services that the company offers to its customers. Simply put, the products and services offered by the company determine many of the jobs. The company has to use its own or external resources to design, produce, sell, and deliver the goods and services. The resources it selects and the means by which it uses them help determine the jobs in the company.

At the same time, the company has a number of alternatives for the processes by which the jobs are performed. In an auto assembly plant, for instance, the cars need to have fenders attached, but there are a lot of ways to design production lines to get the job done. A travel agency has to book reservations for its customers, but the responsibilities for doing so can be parcelled out among the agency's employees in several ways, for example by customer identity and size, customer industry, or reservation type.

Finally, the employees themselves are the third element of the circle—their lifestyles, attitudes, etc. must be considered. Employee attitudes affect how you lay out your production lines and even whether

Figure 16–1
The Jobs Circle

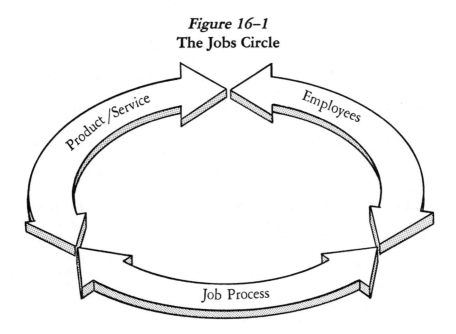

you choose to do parts of the production job in-house rather than through subcontracting.

The Product-Service Connection

In the previous section we identified some industries and companies that will do well in the 1980s and 1990s. High technology, including electronics, biotechnology, materials technology. Goods and services that cater to the new lifestyles, for example, recreation and leisure companies. Also, well-managed companies in less glamorous low-growth industries. And we must not forget well-positioned companies, such as specialty retailers, who have market niches that will behave more attractively than the overall market.

Let's first consider high-growth industries. What influences do growing companies have on jobs? Obviously, they have more jobs available. However, we hope to be able to say more than this, just as we hope there is more of a relationship between declining companies and jobs than simply a fewer number of available jobs.

Most growth companies, the high-technology firms in particular, are trading on recently-acquired knowledge. An employee's formal education may provide a grounding in fundamentals, but the practical knowledge quickly becomes outdated. The rapid obsolescence has a multiplier effect on the number of jobs available. A company may require new people with different knowledge even though the total number of jobs doesn't increase or increases only with the growth of the company. Similarly, the pool of qualified job applicants may drop in comparison to the number of jobs available as individuals' knowledge falls in value. In either case, the relative number of jobs increases.

Let's explore a high-tech job market as an example. How about computer programming? Commercial use of computers began seriously in the 1950s. Instructions for the machines were communicated to them in a binary system machine language of 0's and 1's or through the way their instruction boards were wired by human beings. Gradually, English-like computer languages, such as FORTRAN, COBOL, and BASIC, were developed. Programmers use these languages to write programs. As computers have become more and more powerful, specialized computer languages have been developed to aid programmers in writing certain kinds of programs. Programs that help the computer itself run more efficiently or perform basic functions such as translation of the English-like languages. "Data communications" programs to help one computer communicate with another computer or to remote terminals on the desks of computer users. "Data base systems" that control the storage of data in very complex ways so that an airline clerk can retrieve your reservation by knowing either your name or your flight number, or the person building the airplane can get a printout of all the parts used in the tail section or all parts made of aluminum.

Progress in the computer field is so rapid that even the experts have to educate themselves constantly on new developments. A person who has not stayed current for twelve months is no longer anywhere near the frontier, and a person whose expertise is three years old would probably have a tough time landing a job if he or she had to change companies. Against this backdrop of change, computer power is becoming cheaper and cheaper. The number of computers and users is continuing to increase dramatically. What has been the net result of the confluence of these forces?

A staggering shortage of computer programmers. For many years, computer programming positions have consistently ranked among the most difficult to fill. An experienced programmer makes as much money by being an "individual contributor" (buzzword for jobs in which personal technical skills other than management skills are required) as people in middle to low end of upper management slots. The law of supply and demand is responsible, assisted by the large numbers of technical people who tire of educating themselves constantly and so move into computer management or sales, leaving a vacuum behind them.

At the current rate of job creation, millions of people in the work force would be programming by the turn of the century. Which, despite predictions to the contrary, will not happen. Why? The current shortage of programmers can't be alleviated. How are we going to alleviate it if the shortage keeps growing geometrically or exponentially? Not with people, but with changes in technology. Dramatic changes in technology can wipe out hundreds of thousands of jobs. The calculator killed the slide rule industry. Transistors killed the vacuum-tube makers. Somebody will figure out an easier way to produce computer programs, possibly using "program generators" on chips (primitive ones are already in use).

Most jobs in growing companies have the same general characteristics as computer programming jobs. Change as well as growth in the number of jobs. Emphasis on excellence and good personal performance. Specific knowledge requirements that change frequently. Excitement. A seller's market for the job seeker. Possibility of rapid shifts and obsolescence.

So much for high-growth companies. What about the other companies expected to do well? The well-managed or well-positioned companies in low-growth industries. The story here is a little different. The environment is not exciting. The companies are nowhere near the frontiers of knowledge. We are talking about basic skills in a job market that is stable at best. Marketing skills. Planning skills. Production skills. The functional skills required to develop and implement an effective corporate strategy. Nothing unique about the skills. But, as there is always room for well-run companies, there will always be room for skilled people. Not the magicians who conjure up quarterly earnings out of obscure accounting principles. Instead, the people who produce value for the marketplace. These jobs will carry the traditional trappings with an additional caveat: The marginally skilled need not apply, and people with average skills will have to run fast to stay up with the company. Their alternative will be to catch on with the companies that are losing.

The Place in the Circle

So we have an idea of what the jobs are going to look like in winning companies. How do they fit into our "Jobs Circle"? How well do the job characteristics that we derived from product-service-analysis mesh with our knowledge of worker cultures? And with the processes by which the jobs are performed? And, most important, what can future managers do?

The jobs in growing industries are charismatic. They change rapidly. They're not boring. They would seem to fit in well with worker independence and restlessness. They're not dead-end jobs. Workers can see that they're part of something that is growing. The coming bulge in people eligible for lower- or middle-management jobs can be partially absorbed by productive challenging jobs that do not carry management titles. There's never a dull moment. A team spirit is likely to prevail since people working together can accomplish so much more than single individuals. There's not a 100 percent match. The work demands may conflict with some needs for time off. But the beat of the new jobs in growing industries seems compatible with the beat of contemporary society. Managers do not have to do much except go along with the tide. Trying to fight it would be trying to fight both society and the inevitable shifts in the nation's economic structure.

Job processes provide the glue between the employees and the jobs created by the growing shifting economy. The processes of doing the jobs are just as volatile but management controls the processes. Consider our computer programmers. Tools to assist them are changing every day. They've gone from punch-card processing to timesharing terminals. But management decides which tools to give the employees. Improving the job processes is important in high technology and other growth industries where you have to be on the frontier in as many ways as you can. Managers will have a responsibility to keep the job processes in step with the excitement of the new jobs and the new culture. If a lag occurs, it will be fatal because of the interface problems among the parts of the circle.

If we manage well, we can have a match among the circle components for growth industries. Not perfect, perhaps, but let's see how good it is relative to the other jobs in successful U.S. companies. These jobs will be provided by the companies that will do well because they are well run. Nevertheless, as we discussed above, the jobs will be more conventional than the jobs available in growth industries. That doesn't mean that it will be impossible to make the pieces of the circle fit together, but it does mean that it will occur less frequently. The well-run companies will have success on their side. Their management will need to have the foresight to change the job processes as appropriate to coincide with both market and employee requirements. Since the jobs aren't the same (e.g., usually less exciting), the processes will be changed differently. Whatever the changes, the companies' financial success will be the key allowing them to do so.

The success also can be an instrument for motivation of their employees. One survey showed that approximately two-thirds of U.S. workers are not motivated by their jobs, but that the remaining one-third do generally put work ahead of other things in their lives.[1] In addition, the survey indicated that about one-sixth of the total work force—one quarter of the disaffected workers—are highly motivated by work but not by their current jobs.[2] In well-run companies, these people can be on your side. Combining them with the one-third who are inherently motivated, we find that half the work force may actually be in favor of the work ethic in well-run companies. Statistics aside, this also passes our common sense test; it's unlikely that the work ethic is totally dead. Other studies indicate that half the workforce rates their companies' management critically in comparison with other companies they know about.[3] Obviously these data are averages, over hundreds of companies, and you could do better (or worse) in your company. Managing this half effectively to go with your effective product-service strategies will help minimize the problems accruing from the inability to generate the number and kinds of jobs that growth industries do.

Conversely, if you are being battered by the competition in a slow-growth or declining industry, then work-force characteristics probably are going to compound your problems. The upcoming decrease in young unskilled labor is going to affect you adversely. The bulge in slightly older workers is going to work against you instead of for you.

You are not going to be able to restructure the jobs and the processes for doing them, because you won't have the time or the resources. You will go into a tailspin that will seem to substantiate the long-wave theories. Maybe there ought to be a work-force component to the long-wave theories. It would recognize the tendency of the work force to add to the problems existing in mature industries that are about to enter the downward phase of their cycle. But these thoughts are for researchers and theorists. We are interested in the reality of the next few years. This reality appears to be that the rich will get richer and poor will get poorer. The companies that are not in growth industries will have to do a number of things well, perhaps achieve a "critical mass" in process and people management. The ones that reach the critical mass, as when it is reached in nuclear fission, will be successful. The ones that don't will be unable even to hold their own.

A Subtotal

Let's summarize where we are. The jobs that a company will have in the future are derived from its planning of product/service objectives and how to achieve them. The jobs will vary significantly between industries and among companies in a particular industry; the jobs will have the characteristics that we have just described. Individual workers will have to be matched with jobs that fit their lifestyle and culture. In simple terms, the jobs are determined by the marketplace and a company's efficiency; the workers bring to the jobs cultural requirements and expectations. Management must link the two.

The link between the workers and the jobs are the definitions of the jobs, the way they are performed. This we have called the job process. The process must be compatible with the workers and the jobs when these two factors are consistent, as with high tech jobs and aggressive workers. In other cases, the process must build a bridge over some incompatibilities, such as between old-line manufacturing jobs and workers lacking the work ethic. Influencing the job processes is management's responsibility. We'll now consider some specific ways to do this.

Bigger Is Not Better

We can start the task of improving the link between employees and jobs with the definition of organizational work units in the corporation. To introduce the subject, let's review a bit of history.

"He believed in economies of scale" could be the epitaph of every industrial giant of the nineteenth and early twentieth centuries. The ideas behind economies of scale are simple. If you have a large number of people and machines under one roof, you can coordinate their activities easier. You can more easily match people and jobs. You can break jobs down into simple tasks to assign to individuals, and there will be enough people for all the simple tasks. Administration and other overhead costs can be kept low and spread over a large number of units produced.

The ideas were applied easily in manufacturing companies. Huge factories were built. For example, Ford's Rouge plant near Detroit employed 60,000 workers into the 1950s. But the implementation of the idea wasn't confined to manufacturing. For example, railroads centralized their purchasing and accounting functions, then acquired other railroads in order to spread the centralized costs over larger volumes and take advantage of discounts by purchasing larger amounts from their vendors. No matter what the industry, economies of scale seemed to exist. Financial institutions grew as large as permitted by law. Retailers grew by expansion or acquisition. Size seemed to carry efficiency along with it. And the bigger companies seemed to attract the best people. Efficient operation with talented people—an unbeatable combination that came with size.

This simple view of bigness started changing with the 1960s. The change was partially evolutionary in response to changes in communication and transportation systems. Although the basic technical tools had been around for some time, it took the mass media's embrace of electronics in the 1950s to get business moving in the same direction. With improved communications, some of the reasons for large, comprehensive operating units became obsolete. Corporation executives also were exposed to some comparisons in which their large operations came off second best. Many companies expanded into other countries during the 1960s and 1970s and were unable to build the large plants they were used to. Others acquired smaller companies with small plants during the conglomerate craze of the 1960s. Both kinds of companies discovered to their amazement that smaller plants could be even more efficient than large plants. Plus they were easier to manage; there was less bureaucracy in a smaller plant. Evidently the world had changed since companies had last attempted to use smaller plants.

Today most corporations are functioning effectively with much smaller operating units than they would have thought possible twenty or thirty years ago. New manufacturing plants are no longer million-square foot monsters. Small branch banks dot the landscape in most states. Even the general full-line retailers are building smaller stores than before. The smaller operations are easier to manage and they produce goods or deliver services efficiently. But fewer companies are taking the next step—forcing operations down to absolute minimal size. Managers find that concept difficult to reconcile with the economies-of-scale benefits that they all have been raised with. However, there is ample evidence that becoming as small as reasonably possible is a good idea.

The evidence comes in two forms—hard and soft. The hard evidence is the statistical edge that small companies and organizational units have over big ones in creation of jobs, which is an excellent bottom-line measure of growth. If you prosper and grow you need more people. If you manipulate numbers so it looks like you've grown, but you've added no more people, then maybe you really haven't grown. What if you add equipment instead of people? Then the companies who make equipment have to add people. It would be difficult to construct a scenario of national economic growth without new jobs. So why belabor the point? Because 80 percent of all jobs created in the U.S. are by firms of 100 employees or less.[4] The very largest firms frequently have experienced declines in their levels of employment.[5] These are not new statistics, but they're often ignored as they run counter to the "bigger is better" notion. The most striking data, however, is on the fate of small firms that are acquired by larger ones. Their job growth is considerably lower than their counterparts who remain independent.[6]

This is where the soft evidence comes in. We all understand the potential for less creativity and individual freedom that exists in large organizations. More important, many organization researchers agree with those gut feelings. They believe that new ideas for products, procedures, personnel practices, etc. are more likely to be brought to fruition in small companies. The reasoning supports the data.

So we've come across an important factor to consider in defining jobs for the future—the size of the organizational entity. Small groups are more palatable to individuals and more effective for society at large. Until recently, few practitioners in human resource management recognized this point; most of them have concentrated solely on day-to-day work activities, ignoring the basic organizational unit. If the basic work units aren't defined correctly, nothing that is done within them is likely to work very well. Maybe that is part of the reason for failure of a lot of human resource programs.

So, if you are in a company of less than 100 people, great! You may have a lot of problems, but being too big isn't one of them. If you're not, how can you create a different environment in your company? Or is it possible? Maybe you're doomed to shuffling papers in a bureaucracy. Minnesota Mining & Manufacturing (3M) doesn't think so. The company has almost 90,000 employees, making it one of the largest U.S. employers. It has done well financially, with returns on equity in excess of 20 percent. And the size of its average U.S. factory is less than 300 people. In the 1970s their overall employment increased by over a third, a record that can be matched by only a few other large companies. The philosophy must be working pretty well, especially considering that 3M had not been in high-growth markets. They have more than their share of advanced products, but they get them through good management and support of individuality.

What should the rest of us do? Think small. Bigness is not implicitly present in any of the forms of organization that we have reviewed. You don't have to go as far as 3M, but you can have organizational building blocks that are fairly small. You'll have to judge how small for yourself, considering the requirements of the jobs to be done in your company and the characteristics of your workers—their lifestyles, concerns, etc. But you'll probably be able to make substantial improvements over your present situation.

Subdividing the Units

The next step, of course, is to define the jobs within the organizational work units. The usual U.S. approach is twofold, a combination of the military management model and scientific management, Frederick Taylor's term for carefully planned job assignments to workers. The theory is that the autocratic management model provides the structure and discipline, and the carefully planned detailed tasks maximize the output of each worker.

The theory fails in today's world with employees who demand both responsibility and variety in their jobs. What can be done? The answer—employees can be organized into small, essentially self-governing groups. Where would this approach be effective? How about old-line manufacturing, say an automobile plant? What if you completely abandoned the assembly line concept? Suppose the workers were organized into small groups that worked on certain large portions of the cars, such as interiors. Suppose each car was worked on separately by the group at its own pace. The cars would be transported around the factory on individual carriers. Suppose the groups were given primary responsibility for inspection of their work. Maybe you'll also let them be responsible for maintenance of much of the equipment that they use. It would require a lot of effort. You'd have to redesign the automobile itself in some ways. The traditional manufacturing process builds a car like a giant layer cake, by adding one thing on top of another. That's not going to work very well if you want to give workers responsibility for functional subsystems like brakes or electrical systems. You're going to have to redesign the car so that all work on the brakes can be done by one group rather than piecemeal. That's a big job.

But it's been done. Volvo has a half dozen car and truck plants, built from scratch using this approach. They are the newer plants in the company. Some of the older plants did not lend themselves to the physical redesign that would have been required. In these plants more emphasis has been placed on working conditions, job rotation among workers, and other improvements that could be implemented while retaining traditional assembly lines. Volvo also has been able to export their progress to Volvo factories in Belgium and the Netherlands, where the concepts have been introduced successfully.

It hasn't been easy. There have been false starts in many plants and procedures that had to be modified several times before they worked. But they worked. Volvo has managed to be profitable in years when the U.S. automakers were on death row.

I used Volvo as an example here for two reasons. One, the company is a good illustration of certain approaches in practice. Two, Volvo has an image of coddling workers, as though they're a microcosm of Sweden's paternalistic society. But the key is that Volvo's management actually are realistic business people who recognize that we are in the 1980s, not the 1920s, and they manage accordingly. It hasn't been easy—they've had to completely rethink the design and manufacture of automobiles. And it's been effective where it mattered—the bottom line. In 1980 and 1981 they achieved better returns (measured any way: on sales, equity, etc.) than any of the Detroit automakers.

The Individual Worker

Now we come to the individual worker. U.S. business needs to apply the same attention to an individual's job that it should to organizational units and work groups.

How can specific jobs be tailored both to the employees' concerns and to product/service requirements? Many small products, such as cameras or subassemblies of large products, can be produced completely by one person. The responsibility of the person is similar to that of the old-world craftsman who personally made his product. Clearly the worker has to possess a great deal of product knowledge as well as a sense of commitment to quality work. But such people can be found—more of them, in fact, than the conventional wisdom of U.S. management would allow for. Mercedes-Benz builds many of their major automobile components such as gear boxes using this system. Maybe they know something that Detroit doesn't.

What if the product/service job requirements don't lend themselves to subdivision by discrete components assigned to individual workers? Is there still a way to bridge the product/service-employee gap? Yes. One straightforward approach is simply to increase the complexity of the jobs to be performed by individual workers. In Germany, for example, studies were conducted to determine the degree of complexity in particular jobs that the workers would be comfortable with. In other cases, more tasks were added so that the "cycle time"—time from start to finish of the job that the worker has to perform—was increased, making the worker feel less like an automaton endlessly repeating simple tasks. Minimum cycle times were written into some union contracts, such as that of the metalworkers union in Germany.

The indirect elements, such as the physical environment, are also important. Many office workers have made great strides with "office landscaping" providing an appealing physical place to work—with plants, comfortable furniture, indirect lighting, paintings on the walls, etc. Other workers, especially factory workers, haven't been so lucky. Things are different at Robert Bosch, the $7-billion German manufacturer of auto parts and appliances. Many of Bosch's factories have been designed with workers' comfort in mind, including better lighting, comfortable work benches, etc. The investment has paid off in higher levels of worker satisfaction and output.

Technology's Impact

So far we have discussed redesigning job processes so as to align them more closely with product/service requirements and the expectations and desires of the workers. Necessity certainly has been the mother of invention of new processes for doing jobs. However, to twist the old proverb a bit, invention can also create necessity. If a company invents a new way of doing a job that is more efficient or satisfies other requirements, then it will have a competitive advantage. This advantage will generate a necessity for other firms in the same business. In fact, either necessity or invention can be the catalyst—it depends on the circumstances in a particular company.

Improvements in technology have been the major "invention" in recent years. Consider only the information processing revolution. The revolution has spread from the giant corporate computers of the 1960s through the remote terminals and powerful calculators of the 1970s to the personal microcomputers of the 1980s. Many jobs that have remained the same nominally have, in fact, been totally changed. For example, every organization has people who work extensively with documents. Producing them. Filing them. Retrieving them. Making copies of them. Sending and receiving them. Almost all activities in a company require dealing with documents. And technology has altered every job involved with document processing. Documents used to be typed, corrected when necessary with correction tape or fluid. Now they are produced with word processors that can make changes and corrections easily. Manila folders and file cabinets are on the way out as documents are filed electronically. Multiple "original" copies can be produced. Word processors can communicate with copying machines. The copying machines can talk to each other. Images can be communicated over telephone lines to distant cities instead of through the mails.

Some new job titles have been created, primarily for people in high-volume document production departments such as word processing departments that replaced typing pools. But most administrative jobs have not changed much in title or nominal function even though they are performed with vastly different tools. The surface continuity masks the fact that the jobs have changed significantly. Using the equipment of the past, such as typewriters, the workers were as much tools as the equipment itself, because they were needed to correct errors with tape, maintain indexes to file cabinets, and so on. A mechanically-minded ten-year-old child could have done many of the jobs. Now these chores are done by the new tools. The human beings are able to devote more attention to matters requiring brains and experience, such as document content. In addition, the ease of use of the tools makes it possible for people who would not have used the old tools, such as typewriters, to use the new ones. When it becomes easier to do the job oneself immediately than to ask someone else to do it, explain it in detail, and wait for the results, then only the people who are overly status-conscious will choose to have the other person do it. The overall effect? Transformation of many jobs, although you couldn't tell it from the organization charts and procedures manuals.

Obviously, office jobs are changed by information technology, but the manufacturing plant is equally affected. The production foremen and the industrial engineers (IEs) used to prepare charts illustrating the tasks to be performed each day by each employee at each work center. A lot of time was required to integrate the foremen's practical knowledge of the job with the IEs' theoretical knowledge and understanding of the total manufacturing process. Sometimes not much time was left over for the foremen to supervise the workers and the IEs to analyze the job flow and production layouts. Now the charts come out of the computer 90 percent correct. The foremen and IEs can make the necessary corrections instantaneously through video display terminals on the shop floor. The rest of their time is free to do what their job descriptions say—to act like foremen and industrial engineers, not to make charts. They can spend the time supervising their employees or designing a better flow of materials through the plants. Their nominal jobs haven't changed, but the technological improvements in information processing have changed their real jobs.

Running Away from the Work Place

The office staff, manufacturing foremen and industrial engineers have a common element in their jobs—electronic communication. Their links to important parts of their organizations are electronic instead of personal. This brings up some interesting possibilities for people who use electronic communications in performing most of their work functions. The traditional gathering of workers at the employer's work place may no longer be necessary.

Again, consider the various tasks associated with documents. As we said, they are or can be almost entirely automated. Employees who prepare documents electronically usually commute to an office to sit beside other employees who do similar things. Then they go home at the end of the day. The commuting time and expense add nothing to the employees' or employers' lives. Why not put electronic devices in their homes and let the employees work there? No reason not to. Many computer companies, including Data General and Digital Equipment, have employees working at home. These companies' familiarity with telecommunications has made them natural leaders. Other interested companies include those that have become sensitive to the high cost of providing prime office space in downtown locations for employees who could work elsewhere. Providing adequate workspace and facilities (e.g., supplies storage) can add 40 percent to the cost of maintaining a clerical employee. The employee spends as much or more on commuting, eating, and clothes. Why not put the terminal and desk in the employees' homes? Banks, which are committed to prestige downtown locations for the headquarters offices, have started to do so in banking centers like Chicago.

What are we going to see next? The industrial engineer can do a lot of his or her work at home, coming into the plant perhaps once or twice weekly to interact with other workers and stay in touch with the physical production facilities. The foremen probably can't do most of their work at home. And in some other occupations, workers have to deal with customers. But here we have some intriguing possibilities.

Suppose the employees dealt with the customers by phone or through the ultimate in personal service, going to see the customers at their places of business. Then they could work out of their homes, saving office expenses and providing better services. It's starting to happen, mostly in smaller firms that are less bound by tradition. Several small securities-trading firms in the New York area are run out of the traders' homes. They have easy access to a large marketplace and large financial institutions if they should be needed. And they have the incentive of avoiding one of the biggest commuting hassles in the world. The idea is going to spread, probably more slowly than other uses of technology because it involves some rethinking of the fundamental aspects of the jobs. But it will catch on. It's good for the economy, and it's good for the employees.

Or, is it always good for the employees? Can technology be carried too far? Is it perhaps possible to eliminate too many jobs through automation?

Total Automation

Like spirits from the beyond, automation takes many forms when it appears to us. It is difficult to predict exactly when the technological apparitions will make themselves known and how they will affect our lives. Nevertheless, we can make some estimates on the basis of what has occurred so far.

Office automation, specifically the automation of document processing functions, is our best data point. A reasonable sample of such functions has been automated. Clearly some jobs have been lost, but others have been created. Some workers' functions have been taken over by computers, making jobs duller; but the computer has freed other people from simple tasks, allowing them to use their brains. The overall result is that jobs have changed for the better and that overall employment has not decreased. Basically, we just gave the workers better tools. The next step, as we have intimated, is increasing use of technology in management and professional positions. These people are "knowledge workers," whose jobs are going to be done better, not eliminated, through the use of technology. The impact of technology on these groups will be tremendous. There are many more of them than there are clerical and administrative support workers and the value of their services is higher. Improving their efficiency and job quality will yield benefits that will make everybody sit up and take notice. Of course, there is no free lunch. Some cultural resistance may make implementing new technologies difficult. However, as we noted, there are also powerful cultural factors favoring the automation, and my guess is that it will run more smoothly than the pessimists believe.

The other major potential area for automation is the production and delivery of goods and services. It is customarily thought of as factory automation, but it also includes automated teller machines at banks and food preparation machines that require little human intervention. Machines like these are already in operation. They're sometimes called robots, but they're a far cry from the robots of science fiction movies. They are simply sophisticated pieces of machinery that can weld seams accurately, paint car doors, dispense cash, and make TV dinners. They may have computerized controls and they may be linked to computerized design systems used by engineers. They have one characteristic that sets them apart from office automation and other uses of technology: They unquestionably displace people. They are designed to do so. They're cheaper and more reliable.

Is this cause for alarm? Emphatically, no! First, there will be jobs created to replace the ones that are lost. The new machines have to be manufactured and serviced. Plus their use can increase a company's sales and thereby add jobs. Some research studies support the conclusion that there will not be a net job loss, although of course nobody knows for sure.

The second reason is perhaps more persuasive: There isn't anything we can do to control the spread of low-cost automation throughout the world. Japan already has five times as many industrial robots as the United States. They are exporting almost none of them. They're being used at home to increase the competitiveness of Japanese industry. Nissan body-welding operations are almost totally automated. Some of their manufacturing plants that once had hundreds of people now measure employment in dozens. The trend is clear. The U.S. has to continue factory automation and rely on the increased competitiveness to generate jobs for displaced workers.

Making the Circle Work

U.S. managers need to understand the new professional and personal concerns of the employees of the 1980s. They have to determine realistically the job requirements that will flow from their product and service strategies. Then they have to match the jobs to the employees— and the employees to the jobs—through an intelligent structuring of the jobs and provision of a proper environment and tools for the employees.

The matching process will range from being simple to quite difficult. It will be easy in growth industries that have motivated employees and can afford the new tools. It will be most difficult where it is most needed—industries in trouble that cannot afford worker alienation but that don't want to afford the costs of doing things the right way. It takes time and money to redefine jobs and assist people with their new responsibilities. The problem is partly psychological and partly real. In other words, employees have to feel good and they also have to know what they're doing in their new jobs. U.S. business is still too inexperienced at the process to have all the answers. However, companies such as General Motors, General Electric, and Deere have trained people extensively for new jobs in heavily automated factories. In the short run, the additional costs may be significant; in the long run, the factories will operate more smoothly than they otherwise would have. That's the shape of success—initial high costs followed by permanent improvements in quality and productivity.

Through all of the above, and for long after the jobs have been defined, the managers and the people they manage have to work together productively. We don't do this very well in U.S. business— our people-management skills are poor. But they are not beyond help. It's time to see what we can do about them.

"Men are not altogether bad or altogether good."
—MACHIAVELLI

Chapter 17

The Lost Art of People Management

PEOPLE MANAGEMENT is 'where the rubber meets the road.' You may have the most noble intentions of developing a corporate strategy for products, services, and social responsibility. You may have in mind the best organization structure and job definitions for your company. You may wish to build a corporate culture that works for both the company and the employees. But all your plans will be for naught if you are unable to get people to support them willingly. Everything comes down to effective people management.

We are referring to all the people in the corporation. Workers and managers are driven by many of the same economic forces. Managers are also workers. Managers have jobs to do. As we saw in the last chapter, the structure of their jobs is as important as anyone else's. Managers are also managed. Even the top manager answers to the board of directors.

All this adds up to good people management practices being needed at all levels of the corporation. People management, however, is not something that many corporations are good at. In this chapter we'll review various theories of people management and synthesize a new theory. We'll discuss participative management and team building, with examples of how to do it. Finally we'll cover compensation systems—the do's and don'ts. When we finish, we'll know how to do a lot of things more effectively.

A Synopsis of the Past

Since our interest is the future, we are not going to dwell long on the past. However, in the area of people management it is important to understand the predispositions that people are carrying around with them.

In a previous chapter we used the military as a model to illustrate conventional organization structures. The analogy carries over well to people management. In *The Charge of the Light Brigade,* Tennyson described the duties of soldiers:

> Theirs not to make reply,
> theirs not to reason why,
> theirs but to do or die.

Soldiers are not people. They are cogs in the war machine. As the corporation's employees are cogs in the industrial machine. The essence of this concept is the soldiers' willingness to die for the sake of victory of the army. Most societies have gone to great trouble to glorify soldiers who gave their lives for their country. Unfortunately, we never saw the need to make saints out of the hard-working employees who made corporate success possible while retaining their anonymity and low salaries. When they decided they were being conned, their loyalties changed almost overnight. They now want the corporation to be a partner in their lives, to do as much for them as they do for it. They're not all interested in being four-star generals, but neither do they want to be treated as privates with no rights.

So we have conflicts. Management people are shouldering an impossible burden: their education and training which have instilled in them a master-slave relationship towards their organizational subordinates, in conflict with their personal desires to be treated as thinking human beings by their organizational superiors. They're forced to live two lives. The people on lower rungs of the corporate ladder, with no subordinates to kick, are just tired of having their hands stepped on. However, the traditional master-slave approach still is dominant in most corporations. It casts a long shadow over any attempts to do things in different ways. We are chained to an antiquated management style that is out of step with the times but lingers on to haunt us like the ghost of Christmas past.

Is there hope? Some different management styles have been suggested in an attempt to exorcise the ghost.

A Survey of Management Approaches

Behavioral scientists have been around for a long time. Probably their most well-known contribution has been the Hawthorne studies of five decades ago, in which it was demonstrated that paying attention to employees can have a positive effect on their work output. The conclusion sounds tame but it was unusual because the intent of the Hawthorne experiments was to measure employee efficiency after certain improvements in working conditions. The studies found instead that paying attention to employees while changing working conditions was more important than the actual conditions.

In the last half century, the behavioral scientists have progressed far beyond Hawthorne in their understanding of human beings in the workplace, although few experiments have had the same dramatic impact. Hundreds of social scientists from behavioral science, industrial psychology, social psychology, industrial relations, and other academic permutations have attempted to figure out what makes people tick. They want to determine the management approaches that elicit the most from employees, singly and in groups. They have gone about the task in true scientific fashion: gathering data, forming hypotheses, testing the hypotheses through experimentation. The results have been somewhat puzzling. One would have expected all the effort devoted to the subject to have produced a theory that stands up to testing. Instead, we have three theories, or perhaps "schools of thought," since numerous specific theories have been put forth in each school.

People who we can call the moralists cling to an optimistic view of mankind. This view holds that the desire to achieve is natural in workers. Management's responsibility is to nurture this desire through creation of an appropriate work culture and proper treatment of the employees.

Douglas McGregor's Theory X and Theory Y organizations present one form of moralism. In a Theory X organization, people are managed with force and threats. They are assumed to be lazy and always looking for the easy way out. They are satisfied with minimal accomplishments and need to be coerced into doing any better. Theory Y assumes that work is natural, that people need and want something constructive to do. They are interested in accomplishment for the intangible satisfaction it brings as well as for the money and other rewards. Other people have proposed variations or refinements of the idea. Chris Argyris extended Theory Y to what he called Theory Yb. The b is for the group and individual behavior patterns that accompany Theory Y management. His emphasis is on the human interactions in an organization, the way people work together.

Rensis Likert is on a similar wavelength. He even calls the ultimate management approach by the name Participative Group style. He has three other styles, in decreasing order of desirability: Consultative,

Benevolent-Authoritative, and Exploitative-Authoritative. He also uses a shorthand for these, calling them System 4, 3, 2, and 1, where System 4 is the Participative Group. Perhaps Likert's major contribution has been the recognition that you can't move from one approach to another as though you were simply changing your hairstyle. People have to work very hard at implementing any approach except the unthinking military model.

Frederick Herzberg is more interested in the specific factors that prompt people to do their best. He categorizes motivational factors into two types: hygiene factors and true motivators. The hygiene factors are things that avoid worker dissatisfaction with their jobs. For this reason they have also been called dissatisfiers. Company personnel policies, salaries, and working conditions fall into this category. The true motivators or satisfiers are the kind of work, achievement and recognition of it, and responsibility.

There are other disciples of the principle, but we've made our point. Let's go on to the second school of thought.

Behaviorists take a different tack. They reject the notion that people choose to respond favorably or not, depending on how they are treated. Desire or free will is not in the behaviorists' vocabulary.

Behaviorists, to put it roughly, believe that people try to seek pleasure and avoid pain. If people receive "positive reinforcement" from tasks, i.e., pleasure, they will repeat the tasks. If they receive "negative reinforcement," i.e., pain, they will endeavor to avoid a repetition of the mistake. Positive reinforcement is more powerful than negative reinforcement. Rewarding a dog with a treat for coming to you is better than beating it if it does not come.

The animal training analogy is appropriate, because behaviorism on a grand scale owes its attractiveness to success in experiments with animals. As B. F. Skinner, who epitomizes behaviorism, points out, you can get a pigeon to peck a lever a thousand times for a few seconds' exposure to pigeon feed, and then go back and do it again. Skinner uses the phrase "operant conditioning" to describe the principle that creatures behave in the way that gave them pleasure in the past. He believes that operant conditioning can be applied to human beings in industrial and social settings. In fact, his book *Walden Two* proposed an entire model community based on behaviorism.

Other behaviorists aren't sure that the idea should be promoted to the exclusion of other approaches. George Homans and William Whyte, for example, believe that the principles of behaviorism are sound but that large-scale implementation of them may be impossible. In other words, it may be true that everybody has been conditioned by the innumerable experiences in his or her lifetime and that you can theoretically play on these experiences in order to get people to do what you want. But if you can't do it in practice, what's the difference?

Pluralists are our third group. They believe in free will, that employees choose how to behave. However, the goals of the employees are not necessarily as noble as achievement. There are a few other fundamental goals that people may have, such as social interaction or exercise of power. Management's responsibility is to understand which fundamental goal applies to each worker and then treat him or her so that the employee can achieve the goal while performing effectively for the company.

The pluralists diverge somewhat. Each believes in different basic values. One set of values, developed by David McClelland, is power, achievement, and affiliation. People are motivated by a desire for power, a desire for achievement, or a desire for social interaction. Power and achievement are different things. Power refers to obtaining a better job in the organization, managing more people, etc.—the classic 'getting ahead' in the company. Achievement is related to doing a good job without career aspirations—being the best engineer, for example, without wanting to be the engineering manager. Affiliation or social interaction is self-explanatory—a desire to like and be liked, to enjoy the company of one's fellow workers. Once you understand somebody's type, the person can be motivated properly. You motivate salespeople who like to sell differently from how you motivate those who like to socialize with the customers, who in turn are different from the salespeople who want to be president of the corporation.

Testing the Methods

How well do the approaches work in practice? They appear to work well. There are hundreds of scientific studies documenting the usefulness of each of the schools of thought in improving organizational effectiveness. Unfortunately, in these matters we start to run into one of the disappointing aspects of modern science: the existence of apparently valid studies, based on scientific methods, that come to different conclusions. We see this phenomenon everyday in news reports regarding the effects of drugs, certain foods, or chemical additives. Each side in an argument has its own experts and studies. The same holds true for studies of management styles. The studies performed by the moralists and their supporters tend to validate their theories. Ditto for behaviorists and pluralists.

Studies performed by independent parties have had mixed results, which each school claims are due to poor implementation. Could be. Could also be that the specific theories don't always work. I conducted a research project that compared the three schools of thought in particular business cases. This project was virtually the only one of its kind ever conducted, i.e., head-to-head comparisons of behavior and motivation theories. The results were intriguing. All of the approaches were effective sometimes and not at other times. The outcome seemed to depend on the employees themselves—their concerns, psychological makeup, etc.[1]

An Alternative Theory of Behavior Management

Variety, as the spice of life, applies to people as well as things. People are individuals with individual needs and desires. The data supporting this has been there all the time. It's the reason why the moralists' theories don't always work, why the behaviorists can't figure out how somebody's experiences have programmed him or her, and why pluralists still are unable to identify all the personality types. The permutations of characteristics in people are virtually limitless. It's the only possible explanation for the success of some experiments and the failure of others. When the psychological approach being tested matches the people in the experiment, the experiment succeeds. When it doesn't, the experiment fails. Why? The approach is wrong, not the subjects of the experiment. When the subjects ruin it, the experimenter is actually at fault. We seem to have learned this very slowly.

Let's say that we tentatively accept the idea that people vary in more ways than the pluralists have ever thought of. This would explain the variations in experimental results. Are there any other ways to test it? Yes. In addition to the scientific approach of behavioral scientists, we have available a number of surveys and studies performed by management-oriented people rather than academicians and theorists. What do the surveys and studies show? They show that both autocratic and consensus-building bosses are accepted—by different groups of people, of course.[2] They show that some managers still believe in the work ethic.[3] They show that workers' goals range from living for today to saving for retirement.[4] They show that CEOs look most for integrity and interpersonal skills in their successors, and manage people so as to encourage people with the right traits.[5] How do these fit in with any of the motivation theories? They don't. Trying to develop a general theory of human nature that accounts for all the variations will leave you tied in knots. It can't be done.

An alternative is a new theory of motivation, recognizing that the possible combinations of personal and cultural characteristics is a staggering number. There probably aren't more than a few dozen variations of lifestyle, demographic statistics, and the other factors that we have discussed. But when you multiply the variations together in order to see how many total possibilities exist, you realize that people are indeed close to being unique.

For some people, certain traits are dominant and can be treated as essentially representative of the whole individual. Many high achievers fall in this category. Remember, motivation and the work ethic are not dead. They are just less prevalent than they once were. If motivation based on achievement is appropriate for an individual, however, then by all means use it.

Unusual mixtures of traits are surfacing in our society. One such mixture is an ability to work very hard for a short time to earn enough money to support a non-working lifestyle for a while. This mixture of hard work in order to avoid it occurs in all age groups, although the incidence is higher in younger people. You simply have to go along with it when you encounter it.

Sometimes traditional motivation tools work, even though they are personally distasteful. Fear is such a tool. There are people in this world for whom fear appears to be the only successful motivator. Searching for techniques that are more socially acceptable may be fruitless. People who respond well to fear motivation are found at all levels of management as well as in the ranks of workers. Feel free to look for "better" ways to motivate them, but be aware that you may hurt the company in the process if you fail.

Social issues are becoming important. Employees who are concerned about discrimination because of race or sex may place the matter ahead of all other job-related concerns, including level of responsibility, achievement objectives, work atmosphere, and so on. You will have to deal with it successfully as a manager before you are able to get through to the employee on any other issue.

These examples of specific personal characteristics that must be considered in managing and motivating people illustrate the difficulty of applying generalities to individual human beings. The greatest difficulty comes, however, with the well-rounded personality, the person who has a number of coequal interests in life, of which the job is only one of them. Becoming this type of person appears to be an increasingly popular objective, but our management theories are not changing to cope with the new reality. We must turn ourselves away from the simplistic approach of a single theory of management and motivation. The idea is appealing, but it won't survive the test of reality. As H. L. Mencken said, "There's always an easy solution to every human problem—neat, plausible, and wrong."

We must stop looking at individual differences as impediments to effective management. We must learn to capitalize on the strengths of individuals and not to focus on their weaknesses. Every athletic team coach knows this, or at least every successful coach knows it and constructs the offensive and defensive strategies around the team's particular strengths. A lucky coach can acquire players that tend to conform to his or her personal philosophies. However, coaches know that they cannot build a team entirely of players with only the capabilities the coaches like and none of the weaknesses the coaches do not like. They blend what they have to produce a winning combination. They accept the idiosyncrasies of individual players to get the best from them. The coaches have to do this, because they are measured uncompromisingly on the scoreboard. The day has come when business managers can do no less.

Participative Management

If we agree that employees should be treated as individuals, presumably some employees are going to be able to accept more responsibility than in the past. Managers will have to solicit ideas and share decision making with these people.

U.S. managers are not yet very adept at sharing responsibility with organizational subordinates. However, some progress has been made with formal programs involving groups of employees (as opposed to programs encouraging true individuality). One of the buzzwords used to describe this kind of program is participative management.

Participative management presumes that people can be effectively involved in decisions that affect them. They will feel better and become committed to the decisions, but those are only byproducts. The primary reason is that better decisions will be made. People actually understand their own work lives well enough to contribute to decisions regarding them! Sounds simple when we say it that way. It probably is. Most new ideas aren't difficult to understand; they're just difficult to believe if you are accustomed to a different perspective.

Is scrap a problem in your company? Or rework? Either one or both are probably too high if you're a normal manufacturing company. How would you like to reduce annual scrap costs by over $100,000? Consider the following scenario. You manage an engine plant for one of the Big Three automakers, turning out more than two thousand engines per day. How would you like to have a day when every engine was made right the first time? No scrap and no rework. It's happened at Ford's Lima, Ohio, engine plant. Overall, the plant's reject rate has dropped over 50 percent. We've certainly given the automakers their share of criticism in this book, so we owe them some praise when they do well. Through its Employee Involvement program at many of its manufacturing plants, Ford gives employees a chance to change their work lives. They can focus on working conditions, process layout, or anything else that comes to their attention. Scrap and rework was a recognized problem in the engine plant, so the employees pitched in to help in redesigning the manufacturing procedures for making engines. The United Auto Workers (UAW) Union has supported the program from its inception. In fact, UAW and company personnel run the program jointly.

One of the keys to a program like Ford's is communication and training. Many levels of people must be involved. Executives must support the program. The workers must believe in it rather than see it cynically as another underhanded attempt by management to increase output for no increase in wages. The supervisors and foremen must not conclude that their authority is being undermined. Also, they must be given as much additional responsibility by their superiors as they have "lost" to the workers.

The proper attitudes can be instilled through training and, just as important, through proper administration of the program. People have to see that the program works as advertised. Motorola has taken both steps in their participative management program. The company discovered that management education was a bigger hurdle than employee education. The change in management style from autocratic to participative had to be explained carefully and implemented cautiously. The turning point came when the managers at Motorola were able to see the results of the program: increased output, lower costs, improved morale, and fewer disciplinary chores for them.

More Participation

We've shown that workers can drive down scrap and rework rates by applying their knowledge of their jobs to the problems. What else can they do?

They can become involved in the entire manufacturing process, including the flow of materials and in-process work. They can assist in the design of better work stations for the employees. They can help with the routing of conveyor lines and the location of intermediate storage points. In the last chapter we talked about the importance of the process by which a job is performed. Now we see that a worker can have a say in the process of performing his or her job.

We can appreciate that employee involvement with the definitions of their jobs and work-related responsibilities can have a beneficial impact. What if we go a step beyond that, to let workers participate in the process of being an equal member in corporate society? Maybe we'll take away the time clocks where the workers used to punch in and out. Work out disagreements through discussions instead of grievance procedures. We'll let the workers choose their own hours, or as much as they can do so while maintaining contact with other people. Hewlett-Packard offers this "flexitime" approach to its employees, in both offices and factories.

We'll encourage the workers to understand the production schedule for the entire plant and how they fit into it. We'll let them work together in teams that set their own schedules and assignments within the overall plant schedule. One of TRW's divisions has work teams similar to these. The teams also are responsible for performance evaluations of the team members—probably the ultimate proof of who is running the show. At Eaton Corporation, all workers in the new plants were started as salaried workers and treated as such, including their participation in the salaried pension and sick-leave programs. Many workers are on flexible work schedules and are able to set their own hours. Eaton compares the results at their newer plants with the older plants that still operate with traditional procedures. Their experience has been that workers produce much more in the new environment. Absenteeism has also been reduced to levels far below those of the older plants!

Another way to help both workers and the company is to change the layoff procedure so that work requirements are reduced slightly for a number of employees rather than laying off an equivalent number of full-time people. For example, if five people each work 20 percent less, it might make it unnecessary to lay off one of the five. This concept, called worksharing, is popular mostly in California, Arizona, and Oregon, where the workers can collect unemployment compensation for the time their workweek is reduced. The employees as a group benefit through a kind of job security. The company benefits by avoiding some administrative plus retraining costs when business picks up. The biggest benefits perhaps are psychological—a feeling that the company and the workers are pulling together as a family. It's not perfect, but it's a lot less dehumanizing than layoffs.

General Motors has an interesting approach to the question of results from their Quality of Work Life (QWL) program: They won't discuss it. QWL programs have been initiated in over a hundred of GM's plants. Obviously, some are much further along than others. It is also obvious that GM, like Ford and Chrysler, has so much catching up to do in the field of human relations that it may take years before the issue of results is even meaningful. But both the company and the UAW, which cosponsored the program, are convinced that QWL is right for its own sake. QWL has involved GM workers in design of their own jobs, resolution of quality problems, improving safety procedures, and the like. The company repeatedly has said publicly that its goal is a better life for the workers in their plants. And that's all. No goals of getting more out of the workers; the program has its own intrinsic benefits.

Is that statement a solid one? It sounds like a noble objective, and, in fact, it has fooled a lot of people who expected GM to want something in return. All we can hope is that GM doesn't mean what they say. There are a number of problems in their plants that we have previously delineated—quality, absenteeism, cost, etc. The company, which means management and workers, has to solve these problems if they are going to regain their former position with the U.S. public. If treating workers better is going to help solve these problems, why not say so? The same goes for the UAW. Why go on pretending that they are protecting their members from the evil company that expects the workers to do better if they are treated better? Clearly the company has to do better if it is going to be an example of something other than money wasters.

And, for another sobering thought on worker participation programs, consider General Foods. The company attempted to implement such a program at its Topeka pet-food plant. It worked poorly, and the company won't talk much about it. The reasons were primarily related to inadequate breadth of support of the ideas, or in other words, insufficient participation in participative management. The moral—just because an idea's time has come doesn't mean that hard work won't be required to implement it.

A Logical Extension

Manufacturing companies have been the leaders in worker participation movements. Ironically, their position of leadership is due primarily to the deterioration of worker-management relationships in many manufacturing companies to the point where almost any idea that was not illegal would be tried. It may seem strange to you that the auto companies are as involved as they are. It's really no more unusual than an atheist near death converting to a belief in a Supreme Being and an afterlife. The real test will be the strength of the belief if the disease goes into temporary remission, or if the patient partially recovers because of the belief and has to face the possibility of living indefinitely with the new religion.

What is the implication for service industries? They don't have the severity of worker problems—yet. Should they wait before embarking on programs to increase worker involvement? No—that would be a case of deliberately waiting until the horses were stolen to lock the barn door. Service businesses are as complex as manufacturing businesses to manage. There is the added dimension of the lack of a product. The employees and their customer interactions take the place of a product focus. If there is a difference from manufacturing, it's that the people are more important, not less. The question is: can participative management work effectively in a service company?

I think it can. The principle is a reflection of human nature, not of the product or service environment. It is the nature of many people to perform better if they have a say in the decisions affecting them. Involvement by the workers in defining their jobs and how to do them. In designing working conditions. In designing the mode and procedure for customer contact and service. In contributing ideas to improve the quality of the service. And, in establishing a work environment that is just plain fun to work in. Unhappiness and dissatisfaction, when they exist, are apparent to customers. Not only can you get dissatisfied workers, but you also can get dissatisfied customers who weren't pleased with the service they got from the disgruntled employees.

You kick off a participative management program from the top. Senior management has to show that they care by becoming personally involved. Hyatt Hotels has done this. The president of the company has gone to the hotels to talk personally with the employees about their concerns. Not to circumvent the normal channels, but to strengthen them by showing that the boss really does want their opinions. Then, of course, the conversations are followed up with action. As with all participative management programs, the action is what counts. Employees need to see that their thoughts on better jobs or procedures are taken seriously, evaluated and, where appropriate, implemented. Some ideas are minor; some are major. Of course, not all employees at Hyatt have all their ideas accepted, but enough of them do to make the program a success. And that's what counts.

The Union Position

The UAW has been somewhat cooperative in the QWL program at GM and Employee Involvement program at Ford. Is this representative of their general attitude, or is it an accident? Where does the rest of organized labor stand?

Let's lay the UAW story to rest. The union clearly has changed. They've made concessions in work rules and wages as well as provided support for worker participation programs. Individual leaders among the workers have been as instrumental as the national UAW leadership in implementing the changes. They appear to be committed to taking part in doing things better. It's difficult to say if that will be enough. Given the history of relations with management, the union is justifiably slow about making changes that the company could take advantage of. Company management, in turn, is suspicious of the workers. In the auto industry, the two sides are so far apart that progress may be only an illusion unless it continues for several years.

Where do the other unions stand on the issue of worker participation? Where would you expect them to stand? They've been as anxious as management over the last fifty years to draw a line in the sand that neither side could cross. To define management's jobs as managing and the workers' as doing. They haven't been the least interested in things like profit sharing. This history would lead you to believe that unions would be skeptical of their members being asked to assist in activities that traditionally belonged to management or to strive for work lives loaded with benefits traditionally reserved for management. And you'd be right. The unions have been skeptical. But they haven't shut the door on the idea.

The United Steelworkers started working with steel companies' management in the early 1970s on ways to increase the competitiveness of U.S. steel products. At one point they even signed a no-strike contract. In 1980 the union and nine large steel companies agreed to establish teams of workers and managers at steel plants. The teams would be able to attack any problems or issues in the plants that were not specifically covered by the negotiated formal contract.

That year was also a good one for the Communications Workers of America, the union that represents employees at AT&T and other telephone companies. Both the company and the union entered contract negotiations with quality of work life high on their agendas. By the time they left the bargaining table, the sides had agreed to work together to make the employees' jobs more interesting and less tightly controlled by management.

The United Rubber Workers is another union that is often characterized as traditional. Yet several of their locals have negotiated participative management pacts with management in local plants.

Who else? The International Union of Electrical Workers. The Telecommunications International Union. The tide is turning. All the major unions that we have mentioned have addressed the basic question: What is best for the employees? Once they decided that the employees' long-term welfare was their goal, the rest was easy.

Unions are even beginning to get involved directly. They are assuming some responsibilities that were previously reserved for management. For instance, unions have access to confidential financial data at several major companies, including United Air Lines and Uniroyal, to share responsibility with management for establishing reasonable working conditions, wages, etc. Union officials sit on boards of directors. The well-publicized Chrysler seat may be the most prestigious, but Pan Am and a host of smaller companies also have union representatives on their boards.

Unions have shown that they can be supportive of worker participation programs. Some unions have not moved as quickly and are still stuck in the militant rhetoric of higher wages and more grievances. But the trend is clear. Company managements have a responsibility to work with the unions in good faith. If they do, perhaps the less-supportive unions will change their minds. Eventually union-management difficulties might be as outdated as the armed conflicts with strikers in previous generations seem to us now.

A Summary of Group Efforts

What can we say to summarize the efforts to involve employees actively in the workplace? Basically, that a few formal programs have been established and that the results, as we have seen, have generally been promising. U.S. managers should conscientiously learn some lessons from the discussion and examples in the foregoing pages.

What lies ahead for formal programs? Probably more of the same— the pattern of success has been established by a few companies. But there is one more possibility—worker involvement in the top management of the company.

We've mentioned limited worker involvement on boards of directors in the U.S. However, "codetermination" has been around in Germany since the early 1950s. In those years workers in the iron, steel, and coal industries were given equal representation on the boards of directors of companies in those industries. Subsequent legislation extended the same right to workers in all companies with more than 2,000 employees. Norway and Sweden also have laws requiring worker representation on boards. In Sweden, companies with as few as 200 employees are affected. Japan and the other countries in Western Europe, including Britain, do not require worker participation in top management of a company.

Despite some disparity over worker-directors, there is no dispute in Europe over worker involvement in managerial decisions. Workers are consulted (really consulted, not merely informed) on production schedules, equipment acquisitions, plant openings and closings, and other similar matters in addition to the normal issues for worker involvement such as work rules. Groups called works councils are the vehicle for these discussions. Works councils are composed of worker and management representatives. They are not unions. They are truly a third kind of body, in addition to unions and management, although their interest in employee well-being frequently means that their interests mesh with those of the unions. Works councils exist in every Common Market country except Britain. They meet frequently, dealing with a company's short-term and long-term concerns, in a cooperative fashion that bridges the gap between unions and management. To the U.S. way of thinking, they appear to be an unnecessary appendage. They seem to be an additional bureaucracy for managers and employees who already have existing mechanisms, such as unions, to deal with their problems. Almost all U.S. visitors to European companies, whether in management or union positions in the U.S., return unconvinced that works councils would serve any useful function in this country. Europeans, and Americans who have spent a great deal of time in Europe, would come to a different conclusion. They would point to the necessity to do something to circumvent the confrontations that normally accompany union-management relations. Maybe works councils in the same format used in Europe aren't the answer, but the idea is solid. U.S. managers should look for the good features of the works councils and search for a way to import them.

That concludes our discussions of formal worker involvement programs. We are going to return to the concept of individualism, but first let's consider one more thing that interests every employee and manager—compensation.

Incentive (and Dis-incentive) Systems

Today's effective manager of people is as well-armed as today's champion golfer; both have an arsenal of different clubs to be used in different situations. And, just as the golfer uses a putter on every hole, the manager also has one tool that is used for every employee—the compensation system. Everybody has to be paid. This fact gives you an opportunity to design a compensation system that helps you in the management and motivation of people. You can't ensure that compensation means the same to everybody, but you can create a system that optimizes whatever effect compensation has on an individual.

Fundamentally, the current compensation system is based on marketplace supply and demand. Corporations pay people enough so that they will not defect to the competition, loaf in their jobs rather than strive for promotions, or decide to bask in the sun rather than work. Of course, if you pay someone too much, the person may decide to retire rather than work.

Senior executives typically have a large discretionary component to their income, which is intended to act as an incentive. The incentive portion may be well over half of an executive's total compensation in a good year. The exact form of payment varies with the tax laws that are in force at any given moment. The tax laws influennce both the executive, in terms of tax liability on compensation, and the corporation, in terms of the amount and timing of deductibility of compensation as legitimate business expenses. Depending on how the laws read, executives may be paid in cash, various kinds of company stock, or through such exotic means as phantom stock or stock appreciation rights.

Lower and middle-level managers may also be eligible for incentive compensation. Both the size and form of the payments vary considerably less than for senior executives. Cash payments and small awards of stock are common. These bonuses would seldom exceed 20 percent of base salary.

It is not unusual for incentive payments to be deferred, i.e., spread over several years from date of award, to be paid only if the person remains with the company. A three-year plan might pay 40 percent of the award at the end of the first year and 30 percent at the end of the second and third years. These "golden handcuffs" are a recognition of the declining company loyalty among U.S. managers. Surveys indicate that as few as a quarter of U.S. executives believe loyalty to their companies is important.[6] Even blue-chip companies like AT&T report significant declines in loyalty among younger managers.

People in non-management positions usually are paid straight salaries or wage rates. The compensation is far from arbitrary. Salaries are set on the basis of job level, usually within a pre-established range for the level. The rules for setting hourly employees' compensation may be quite complex, considering seniority, work content, the shift worked, etc. But incentives for good work are rarely part of the system. They used to be more common, but they were abused. By management who set performance standards so high that incentive pay could not be easily earned. By workers and unions whose nitpicking over minor inequities resulted in administrative burdens and/or full incentive pay for everyone, destroying the usefulness of the system.

Some companies have profit sharing or stock purchase plans that reward employees for good overall company performance. These are group incentive rather than individual incentive plans and therefore are less intended to affect the performance of specific employees.

What's Wrong?

There are a lot of things wrong with this system. In practice, executive bonuses often are not related to the executive's performance in a clear way. Many CEOs receive big bonuses in years when their companies do poorly. The argument in favor of this, of course, is that the company would have done far worse without that executive. Also, executives usually retain their perquisites (cars, country club memberships, etc.) regardless. When the bonus is clearly tied to performance, it is tied to short-term performance. The auto companies are good at this. In bad sales years, the top management of General Motors can lose up to half their compensation compared to good sales years. But there is nothing in the system that rewards planning for the future or penalizes for the lack of planning when current sales are running at a high level.

Bonus payments for lower and middle managers are often perfunctory. They come to be expected by the people. Furthermore, the cap on them precludes high bonuses for truly outstanding performance. Consequently, their role as motivators is not as strong as it might be.

Non-management salaried people have limited incentives—they can receive merit raises and be promoted. However, hourly workers have virtually no financial incentive to do better. In fact, in many cases they benefit by doing poorly, causing the company to hire more junior workers which, over time, bumps up the labor grades and pay of more experienced workers. This practice eventually backfires, but it can work for a short while. In addition, the presence of financial incentives for higher-level people can be a negative factor. Many non-management employees feel it would be more fair if nobody were on an "incentive" system. The situation has been exacerbated by the recent emergence of "golden parachutes," financial cushions for executives if their company is acquired by another. Workers have no such protection and are justifiably resentful.

On a broader scale, the system institutionalizes discrimination and unfair practices. As long as everybody discriminates, the demand lever in the supply/demand system fails to function. Bank tellers are a good example. They are paid far less than people in other jobs demanding similar skills. But almost all banks pay the same, so there is no balancing force. Tellers who want to make more money go to different kinds of jobs. Some non-bank companies routinely look for bank tellers to fill job openings. The tellers are trustworthy, presentable, articulate, often college-educated, and have been exposed to the business world. And they don't cost much. Quite a bargain.

Not everything is wrong with the system. The chance to get rich through stock options has motivated many managers. But, in summary, it could be a lot better.

Making The System Better

How can the system be improved? Integrate it with long-term corporate objectives. Don't throw out the link to short-term performance, but complement it with a piece focusing on the future. Pay for team contributions as much or more than for individual effort. Extend it to all employees, so that all people for whom financial incentives are important can share in the wealth. For some people it's not important. That's okay, too, if the incentives are provided for the people who want to do more than the minimum without penalizing the average worker.

Give workers a share of the financial rewards that are derived from better performance. Share them directly, through compensation or fringe benefits. It's a perfectly logical approach. Isn't it strange that this approach is so rare in U.S. industry or, for that matter, in business anywhere in the world? The historical reason is obvious. Business managers were the owners of the business when capitalism was born. The owner-manager business person in the U.S. existed until well into this century when the "professional manager" began to fill the executive suites. The owner-managers had their own capital, lives, and reputation at risk in the company. They deserved the fruits of success if they came. The workers did not share the risk, so why should they share in the rewards? Things have changed since those days. Business managers today usually have virtually nothing at risk. The workers always really had something at risk—their jobs were at risk—but today they are certainly on a par with the professional managers. The shoe may even be on the other foot. A Chrysler worker would probably have more difficulty in locating a comparable job in a different company than a Chrysler manager. Management skills are more easily transferred to different environments than auto-assembly skills. Historical reasons for not rewarding the workers no longer apply.

Profit sharing is also a form of reward sharing. It's a valuable tool and probably should be in the compensation arsenal of most corporations. Its implementation, however, has been less than ideal. Typically, a preset fraction of total corporate earnings above a "floor" level is distributed to employees proportionately on the basis of their base compensation or job level. This does encourage employees to work for the overall good of the company, but it's just a little too far removed from an individual employee to motivate him or her strongly. Also, it does not eliminate the effects of external influences such as a general economic malaise in the country.

A better approach is to link the payments to employees to things they can affect directly, such as specific costs or elements of sales that are not beyond their control. Large categories, such as operating costs for a particular factory, can be established so that people will have a broad enough objective to minimize suboptimization. Such an objective, while large, is still specific enough for people to focus on in their own jobs. The second requirement of an effective reward system is to make payments frequently, with the amounts based on the improvements made, in cost reduction, for example. People will be able to see a direct benefit in their paychecks. This kind of approach is sometimes called a Scanlon Plan after a specific version of the approach developed by Joseph Scanlon of MIT over forty years ago. Implementation of a true Scanlon Plan or your own version will give you a leg up on the competition. Most of them will still be struggling to get the sincere commitment from management to the idea that workers should share in the success they bring to the company. Caterpillar Tractor Co. took this step in 1983 by agreeing to a profit-sharing plan as part of settling a strike with its union, the UAW. Cat, as it is known, is in a tough business, and the move, while not a panacea, should help strengthen their ability to be competitive.

Be adventurous. Explore new concepts, such as a "cafeteria" approach. Maybe some employees would like their bonuses in cash and others in stock or in additional time off. Don't try to design one reward that fits all people.

Above all, be fair. Eliminate discrimination. Don't pay unearned bonuses. Correct inequities in pay among employees and jobs. Correct the salary compression that tends to occur in inflationary times. Fairness will go further than anything else toward improving morale. The sense of justice of many people is more powerful than greed. If employees see that the company is on their side, they will be glad to shoulder their share of the burden.

And make the compensation system just one part of your reward system. Add non-cash awards and other forms of recognition. For many people, formal recognition of a job well done (perhaps in the company newsletter) is more important than an extra $100 in the pay envelope.

And there are numerous other possibilities. Perhaps extremely flexible working hours that let employees work at home if they want to in order to do personal things at convenient times during the day. Partial or total payment for adult education courses that are not related to the jobs and time off, if necessary, to take the courses. Planned communities to minimize the time and hassle of commuting to work. Availability of leaves of absence or sabbaticals for employees to do anything they want for a few weeks or months. Employee health and fitness programs, including exercise facilities maintained by the corporation. Sponsorship of cultural events.

No single corporation has become involved in all these things. That's probably good—it would smack too much of the old company town where a benevolent interest in employees' lives could slip too easily into interference. But some companies have taken a few of the steps. Rolm, the telecommunications equipment company, built a multi-million dollar recreation center for its employees. They also offer employees sabbaticals every seven years. At Research Triangle Park in North Carolina, such companies as Data General have flexible hours for many employees. Sentry Insurance and other companies have sponsored "wellness" programs to assist employees with health improvement. The success of these programs is supported by the facts: the National Institutes of Health estimate that corporate programs reduce per-employee medical costs by $500 annually, far less than what it costs to provide the programs.

Blending Theory with Programs

We have discussed two major thoughts in this chapter. First, individuals can be motivated and rewarded according to the new theory of individual uniqueness. Second, formal programs involving large or small groups of employees in their jobs can be successfully implemented.

U.S. companies need to adopt policies for dealing with individuals, extending to them on an individual basis the freedoms that are found in formal group programs. To design jobs, pursue interests, choose one's form of compensation. To take part in decisions. Or simply to sit on the sidelines. Whatever will encourage employees to contribute to their maximum. No company has taken this step, but it's the only way the U.S. will be able to compete in the future.

James Beré, chairman and CEO of Borg-Warner Corporation, has said that "the real untapped asset at most corporations is the energy of the human spirit." I would add to this that U.S. workers and managers are unique in the world in their cultural backgrounds. We have a history of being much freer as individuals than people in other societies. The freedom and individuality built this nation. The last century's forced acceptance of group thinking is only a transient phenomenon. The individuality is now bursting out again all over the country, driven by the twin engines of economic success and individual self-actualization.

We can never create teams composed of individuals who strive solely for the common good, blindly assuming rewards will follow. Such selflessness is not part of our culture; Kamikaze pilots could not have been produced from the U.S. system. We have to build teams on the premise that everybody will gain personally by contributing to the team. Our professional sports teams are a pretty good model. We don't discourage the emergence of stars on the teams, and we expect individual players to negotiate their contracts rather than receive an equal part of a large pool earned by the team. But we also expect the players to behave like a cohesive unit on the playing field. The model has to be applicable to business, as well. Otherwise the U.S. won't win the global management battle.

"It is safer to change many things than one."
—FRANCIS BACON

Chapter 18

The Productivity Problem

MANAGEMENT always has its hot topics and trends. Executive time management. Merger and acquisition analysis. Strategic planning. Productivity is one of the current hot topics. We already have touched on several aspects of management that affect productivity, but it is important that we address it as a specific topic.

First we will develop a common understanding of what productivity is and why people think it's a problem in the United States. Next, we'll briefly review the explanations from "experts" for the existence of the problem, and their suggestions for potential corrective action. We'll show that these have serious flaws. And then we'll develop some new and different approaches for analyzing and improving productivity.

What Is Productivity?

Productivity is really a measure of efficiency. How much you can produce for a certain amount of effort. Or how many resources are required to produce a certain amount of output, say a specific good or service. If your company is more efficient than the competition, you can sell your wares for less or have a higher profit margin, or both.

Beyond that general definition things get complicated. How do you measure output? In units (of goods or services, e.g., hamburgers)? Dollars? Where do you get the information? How do you account for quality and functional improvements? How do you measure the input, i.e., the resources consumed? Labor hours? Dollars? Using what data? Over what time period?

Dollar output per labor hour, deflated, has emerged as the consensus choice for the definition of productivity. The usual measuring period is a year. Why dollar output instead of units? And why deflated? This approach appears to be a good way to resolve three problems: inflation, changes in the goods and services produced in the economy, and the difficulty of collecting unit data. On the input side, why labor hours? Because this measure, although simple, has some important components. It implicitly considers capital and equipment resources, since their substitutions for labor would lead to higher labor productivity. In other words, the trend would come out correctly, assuming that nobody would ever displace labor with a machine that was less efficient than human beings. Second, it gives us a good society-wide measure. We have to be concerned with the well-being of the citizens of this country. We are unable to control the supply of labor, i.e., the number of human beings. Therefore we had better be able to figure out how to make them productive. Labor productivity rates in conjunction with unemployment rates will tell us how well we are doing.

There is a potential conflict between a good productivity definition for society and a good definition for a particular company. A company increases its productivity and competitiveness whenever it uses fewer resources of any kind to produce the same amount of output. It may replace people with machines. However, if every company did this, society would probably not be better off. With the current measures, productivity improvements would show up for both the company and society. If we factored in unemployment costs, tangible and intangible, we would get a different answer for society although the company's answer would not change. At the moment we don't know how to calculate unemployment costs, so this difference remains hidden. But it gives us the first clue that perhaps society and individual companies must be treated separately when we're dealing with productivity. As we'll see, this approach is somewhat novel, running contrary to conventional wisdom.

Measuring Productivity

We all know that the national productivity problem is serious, but it's important to determine the extent of the problem.

Output per labor hour, as we said, is generally the yardstick that is used in productivity measurements. Using that yardstick, is U.S. productivity increasing or decreasing relative to the rest of the world? In other words, regardless of our absolute levels of productivity, are we moving ahead or falling behind? Figure 18–1 answers that question pretty well. Our annual productivity increases for the past two decades have been a quarter of Japan's and half of West Germany's and France's. Our nearest competitor is Great Britain which manages to beat us out by almost a percentage point.

Not a pretty picture. We'd like to know more though. Have we been on a steady decline or have we been operating at low levels consistently? Figures 18–2 and 18–3 give us the bad news. We've been running at low rates of productivity increase since the mid-1960s. In Figure 18–2, we've included the statistics on total (i.e., capital plus labor) productivity, a calculation that is preferred by some economists. As we can see, the numbers and trend are basically the same as for labor productivity, so our conclusions don't change.

Interpreting the Numbers

Numbers induce a false sense of security. They are precise and therefore give us a feeling of certainty. Certainty, unfortunately, is the last thing we have with productivity numbers. Consider just the arithmetical derivation of the output per labor hour in a particular year. The numerator is the deflated value of all goods and services produced.

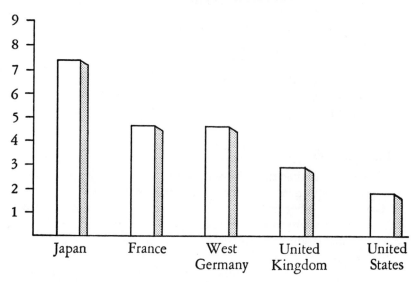

Figure 18–1
Annual Percent Improvements in Total Labor Productivity
Over the Last Two Decades

Source: Data from American Productivity Center

Figure 18–2
U.S. Labor and Capital Productivity Improvement
(Annual Percent)

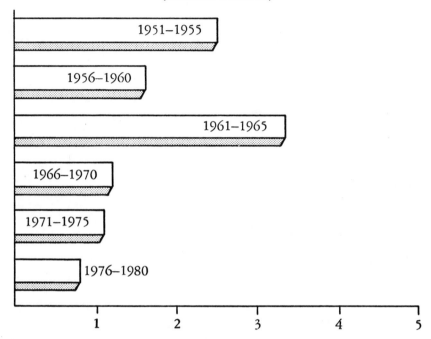

Source: Data from American Productivity Center and U.S. Department of Labor

How do you determine this, starting with the un-deflated value? There isn't any nationwide system to report it to the government? The Department of Labor (DOL) has to make estimates from a variety of reporting sources. The total is only as good as the worst estimate. In addition, we have the "underground economy," which may be over $300 billion. DOL simply guesses ("estimate" is too generous a word) about that. The overall result is a very fuzzy number. Then there are several possible ways to deflate the number, just as there are several ways to compute consumer inflation. The department simply chooses one. The denominator of the number is labor hours worked. Same problem. They have to obtain the labor hours worked for everyone in the country. Self-employed people, for example (five million of them). Small businesses. College students with part-time jobs. The Labor Department ends up making a lot of guesses.

Figure 18-3
U.S. Labor Productivity Improvement
(Annual Percent)

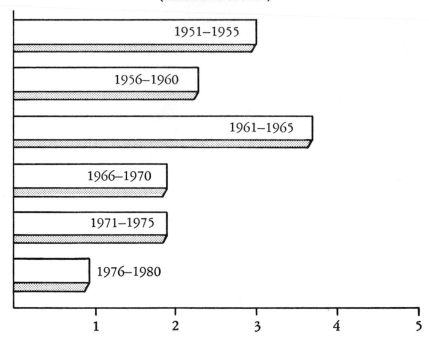

Source: Data from American Productivity Center and U.S. Department of Labor

In fact, the more you dig, the more problems with the data arise. If the U.S. Department of Labor or similar bodies in other countries are off by even a couple of percent on total output vs. input or don't use uniform reporting procedures, then the information we've just looked at could be very wrong. Is that a real possibility?

If we were to examine the U.S. quarterly data (every three months) we would see wild fluctuations. However, the fluctuations cancel out over a year or more. So the data is okay. The international problems are more real. The reporting systems of the various countries aren't uniform, making comparisons difficult. Nonetheless, there is consistently a great disparity between the rates of the U.S. and other countries. It's difficult to believe that there isn't some truth to the numbers if they are as far apart as they are.

And some other calculations of productivity increases do support the DOL figures. Private researchers have reached similar conclusions.[1]

Their precise figures differ, but the conclusion is the same: U.S. productivity increases trail other countries'. A wholly different calculation, gross national product (GNP) per capita in the U.S., shows exactly the same phenomenon as the labor productivity numbers: a falling rate of increase from the mid-1960s onward. So we probably are on to something.

Identifying the Winners and the Losers

You may be wondering why we are dealing with rates of increases or decreases in productivity? Why don't we go right to the heart of the matter—absolute values of productivity in specific segments of the economy? For instance, exactly what is the productivity of the Japanese steel industry vs. the U.S. steel industry?

The answer is, nobody knows. We can figure out how many tons of steel the Japanese produce per worker or hour. We can attach a value to the steel and develop a "pro forma" productivity value according to our standard measure, deflated dollars per labor hour. But that value is not really what we're looking for. We'd like to know the total costs of the Japanese to produce a dollar's worth of steel, so we can determine the net difference in efficiency between our industry and theirs. Hours aren't adequate—it's important to know how much their workers are paid, considering all forms of compensation and benefits, such as company housing. And we would need to know all the other costs of making steel—the equipment costs, value of government tax incentives, etc. The information isn't available. So we measure only output per labor hour. We call it "productivity" because it fits our definition, but we know that it can't actually be used to compare the efficiency of the same industry in different countries.

The sad truth, of course, is that the best isn't very good if we can't tell how much better or worse the Japanese steel industry is than ours. Is it good enough to tell how different industries in the U.S. are doing relative to each other? No—the problem is compounded if we try to make comparisons across industries rather than within the same industry. If we compare two industries, we have to worry about new concerns such as whether the uncounted labor hours (part of the denominator in the productivity formula) are liable to be higher in one industry than in another. Or whether deflated dollars is a good measure of changes in intrinsic value of goods and services. For instance, take memory chips for computers, which have shown actual price declines accompanying improved performance. That amazing accomplishment can show up as a productivity *decrease* for the chip makers (although sometimes as an increase for their customers in other industries).

Figure 18–4 shows some recent productivity increases in selected industries. What can we get from this chart? It tells us that there are some wide variations and that the variations confirm our common sense. For example, the communications industry, which has recently had new technology improving its effectiveness, shows higher increases in output per labor hour than other industries not quite as affected by technology. But we don't know the cost of the technology that replaced

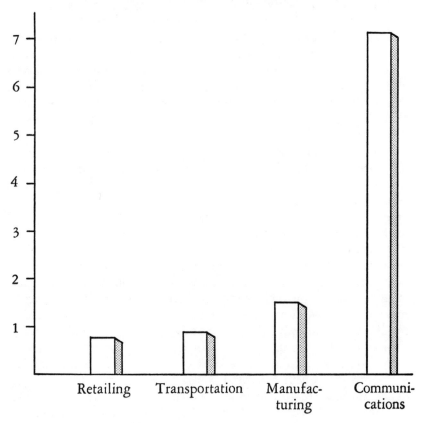

Figure 18–4
**A Sample of Recent Labor Productivity Increases
in Selected Industries (Annual Percent)**

Source: Data from U.S. Department of Labor

the labor, so we don't know the real net productivity increase. And we don't even know if the new technology costs more or less than the equipment used in other industries. So we are unable to compare the net efficiency of various industries, although we can conclude that the significant productivity variations are probably somewhat representative of the situation as a whole.

The Real Reasons Productivity Has Declined

To summarize, the conventional ways of thinking about productivity appear to be valid only on a grand scale, and only when quantitative accuracy is not very important. We are starting to get the idea that new approaches are needed if we are to deal successfully with productivity in our own companies. Some productivity "experts" have a different suggestion. They say that we *can* achieve our objective by analyzing the productivity problem on a large scale using labor hour measurements. In essence, their argument says that the large-scale phenomenon is only the sum of specific companies' actions. They also feel that labor-hour efficiency implicitly considers all other efficiencies. Therefore, we can understand specific companies' problems by understanding the causes for the national labor-hour productivity problem.

Your intuition tells you that there's probably something wrong with this line of reasoning. And you're right. But we owe it to ourselves to review the experts' ideas for the overall productivity problem. Even if the ideas ultimately don't lead to the solution, they represent an interesting insight into the variety of ways that people think about productivity.

There are eight major reasons advanced for the decline in productivity growth.

1. One idea is the disproportionate reduction in capital investment in the United States. Or, to put it another way, the increase in capital investment has not kept up with the increase in employment. We noted previously that employment actually has grown at a pretty good clip in this country. The capital investment hasn't grown as fast, so the investment per labor hour has declined. The experts' idea isn't factually in error (on a national scale, of course; capital investment per employee has behaved differently in different industries). Various reasons have been advanced, such as substitution of cheap labor for equipment, or inadequate government tax policies to encourage capital investment. The real issue, however, isn't the fact. It's whether the fact should be interpreted as automatically leading to lower labor productivity. For a

subsegment of society, of course, using people within the subsegment rather than machines from outside of it would create "lower" people productivity because of the increase in labor hours used. However, reality isn't that simple. Nobody ever has proved that capital investment always eliminates more labor hours than are used in its creation. And some capital investment, e.g., pollution control equipment, adds no productive capacity. Or maybe the fall-off in capital investment rates is perfectly natural and merely the result of analyses that showed additional capital investment wouldn't be cost justified, i.e., wouldn't be more productive than people.

The second part of the real issue is the meaning of capital investment levels in specific companies. Even if the capital investment in the entire U.S. economy, or even your industry, is too low, maybe your company's level is fine. You can't be certain without understanding your unique capital requirements in detail. If you are *significantly* under average investment levels, then there may be a problem. But you can't simply go on a capital investment binge—you have to know precisely where, when, how, etc., to invest. So this productivity idea has some merit, but only in abstract form. Accepting it won't tell you what to do or where to do it.

2. Work force composition is another possibility. This hypothesis holds that the large expansion in employment accompanied by first-time employment of minorities, women, and more young people has generated a less experienced work force. This work force can't be expected to perform as well as the smaller work force of previous years, composed of a higher proportion of experienced workers.

The hypothesis is unprovable. Even if its validity could be proved or disproved, the fact would be useful only as a sociological phenomenon. Popeye said, "I yam what I yam." The work force is what it is. There's nothing we can do about it. Individual companies can do something about their employees—but that's one of the points we're making: individual companies, not national statistical populations, are where we have to focus.

3. A companion of this work force theory is the "decline in the work ethic" theory. This is otherwise known as the "when I was a child I walked ten miles through snow to get to school, so why can't you?" theory. The young generation is no good. People today want somethin' for nothin'. Et cetera.

As we've seen earlier, the work ethic is not dead, but it certainly has changed. People *do* want things different from what previous generations wanted. And that's good, not bad, if we look at it the right way. The new energy can be harnessed to improve productivity. Harnessed in traditional ways, however, it may well be poorly utilized and contribute to the productivity problem. There is insufficient data to know how productivity has been affected. But there is a wealth of experience, as we discussed about Silicon Valley, indicating that changing employee attitudes can be constructively integrated into a work environment to produce high levels of output.

4. Research and Development (R&D) spending levels have come in for their share of criticism. It is a fact that R&D spending as a percentage of GNP has been falling since 1967.[2] Several economists have seized upon this fact to explain the slowing in productivity over the same time period. The connection presumably rests on the assumption that some portion of R&D spending results in procedures, processes, or equipment that make employees more productive. The assumption is probably sound, although nobody has been so bold as to attempt to quantify the relationship. What is not sound is the connection. R&D spending is by nature concerned with basic matters of science and engineering, not specific products and processes. It takes years or decades for R&D spending to have practical effects in the overwhelming majority of companies. However, the statistical decline in R&D spending occurred in parallel with the decline in productivity growth. So much for this theory. There may be some kind of link that nobody understands between R&D and productivity, but it certainly isn't a simple cause and effect link.

5. Movement of labor from high productivity industries to low productivity industries is offered up by the federal government. You might think that the opposite has been happening, with labor moving out of old inefficient industries into new ones like high technology that have higher productivity. It has. The proponents of this theory, however, state that this shift had its beginning and major influence on productivity in the 1950s and early 1960s. Since then, the rate of the shift has slowed down, causing a decline in productivity increases. Interesting thought. And impossible to measure. Or to use if you're worried about productivity in your company. The theory describes strictly a national phenomenon that occurred (supposedly) even though specific companies (such as yours) were improving their productivity.

A variation on this is the notion that the increase in service jobs has been a factor. The presumption is that service jobs require less skilled labor, sopping up the people in the work force who would otherwise be unemployable. Is this a valid presumption? Certainly makes sense that many service jobs—pumping gas, for example—are lower-skilled jobs. But what is the effect of high-skilled service jobs such as computer programming for independent software firms? The American Productivity Center thinks that the high-skilled jobs outweigh the others. Their analyses indicate that productivity increases in the U.S. have been helped, not hurt, by the service sector of our economy. Who's right? I don't know and neither does anyone else. Pick your expert; you can have the conclusion that you'd prefer.

6. Excessive government is named frequently as the villain. The costs of government regulation borne by industry run into the billions, estimated by some people to be as high as $100 billion annually.[3] The argument says that the majority of these costs do not contribute to increased output. They may indeed lead to worthwhile social achievements, but they retard productivity because the actual output of goods and services isn't increased proportionately to the increased expenditure of resources.

The scope of this viewpoint can be expanded to include government policies in general. Tax and income distribution policies that discourage individual incentive. Defense spending that is inherently inefficient (remember all the well-publicized cost overruns on weapons systems?) and robs resources that would be used more efficiently in a competitive environment. You name a government policy, and I'll bet it has come under criticism for contributing to low productivity.

This theory has some hard data behind it. Regulatory costs have been estimated by people and groups with opposing interests, yet the answer always came out that the costs are very high. Defense overruns have been quantified. Et cetera. So this theory probably passes the validity test. Unfortunately, it fails the relevancy test. Except for taking one's rightful place in the political process, there isn't much that a corporate manager can do. This truth doesn't minimize the political process—in fact, the process is very important—but simply recognizes that active political involvement is somewhat limited as a day-to-day management tool.

7. Energy costs are assigned a lot of the blame. The increases in energy costs—primarily oil—have added no real value to companies' output, but have pushed up their costs. Some economists even think that energy costs are the single biggest factor affecting U.S. productivity. One of the biggest problems with this argument is the appearance of low productivity increases almost ten years before the Arabs took their major action on oil prices. In addition, Japan imports far more oil than we do, and they managed to keep their productivity gains at high levels. The connection between oil costs and productivity must not be as obvious as it seems.

8. Finally, we have various theories of inevitability. Kondratieff waves. Club of Rome scenarios of worldwide economic stagnation and

possibly collapse. Laws of diminishing returns, i.e., the second round of productivity increases is always harder to get than the first. Various arguments supporting a thesis that the fundamental forces of nature are against us. Maybe they are. Some of the product and service strategies that we discusssed in the middle of the book should be useful if this possibility starts to look real to your company. If it doesn't, the argument can be viewed as, at worst, defeatist and, at best, as intellectually profound but not terribly useful.

Where Are We?

We've examined the productivity theories and come away empty-handed. Some of the theories just plain don't hold water. Others are issues of national policy, sociology, or otherwise irrelevant to the hard-pressed executive worried about productivity.

The productivity researchers have basically done two things wrong. One, they've focused almost exclusively on "macroproductivity" issues on a national scale. Perhaps this isn't wrong, but just the natural inclination of the economists and academically-oriented people who have been predominant in productivity research. Secondly, they've been lazy. Just as the philosophers' stone was sought by medieval alchemists because of its properties of turning ordinary metals into gold, researchers seem to be embarked on a quest for easy answers to the productivity problem. There aren't any, and the search for them in many companies is inhibiting real progress on productivity. Productivity doesn't lend itself to easy answers any more than any other management problem, and we have to stop looking for them.

Reversing the Trend

The only hope is to examine every aspect of the goods or service creation and delivery process in your company. To look at all the little things as well as the big picture. The key is developing a detailed understanding of the corporation's activities. It is a rare company that understands the minutiae of its operations. But you can't spot potential improvements by flitting over the surface of things. Obviously you need to be able to make the important policy decisions or sweeping changes that make big dents in a productivity problem. However, these are about as plentiful as pearls in oysters. Digging into the details of things is the road to success. Don't misunderstand. We aren't suggesting that only minor changes come out of detailed understanding. Some improvements are minor. But others are major—the distinction is that they are made up of a number of related smaller improvements that come only after corporate functions have been analyzed in detail.

Who is responsible for a productivity improvement program such as this? Top management, of course—it's a big job, requiring a lot of time, effort, and cooperation among corporate units. Top management needs to ensure that the horses are all pulling together in harness. In fact, this may be the most important factor in improving productivity. Lack of a coordinated planned approach, supported by top management, led the list of reasons for poor productivity performance in a 1982 survey of U. S. corporations.[4]

We already have talked about the value of a comprehensive approach in business and marketing planning. We now have to turn our attention to productivity. What are the areas that should be investigated? Let's start with the product or service itself.

Product and Service Design

How can product design considerations contribute to productivity improvements? In two ways. One is the process by which a new or modified product or service is designed. Computer assistance is one possibility. For another, standardized mathematical formulas to achieve design objectives have been used by many companies. Airplane designers, for example, use computerized systems that can turn functional parameters (strength, dimensions, etc.) into complete designs for parts and the tooling required to make them. The systems can even determine when existing parts can be used, with little or no modification, instead of new parts.

The second consideration is the result of the design process. The process should culminate in products or services possessing characteristics of simplicity, reliability, quality, and customer satisfaction with performance. We've discussed these characteristics in marketing terms. They're also important for productivity because of the implication for future costs of the company. The concept is called the "life cycle" approach. Companies will incur far lower future costs if products and services are designed correctly from the beginning. Consider our airplane example again. Commercial airliners are incredibly complex, with almost a million parts in them. Yet they have serious operational failures less often than your toaster or TV set. The manufacturers simply design airplanes to last because that's a lot less costly than redesigning them after serious problems occur. Of course, they have the incentive of poor public relations after crashes, but other companies could do the same if they developed the proper management attitude.

The design results also have an immediate impact in addition to the "life cycle" impact. All products and services have to be manufactured or created and then delivered to the customer. The simpler the product or service, the easier it is to make and deliver. Continuing with our airplane example, the cost and ease of building an aircraft are affected by the use of exotic materials and electronics, and by high performance criteria. That's why fighter planes cost more per seat than commercial airliners. This also leads us into the next area of productivity analysis.

Production/Delivery Procedures

Here we are getting into some areas which have been receiving a fair degree of attention from productivity analysts—the how, where, and when of providing a product or a service to a customer. Many of a company's resources are consumed in this fashion, and efficiency experts have been working for years to improve resource utilization. We are not going to duplicate their efforts. You certainly should become familiar with the work that has been done by the experts in companies similar to yours. But you should also recognize that although many of the experts' techniques are interesting, their basic premises have become part of the conventional wisdom and are seldom challenged. Your mission (and you should choose to accept it) is to look for new ways of doing things that may improve productivity while running counter to conventional wisdom. A Ph.D. isn't required—usually common sense will do. You should look at facilities, equipment, transportation, and factory layout. Inventory and production control systems. Scheduling procedures. Customer service procedures. You are looking for assumptions that haven't been challenged.

Take retailing, for example. I know many companies that have independently addressed the issues of warehouse inventory and store inventory. The assumption is that there are two inventories, each of which can have optimal control procedures. That's wrong. I have helped a few retailers develop integrated inventory control systems that controlled each item (SKU in retail terminology, for Stock Keeping Unit) on the basis of its total inventory and allocated it to stores or warehouses as appropriate. Usually a 30-40 percent reduction in inventory is possible by treating the inventory as a whole. But doing so requires challenging the assumption of two independent inventories. It also involves organization issues, since you can no longer pretend that two individuals each have independent authority over their inventories. And it changes financial reporting and measurement systems. So you can see why people shy away from it. But the winning companies don't shy away—it's worth the effort.

You can get help with your analyses from the customers. You have a natural customer contact at the point where the good or service is actually delivered. Solicit their ideas for better performance. The few companies that have tried this technique are totally sold on it. Naturally they haven't broadcast their success to the rest of the world. But understanding what the customer wants, straight from his or her own mouth, can make you much more efficient in providing the good or service, as well as in designing it. The Japanese, incidentally, are very good at this, although they've used the approach more in industrial sales than in consumer sales.

Company Management

Earlier chapters have dealt with worker motivation and improved techniques of people management. Success in these areas will lead to higher employee productivity. However, rather than rehashing the ideas from previous chapters, let's focus specifically on managerial productivity.

In many companies the most important contribution that management can make is to leave the company or at least to stay out of the way. Overhead costs can run from one-third to one-half of a company's total costs, and a quarter or more of the overhead is likely to be management people. U.S. corporations have become top heavy. The Japanese auto companies operate with several fewer levels of management than their U.S. counterparts.

So, take a look at your management staffing levels. If reductions don't look promising, than examine what your managers are doing and whether they are doing it efficiently. You can ask the same sorts of questions that you did for the workers, only in terms of managerial activities.

Planning for the future and providing continuity for the corporation as it moves through time are key tasks of managers. They need the right tools and information to do both. Computers are an inevitable implication. So are staff support, libraries of information (data bases) and links to the outside world. I've seen companies spend $500,000 on a computer-controlled warehouse storage and retrieval system to improve productivity and then turn down a $20,000 request from the planning department for more microcomputers and access to economic data bases provided by time-sharing companies. Or refuse to replace typewriters with word processors. That's dumb—staff productivity is as important as worker productivity.

Managers make decisions. They need decision support tools—computerized simulation capabilities, for example. They need to attend courses on decision making. As they do on their other activities, such as personnel supervision, organization development, interdepartmental communication, etc. Managers' activities are no secret. And improving their productivity is no secret—it comes from analyzing activities in detail just as you would on assembly lines.

One more thought regarding management: Management has the power to organize itself as well as organize the workers. You can, if you wish, specifically assign responsibility for productivity. General Dynamics has done this. The company has a vice president of productivity and quality assurance. I don't generally recommend this, because it tends to cause managers outside the designated function to think somebody else has been assigned to fix the productivity problem. But when a temporary focus is needed, it can work. Only you know which condition your company is in.

What Productivity Isn't

To summarize the views of the foregoing pages, productivity is the efficiency by which people (workers and managers) design and deliver their company's product or service to the customers. Productivity is not usually related to the management control systems that are in place and, when it is related, the correlation is usually inverse. There simply is no evidence that massive control systems do anything but hinder getting at the roots of problems. So, when you go to attack productivity in your company, don't do it by creating an administrative burden for the people involved.

There is one more important thing that productivity is not. It is not financial management (unless your business is financial services, of course). Accounting in financial terms is essential for measuring your relative and absolute success—one can't quarrel with that. But you can't carry things to a point where you think of your company exclusively in terms of financial returns (whichever ones you use:) return on investment (ROI), return on equity (ROE), earnings per share (EPS), etc. The financial returns are only part of the total corporate score, as we've stressed throughout the book. But the reasoning goes beyond that. You can't win at running a corporation by focusing on the financial returns any more than you can win at athletics by focusing on the score. If you are a football team, you have to concentrate on moving the ball—blocking, passing, running, etc. Those are the things that you practice. The score is the result of doing those things well. The same is true in business. The financial returns are only the score. Productivity improvements come from concentrating on the fundamental details of making and delivering your product.

And there is also another reason why productivity is not financial management. Financial management at the corporate level is concerned with aggregate performance of the corporation. Many things besides productivity are involved in being successful. Sales strategies, for instance. Some empire-building productivity experts have tried to expand the notion of productivity to include everything a corporation does. That's nonsense. Maybe everything in a corporation can be done more efficiently, but in many cases efficiency is a secondary or tertiary concern. For instance, you have to have the right sales strategy before it makes any sense to worry about its efficiency. So beware of the people who want to toss everything, including the kitchen sink, into the category of productivity.

Productivity Improvements in Practice

By focusing on specific companies and productivity issues—manufacturing productivity, office productivity, professional productivity, and service business productivity—we can add to our repertoire of productivity improvement ideas.

Huffy Corporation is the country's largest bicycle manufacturer. They have been concentrating on productivity for years. Huffy streamlined all the operations for making parts and assembling bicycles. Analyzed the costs of making vs. buying parts to make sure each part was obtained in the most economical fashion. They now make some tubing parts that they used to buy. Employed new machines when they would do a quality job and add to productivity (they didn't always do so; some automatic painting machines couldn't do as good a job as people and their use was discontinued). Kept up morale by preserving jobs, not using productivity as a lever against workers. Simplified work rules and eliminated rigid assignments so that employees can use their skills most productively. Workers go where they're needed, with a lot of responsibility. Sound pretty prosaic? That's the whole idea. No magic formula, just hard work. The results at Huffy: annual productivity improvements five times the national average while producing more models that last longer than ever before.

Office Productivity

Office productivity offers an ideal application of the detail approach. All the people who work in offices are painfully aware of the extent to which procedures could be streamlined. Fewer forms to fill out. Fewer file copies of documents. Fewer steps in the approval process of any decision. The situation is analogous to the days when the "Scientific Management" of Frederick Taylor and his cohorts was capable of bringing about efficiency improvements in manufacturing companies. However, there are lessons to be learned from this analogy other than productivity improvements. First, you can't improve procedures at the expense of people. A typing pool may be more technically efficient than personal secretaries, but the dehumanizing effect may cause it to backfire. Two, technology may allow for better processes rather than improvement of existing processes. Five-axis milling machines and computer-controlled lathes did more for machine shop productivity than any of Taylor's improved procedures. The same revolution is taking place today in the office.

The electronic devices becoming available are truly amazing, as we discussed earlier in the book. Word processors are commonplace. Newer products include photocopiers that are also printers of offset quality and can communicate over telephone lines to each other. Electronic filing systems to replace file cabinets. Electronic mail. Et cetera. These devices are going to revolutionize office jobs of secretaries and executives. We have seen how they are going to help society deal with the problem of too many management-age people and too few younger people. They are also going to improve productivity, for one simple reason. A tremendous amount of paper shuffling and delegation of tasks from higher-level people to lower-level paper pushers are simply going to disappear. Gone. Kaput. Replaced by direct access to computer files by the person who needs the information or wants something done with it. It's not going to happen overnight. But it's going to happen a lot sooner than you think.

Some corporations have attacked the problem of office productivity. Intel Corporation, a high-technology manufacturer of integrated circuits, followed the detail approach, analyzing all procedures in depth. They identified necessary steps in office tasks, and eliminated unnecessary steps. They looked at all details, such as numbers of photocopies. The results of Intel's efforts were increases in administrative productivity, worth several million dollars annually.

Professional Productivity

Who are professional people? We used the term earlier to mean accountants, physicians, attorneys—really the independent professionals. We are going to expand it here to include engineers and other such people in a company who are working in a recognized technical discipline with a body of knowledge.

People in these areas don't engage in repetitive processes. In this respect they are more like management people. In other respects they are different. They are personally responsible for their output, rather than working through other people. Their activities often carry a high degree of creativity or imagination, i.e., they are more often confronted with new problems that require new solutions. They frequently are not career-oriented in the sense of looking for promotions out of their fields.

Tools are very important to professional people. Today's tools are electronic—computers, calculators, electronic research libraries. These sorts of things make life much easier. High quality tools, e.g., simulation capabilities, can improve the quality of results. The kinds of tools that are provided are also important contributors to the professional's status and self-esteem, which in turn contribute to productivity.

The management of the professional is important. No-frills management is essential. A supportive but hands-off attitude. You'll benefit in two ways: reduced administrative costs and more output from the individuals.

The general guideline is to let the person do his or her job with the best tools and minimal interference. Don't burden the person with responsibilities outside his or her central responsibility. If you have to hire some lower-paid clerical support people, do so. You don't put a race horse behind a plow, and you don't get the best tax advice from a lawyer who fills in forms instead of practicing tax law.

Validation of the success of these suggestions exists. Hughes Aircraft conducted a six-year productivity study that encompassed thousands of people in technical organizations, both within the company and in other companies. The objective was to determine the key factors influencing productivity in technology-based organizations. The study concluded that the management approaches we have discussed are necessary for high productivity. In particular, it found that people-oriented management which minimized the administrative load on technical people was important. Preserving technical competence was also important—for instance, rewarding individuals' contributions in their fields through the availability of career paths in their disciplines as well as into management. In addition, providing comprehensive support to the technical people, including technical tools, was identified as crucial. Overall, the study results were just what would be expected.

Productivity in Service Businesses

We are advocating an approach that calls for a comprehensive review of everything that a company does. The application of this approach to manufacturing environments seems logical, partially because the principles are consistent with industrial engineering and other traditional manufacturing management practices. Will it work in a service business?

American Express identified the activities involved in providing services to customers. Then they established service objectives for various functions such as issuing a new charge card or replacing a lost card. The objectives were quite specific in terms of response time, error rate, and other key factors. Then they analyzed all the steps to perform the functions, eliminated unnecessary ones and speeded up the critical ones. The changes yielded customer service improvements of up to 70 percent reduction in service times. Error reductions and added revenue from putting cards into customers' hands faster have added a couple of million dollars to the net profit line.

Conclusion—the approach works in service businesses. Note that American Express did not fall into the trap of analyzing and measuring in terms of dollars. They knew their services weren't dollars, but rather, activities like prompt issuance of cards, which can't be measured in dollars. Of course, when all the dust had settled after the improvements had been made, the payoff was a big increase in profit. But, as we said before, that's only the final score, which has little to do with how you play the game.

There is, however, a need for scorekeeping of a different kind, the kind that tells us whether we are making progress in our individual productivity improvement programs. American Express, as an example, had to measure their response time to customer billing inquiries. How do we go about measuring useful things and not measuring useless things?

The Right Way to Measure Productivity

First, a disclaimer. We've discussed the problems with measuring relative and absolute productivity on a national scale. The American Productivity Center and other organizations are working on this problem, but in this book we're not going to deal with the issue further. We've made the point that the measurements don't help a particular company. The only national measurement tool that a company needs is the marketplace. It is an excellent way to determine winners and losers. It determines whether company A has been more productive—efficient—than company B. But, of course, the marketplace can't help with details. It doesn't care whether we use particular resources, say equipment or labor, more productively. It cares only about the net efficiency. Therefore, we need to measure productivity in a specific company in ways that are meaningful to it and will help its management to improve.

A simple approach that has its roots in the discipline of project management can help managers measure. Two key rules of project management are: Divide the project into a number of small activities ("chewable bites"), and define measurable output from each activity. Build your project control system around measuring and documenting the activities' output. In other words, a one-to-one correspondence between activities and results. No activities that don't have tangible results. Project success is then made up of a number of small, discrete successes. (If the concept seems obvious, think back over all the projects you've been associated with.) Applying this to productivity, we can see that the things to measure will be determined by a company's detailed diagnosis of its problems and the characteristics of its business. Huffy measured (among other things) the hours to make a bicycle frame. Intel measured the speed to process an accounts payable transaction and the percentage of payments that were made by the due dates. American Express measured response time to customers.

The real beauty and power of this approach are that anybody can do it. It gets at the very heart of what any department in a company is trying to do and measures progress in terms with which the people are familiar. It does *not* convert everything to financial or accounting terminology. Many experts, including the American Productivity Center, take the accounting approach. This merely confuses the issue and invites wasted effort. A good accounting system can unquestionably be an asset in a productivity improvement program, for example, by assisting in setting priorities or by providing verification (score-keeping) that the efforts are paying off. But you don't know very much about your business if you have to rely on the accounting system to tell you which activities are crucial to your company's success. And you're muddying the waters, as well as building an unnecessary control structure, if you insist on converting the crucial activities into dollars in order to measure whether you're doing them more efficiently.

The Final Scorecard

We've discussed detail measurement tools and their use in obtaining productivity improvements. But we are still stuck with the company's total scorecard calculated according to traditional procedures. Rates of return are measured on capital, inventory, equipment—everything but people. But that can be changed.

One approach is the old "If you can't beat 'em, join 'em" approach: Treat people costs identically with other costs. To measure profits or something else per employee expense, calculate a "return on employees" to parallel the return on assets or return on investment for equipment. It's not inconceivable that you could capitalize employee costs to more closely resemble an asset purchase price (same principle as capitalizing equipment leases). Or you could take an entirely opposite approach and calculate the net present value of future cash flows. Both approaches are commonly used to evaluate equipment investments. Upjohn Corporation has followed this straightforward approach to productivity measurement. They measure employee contributions to profit and value added in much the same way as they measure capital contributions. (So far, they use expense figures rather than capitalized figures, however.)

The other extreme, conceptually, is to focus on measurement procedures unique to human activities. This is basically an industrial engineering approach that is more closely related to specific improvement steps. It involves comparing actual time expended on activities with theoretical standards or past performance. IBM has implemented such a system throughout the world. It goes by two names, the Common Staffing System and the Functional Performance System. It operates by breaking down work into standard activities and calculating average staffing levels for workload levels of the activities. Each IBM location can compare its performance to the average and to its previous performance. IBM has not fallen into the trap of setting standards. They rely on peer pressure and natural motivation to improve on past performance. The system has been successful: The rate of employment growth compared to sales growth has been slowed considerably, reflecting higher productivity of the people. The systems, of course, has no way of measuring the costs of displacing this labor, either one-time costs or recurring costs, e.g., of automation.

So there are a couple of alternatives for improving the final scorekeeping. Whichever you choose, I encourage you to make it the last thing you do. That will help you keep it in perspective, i.e., that it is of limited value in actually determining and implementing the detailed things to do differently in improving your productivity.

Turning Suggestions into Actions

"Well Begun is Half Done."
——HORACE

Chapter 19

Putting It All Together

IN THIS CHAPTER and the next we don't need to introduce any more new ideas. We're going to pull together a few overall conclusions about management in the future. Then we're going to discuss what you can do after you put down this book (besides placing it on the shelf, that is), so that you'll be ready to begin using some of the ideas from it.

Signposts Toward the Future

Despite appearances to the contrary, we really haven't been predicting the future. We've been describing what is likely to happen on the basis of trends and recent events in the U.S. and elsewhere. Bearing in mind that all guesses, even informed ones, are still guesses, let's review our thoughts.

The corporation as an entity is undergoing many changes. Society is performing plastic surgery on it to make it more to society's liking. The corporation was an infant in the 1800s and a child in the first half of the 1900s. It had the simple desires and limited responsibility associated with childhood, as well as the requirement for occasional parental restraint. In the recent past, the corporation entered adolescence and is now emerging into the adult world. It's in its teenage years, getting a taste of increased responsibility that it does not know yet how to handle. It is ill at ease socially, interacting with forces that were shielded from it in the past. It requires additional discipline sometimes when it does unthinking or careless things. Society is an anxious parent wondering whether the corporation will become a contributing citizen or a permanent juvenile delinquent.

301

The corporation has to grow up. The board of directors will have to assume new responsibilities and constitute itself properly to do so. Organization structures more attuned to the realities facing each company will be needed. Managers' jobs will change. Both specialists and generalists will be more in demand than ever before, because doing some things well will require expertise and doing other things well will require a sense of the big picture.

The days of easy pickings for U.S. industries are over. Each company will have to differentiate its products and services from its competitors' or offer them at lower prices. This will be difficult, although not hopeless, in the veteran U.S. industries. It will be easier in high-growth industries, although such industries have a way of attracting a lot of attention from tough competitors like the Japanese. Success will come to the corporations that position themselves to provide long-term satisfaction of marketplace and customer desires. That understand who they are and what they're good at. That work with, not against, the government. That analyze international markets, customers' changing tastes and expectations, and other factors related to their companies. Failure will leave its mark on corporations that focus only on the next year or try to attract customers through gimmicks rather than through value of their product and service offerings.

And the corporation must make better use of its main resource—people. It must care about them, singly and in groups. Jobs must be changed to utilize people's talents and to increase productivity. Workers must be more involved in decisions that affect their lives. Above all, we must stop putting labels on people and then managing the labels according to predetermined policies. We must learn to deal with people as individuals.

Total Management

Clearly, all corporations do not have to change everything they're doing to survive in the future. But most will have to change in one way or another. It is questionable whether a company can do more than merely limp along if it ignores any of the major changes in the world that are occurring or going to occur. This means a fundamental change in the management ideology of most companies. The old ideologies are dying. Every one of them has one or more pieces that are in conflict with the direction the world is taking. More precisely, the ideologies are incomplete. They just don't address the major changes that are happening all around us. We need a new ideology that encompasses the changes and recognizes the comprehensiveness of the new responsibilities and activities of U.S. business. With apologies to Izaak Walton, perhaps we could call it the philosophy of the Compleat Capitalist. We are not throwing out capitalism. We're expanding and strengthening it. It's the most effective economic system the world has ever seen, but it's showing its age. However, it can be rejuvenated if we follow the rehabilitation program that we've laid out.

The new philosophy doesn't have to be viewed as a rejection of previous philosophies. In fact, we've really started with the old ideologies, taken them apart, discarded obsolete pieces, refurbished some pieces that could be saved, and put them back together again into a unified whole. If we look at the situation this way, we'll all come out as winners. We can build on the things that we're familiar with. If we look at it negatively, we'll be losers. We'll be overwhelmed by the changes in our lives that will be necessary.

Profile of the Future Manager

We've already said that numerous kinds of skills will be required in the management ranks of corporations in the future. How, then, are we going to describe a profile of an average future manager? I'm not sure that I have a good answer for this question, so I'm going to dodge it. Instead I'm going to try to draw the profile and hope that something useful is communicated in the process.

As for character traits, the manager can't be a corporate isolationist. Like all of us, the person will have varying degrees of interest in topics both internal and external to the corporation. However, a complete lack of interest in external matters is not likely to be found in many successful managers. There are too many important things going on for isolationism to be effective.

The person must be pragmatic and adaptable. Tuned in to change. Change isn't going to stop or the world freeze in its current state because we've written a book about it. Some people are psychologically unsuited to change. They're uncomfortable with it. These people will be better off in lower management jobs or perhaps non-management jobs.

Managers will have various backgrounds. They won't all be preppies or, conversely, all graduates of public schools. They will be well-educated, but not just in the sense of schooling. There has been a trend in U.S. business in recent years toward recognition that the M.B.A. degree does not confer instant wisdom on its holders. Companies are starting to reduce M.B.A. hiring or to require business experience as well as the degree in the people they hire. This trend will continue and probably accelerate. Future managers will undoubtedly need many skills that can

be taught from books or course work. However, they also need knowledge and skills that can only be gained through living with an open
mind and alert senses. The ability to focus on the true needs of society,
customers, and employees. To deal with international markets. Or the
government. M.B.A. should stand for Minimum Business Acumen—
that's all its holders bring to the party. It's better than the N.B.A.—
No Business Acumen. But it's still only one ingredient in a complicated
recipe for turning out a seasoned manager.

The opposite of education is intuition, the ability to make the correct
judgment without all the relevant facts or tools. All good managers
operate on intuition, probably more than they or their colleagues would
like to admit. This will, of course, continue. I mention it here not to
suggest that it's anything new. However, there is always a danger with
a new philosophy, as we are espousing, that poor literal interpretations
can improperly outweigh good intuitive judgments. We don't want
that to happen. Intuition will remain in the manager's bag of tricks.

The manager's style is likely to be perceived differently by different
people. Since he or she will treat people as individuals, they will see an
autocrat, a consensus builder, a leader, or whatever style is projected to
them in their personal dealings. Publicly or in groups, the manager will
appear to be a strong figure who communicates well and accepts ideas
from those who are willing to offer them, but is always ready to make
the decisions that go with his or her title. Privately he or she will
emphasize the things that are appropriate for the individuals involved.

Specific managerial positions will, of course, require specific skills.
Here we will find the diversity of technical skills that we mentioned
earlier. We will also find the generalists with a potpourri of skills. We
will find managers with small groups and other people who are comfortable managing larger groups. There truly will be a lot of differences
among the numerous managers in a corporation. But they—or at least
the effective ones—also will share some common elements.

The New Complements the Old

Clearly the future and the people who will successfully manage
through it are different from the present in many ways. However, we
must be careful not to paint a picture of a world turned completely
upside down. Many of the new management approaches and skills
must be viewed as additive to conventional management methods. The
forward pass revolutionized football, but it complemented rather than
replaced the running game. There are some traditional management
techniques that are analagous to the running attack.

Thoroughness and detailed planning are not exactly management techniques, but they're so important that they're worth mentioning. There are no new insights, whether gained from this book or elsewhere, that entitle you to go off half-cocked before you've thought things through. The best new product in the world still has to be sound when it hits the marketplace. Airplanes have to fly. Checking accounts have to balance. Organization changes have to be planned and executed carefully. *All* improvements have to be planned and executed carefully. Worker participation programs can't be allowed to fail because management wants to go too fast. There is no person more zealous than a converted pagan. But some things take time. And all changes require caution.

Functional skills will still have to be strong in many traditional areas. For instance, sales and marketing. You need salespeople who know how to make a pitch. How to close a deal. How to communicate to the customers. Market research to categorize the customers and develop advertising programs. You have no less of a need for a good advertising agency. You do need to make sure you've done all the other things discussed earlier, such as having a good product to sell that the customers will want. But people are not going to beat a path to your door, regardless of how good your mousetrap is. You have to show it to the world.

And you have to make some money on it. You have to price it correctly. That means understanding the market, price-quality relationships, and several other factors that we covered in previous chapters. It also means some good old down-home common sense. You have to make a reasonable profit without gouging your customers or driving them away. That often is a gut-based rather than scientific decision.

You also have to control your operating costs. Presumably if you've read this far you understand the need for low-cost operation. We've identified a number of ways for doing this and concurrently improving productivity. But you have to get people who understand the best techniques in detail. Then you have to implement them. Maybe you need production control or inventory control systems. Better warehouse or distribution procedures. Overhead reductions. The normal advances in management methods in conjunction with the recent economic hard times have made many companies experts at operations management. They may be doing other things wrong, but when they fix them you'll be in trouble if you don't have your operating costs under control. Don't underestimate the improvements that can be made; they're often so dramatic as to be almost unbelievable.

And don't be afraid of breaking new ground. For example, many companies have involved their employees, and their unions, in cost-reduction programs. That's not as silly as it sounds. Cost reduction is preferable to company bankruptcy. You also need to measure your progress on cost control. Perhaps you can develop a whole new approach. Westinghouse broke down many of its departments into specific tasks that contributed to efficiency and operating performance. The departments included engineering, personnel and other indirect departments in addition to manufacturing. People in the departments measure the performance on the tasks, which then permits a determination of how to do better in terms of specific tasks. Sure beats the old dictatorial approach of reducing costs across-the-board without knowing where inefficiencies are being incurred.

Retaining Financial Controls

Financial controls aren't new; what is new is the extent to which they are going unused. Perhaps "unused" is too strong. Let's just describe the situation, and you can draw your own conclusions.

The fundamental financial objectives are liquidity and balance sheet strength. One measure of liquidity is a simple ratio of liquid assets to short-term liabilities. This ratio has been in a general state of decline for U.S. business for the last twenty years.[1] Part of the decline is due to increased investments of types other than liquid assets. This is supported by the fact that very few companies have actually run out of cash. However, part of it results from corporations simply not having the cash to retain as liquid assets. Many business people are operating far closer to the edge than they would like to be.

They are also nervous when they look at their balance sheets. The "quality" of assets has been declining in many companies, for example, obsolete equipment carried on the books for more than it is worth to anybody. However, the real problem is liabilities. A corporation usually likes to minimize its loans from banks and maximize the money from shareholders. It can frequently pay lower rates to shareholders and it has the flexibility of suspending dividends altogether, whereas banks prefer to be paid in accordance with loan agreements. As we all know, in recent years interest rates have shot up, making borrowing very expensive. In this environment, adding debt is unhealthy. Yet that's exactly what has been happening. About fifteen years ago U.S. business doubled the rate at which it was adding debt, compared to how fast it was adding equity, e.g., stock sales.[2] That trend has continued to a point today that almost one-half of corporate pretax profits in the U.S.

goes to pay interest charges on debt.[3] That's money unavailable for anything else, including dividends to stockholders.

What has caused the balance sheet and liquidity problems? First, the fundamental problems of U.S. business that we have discussed in this book. Corporations simply aren't making much money and their future prospects don't look good enough to entice investors to buy stock. No money and no investors lead to liquidity and balance sheet problems. The second is the lack of financial discipline. You can't allow yourself to go borrow more money whenever you run out. You have to have budget controls, cost controls, capital expenditure controls, and so on. The people in operating functions are responsible for making the controls work, but the financial people have to take the lead in establishing controls. Perhaps zero-base budgeting. This is not just a legacy of Jimmy Carter. Texas Instruments began using it in 1962. The basic idea is to start from a "zero base" during each budget cycle, i.e., justify everything in the budget, not just changes from last year's budget. A lot of unnecessary fat gets trimmed this way.

Maybe you need higher "hurdle rates" for new capital expenditures or other uses of funds. If your required rate of return isn't high enough, then you're not directing funds to the right places where you can earn enough to avoid borrowing. Maybe you need better cash management. Control of receivables and payables. Better investment strategies for your idle funds. Negotiation of better billing and payment terms with your suppliers and customers. Whatever is appropriate for your company and type of business. You know what to do. If there's one thing that U.S. managers are well-trained in, even over-trained, it's financial controls. But they've caved in under the pressures of circumstances. This can't continue. You have to re-implement basic financial controls. If you don't, doing the other things that we have discussed will have much less impact than they could.

Does Size Matter?

We haven't said much about how to apply the ideas in this book to various sizes of companies. Does size matter? Clearly, our comments about setting up small organizational units aren't applicable if you are already one by virtue of being a small company. You can probably think of additional ways in which company size could be a factor. However, the size issue can mask the overwhelming number of similarities among U.S. companies. Not that there are not valid characteristics of large and small companies (mostly favoring small companies, as we said earlier). It's just that the size issue has to be secondary to the problems and solutions that all of U.S. business is wrestling with. When you or I become physically ill, the dosage of medication prescribed for us takes into account the size and strength of our bodies. But it's more related to the illness we have and the extent to which it has afflicted us. The same is true for business ailments. Size is a secondary concern.

The problems of U.S. business also do not respect geography. Obviously, Silicon Valley is very different from Houston, which is very different from downtown Detroit. But Detroit has problems because of the problems of its businesses, not the other way around. We have to understand the business problems first, then worry about the considerations imposed on us by geography.

No Standard Solutions

Each specific business problem described in this book was accompanied by a specific solution, in the same way that the science of medicine understands how to treat specific illnesses and diseases. But—continuing our medical analogy—individual patients will have different problems. The treatments to be prescribed will depend on the problems. The details of surgery, medication or whatever (within the bounds of the overall accepted treatment for the specific problems) will be determined individually for each patient.

The general form of solutions and the implementation details must be based on the unique business problems and problem-related characteristics of a specific company. The problems are easy to understand. By "problem-related characteristics," we mean the company-wide characteristics or traits that have allowed the problems to flourish.

Consider the stage of maturity of the corporation. We said that U.S. corporations are struggling with the same sorts of anxieties that plague teenagers. But teenagers have very different levels of personal maturity. The same is true of corporations. If you have a corporation with a culture and maturity level still in the 19th century, you've got a different problem from a corporation that has a 1950s or 1960s mentality. Neither will make it through the rest of this century if it doesn't change, but the approaches to helping them will not be the same.

The problems and alternative treatments also will be influenced by the people in your company, their preferences and prejudices. This is not only unavoidable—it's good. Anything else means that people don't play an important role. But the influence can be very strong in certain directions. Sometimes one individual has the power. ITT under Harold Geneen was a company that emphasized financial controls. His successors have been different, but each had his own style. On the other hand, sometimes the group is more important. Caterpillar Tractor has a corporate mentality that discourages acquiring people or expertise from outside. We are not passing judgment on these companies. We are simply saying that circumstances and people play critical roles in determining how a company operates and how it implements solutions. They may even influence the acceptance of a new approach. Geneen, for example, was not inclined to listen for very long to ideas that contradicted his ways of doing things.

So you have to understand the problems and the environment in which they exist in order to determine the appropriate solutions. That seems logical enough. Another way of saying that is that you have to start narrowing down the range of problems and solutions in the world to ones that fit your company. As a result, you'll get closer and closer to a plan of action for your company. And that's what effective management is all about—doing something to make things better.

"Action is Eloquence."
—SHAKESPEARE

Chapter 20

What to Do on Monday Morning

(Getting There from Here)

BEFORE we turn out the lights we need to figure out how to make this book work for you. How? First, determining specifically what to do at your company. Then, getting yourself launched into action.

Taking Stock

At the risk of wearing out our medical analogy, let's say that you have to start with a corporate physical exam. This idea builds on the thoughts with which we finished the previous chapter, tailoring the business solutions and implementation approach to your particular situation.

The first step is the diagnosis. Make a list of all the concerns you have about the business you manage. Or list all the issues that we've raised and leave room for three columns entitled Applicable, Possibly Applicable, and Not Applicable. The point is to create a checklist for the diagnosis, similar to the forms that physicians fill out during your annual physical examination.

Then you have to perform the diagnosis. Carefully and completely. Evaluating your current position, strengths, and weaknesses regarding each area that you're concerned about. You'll want to do this as a formal effort within the company, not as a project to fill up time when people aren't busy with other things. It's important to take enough time to do a good job. The results should be clearly documented, not as a report that nobody will read, but as a communication tool. The written word is imperfect and needs to be supplemented by verbal communication, but it's the best starting point. If you find that it's tough to take the time to research your situation carefully and prepare readable documents, you're in too much of a hurry. You should also monitor your findings carefully. As the analysis proceeds, you should notice that you are getting deeper and deeper into fundamental issues of corporate policy and behavior. If not, you are probably still at the surface level, dealing with symptoms rather than the actual problems.

Your best people should conduct the evaluation. Naturally, it makes sense to involve a cross-section of the people in the company. You have to draw on people at different vertical levels in the corporation and from different horizontal levels, i.e., peers across the corporation at a particular vertical level. You probably have talented people throughout the organization; make use of them. Many of these people will have dual roles in the evaluation. They'll take part in the process of performing it. Then they'll assist in making the decisions of what to do about the problems that are identified. These people require special treatment.

Involving the Decision Makers

Maybe you are a decision maker. Maybe you're the head decision maker. Either way, you know that you have to be personally committed to a course of action before you'll support it very strongly. You also know that you don't like to be exposed to a proposed course of action only after it's been developed by someone else. You like to be in on the process of developing the recommendations for what to do. You like to have a chance to examine the information and conclusions on which the recommendations are based. You're not alone. Most decision makers feel as you do. So it's important to make them part of the evaluation of the corporation's problems, and not only in administrative roles. Ensure that they contribute to the evaluation. But choose a way that is commensurate with their experience and skills, e.g., don't assign a senior vice-president to perform low-level data gathering chores just so he or she is part of the team. Some people like to work in a "shirt-sleeves" mode; others don't. But you can take advantage of the knowledge and interest of all of them.

As the evaluation runs its course, the decision makers will get to do what they're paid to do: make decisions in their areas of responsibility. They'll have to participate in developing conclusions and then in formulating a plan for corrective action. Their seal of approval on the plan is important to ensure the general acceptability of the plan as well as for the improved odds of success due to the decision makers' commitment to it. You'll also find that good managers will want to have some responsibilities assigned to them in the plan. This is, of course, entirely consistent with our description of managemennt approaches that will be successful in the future. It also increases even further the individuals' commitment to the plan.

By the way, what is this thing that we're calling a plan? I can tell you more easily what it is not. It is not a detailed blueprint for fixing everything that is wrong in the corporation. It is not a timetable for developing new products that are missing from the product line, reducing operating costs or doing anything else that would appear to eliminate deficiencies identified by the evaluation. It is instead a plan for developing a management process or methodology that can be effective in correcting specific problems. Just as the evaluation has to get at the underlying causes of such failures as inadequate new product development, so the corrective action plan has to eliminate the causes, not just make the symptoms go away. Subsequent steps can deal with things like specific new products. It is up to the decision makers to understand this point and communicate it during the evaluation and development of action plans.

The Rest of the Organization

While all this is going on, the rest of the company is involved, too. Perhaps not in the same way as the people who are contributing full-time, but they're doing their share. As we have discussed before, it is important to have people participate in anything that affects their own jobs. That takes care of a great deal of the participation question, since sooner or later you're going to get around to just about everybody. But there is more to it than this.

The corporation will have to create a culture of change for employees to be comfortable with. Change is a fact of life. People have to deal with it in their own ways, including through conflict or denial in a few cases. But the overall culture of the company has to become one that supports and encourages change. People can make their peace with it in whatever ways they wish. The great majority have to find a way to accept it. They need help in doing so from their peers and from top management of the company. It's part and parcel of good people management—no more, no less—to help people become familiar with change.

Management can assist in the creation of this culture by communicating. Formally and informally. In large and small groups. Build it into everything that people are asked to do and into their reward systems. Remember, change is just another word for long-term thinking. If you think very far into the future, you are thinking about change. If you're not thinking about change, then you're just extrapolating the present, which isn't thinking about the future at all.

Once again: caution. You're trying to turn around a large slow battleship. It takes time. Don't try to force change too rapidly on the organization and the people. Initially it has to be spoon-fed. People have to see and understand the benefits of thinking differently. It has to become a way of life. The best way to do this is to concentrate first on changes that you can make easily and still will have significant impact.

Deciding What to Fix

Let's drop back for a moment to the development of a plan for corrective action. We didn't talk about how to set priorities for the things that had to be done. What to do first, second, third, etc. We'd like to take things in some order of importance, but we'd also like not to take a chance on failure. Therefore, it seems logical to work on something that has a blend of importance with potential for success. By a happy coincidence, this sort of thing is also going to help us build confidence in the minds of the people in the company. We'll demonstrate that the culture of change can work.

Believe it or not, you're probably going to have to use your skills of persuasion to get some people to buy this approach. Why? We can name at least two alternative approaches that may be appealing. One is the "leaky roof" problem. Fix the hole where the rain is coming in the heaviest. A noble idea if it's possible. But what if you really need a whole new roof or a new house? You don't want to bite off more than you can chew in your first attempt.

You also have to fight the urge to do something dramatic. To attack something in a flashy fashion when there really isn't a problem worth going after. Or to leave a bad taste in everybody's mouth by expending more effort on the hoopla than on the solution. Or hogging the spotlight on a problem of personal interest that really isn't the right problem for the corporation as a whole to be working on. There are a lot of ways to commit this particular sin. Try to avoid all of them.

Choose a goal that the company probably can reach. Maybe it's a certain social obligation. Or a way to get workers involved in the design of their jobs. It could be anything that we've talked about. But make it something that can be accomplished in a reasonable period of time. For scheduling purposes, estimate the maximum time required and then double it. You don't want to fall behind right out of the blocks.

And lead from strength also in the people you select. The people that you'll be working with may even be one of the primary factors in your selection of where to go first.

Remember that you have to control the process, not let it control you. The process of doing things differently takes off just like a rocket. After ignition, it just sits on the launch pad and rumbles for a while. Then it begins to lift slowly, and before you know it the rocket is moving at thousands of miles an hour out of your sight. You have to carefully program the flight before it commences, because the only option you have later is a destructive abort. And that's no more fun in running a corporation than it is in launching a rocket to the moon.

Learning from Others

Experience is a wonderful thing. It enables you to repeat successful strategies and to avoid approaches that, no matter how brilliantly conceived, failed under battlefield conditions. It's even more wonderful when you don't have to make the mistakes yourself in order to learn from them. You can benefit from both the victories and misfortunes of others.

Many companies have attempted to change the way they do business to accommodate the changing world. Their organization structures. Their product planning systems. Whatever has appeared to need the most attention. Some of the companies are not willing to share their experiences, whether they were good or bad. Others are. Except as specifically noted in one or two cases, all the companies that we have used as examples of progress have publicly expressed interest in talking about their situations. Requirements of brevity have forced us here to take a snapshot of the companies' problems and solutions. People in the company will be able to fill in the details and provide the total picture that you'll need in trying to apply the lessons to your company. (Of course, there is always the possibility that the companies' current management will have perspectives different from previous management.)

Other sources of information are associations of people and companies with interests in specific problems and business functions. The American Productivity Center in Houston studies productivity. The American Production and Inventory Control Society can provide information on operations management methods. The North American Society for Corporate Planning and Planning Executives Institute can help with planning. The people in your company with problems or functional assignments will know which associations to contact. But they may not have the top-level commitment and support required to derive anything useful from the contacts. Some effort and expense on the company's part will be required. Learning is a two-way street. The student has to meet the teacher at least half way.

Along the same lines are industry associations. The Bank Administration Institute (BAI). National Retail Merchants Association (NRMA). Again, your experts know the right associations. Use them. You also may be able to draw on information from that very general group, the American Management Associations. They produce so much material aimed at various levels of management that only a fraction of it can be of use to any one person. But in recent years they have begun addressing many of the issues we've raised in this book. At a minimum, some of their material is good background reading.

And don't forget universities. While the material universities produce is not flawless, it can be of value to those who prefer the rigorous scientific approach to problems. You should probably get to know who the university experts are in the fields in which you are interested and read some of their material, or talk to them.

Speaking of reading, we are all aware of the "information explosion." More material than we can possibly read already passes over our desks. Surely I'm not going to suggest that you should receive more things to read! Unfortunately, I am. You'll have to figure out for yourself how to get through it. Maybe one of the things you should read is a book on time management. Seriously, there are a number of general management journals, as well as the specialized journals, that carry articles on the issues facing the modern corporation and manager. A number of them provide case studies of the author's or someone else's experience. They're worth reading, as are the books that are published each year on the business issues of today.

As you can see, learning from others' experience is actually a lot of work. That explains, of course, why so many people make mistakes that others have made before them, why we say that history repeats itself. The phenomenon clearly is bigger than U.S. culture, but it manifests itself strongly in this country. U.S. business has a short-term go-go-go mentality. It's difficult to break through this mentality in order to take the time and spend the effort to see what other people have done. It's often more acceptable to rush off in ten different directions at high velocity than to steadfastly pursue the course of greatest reward. This is part of the corporate culture that we have to change. Investing the resources required to understand the experience of those who have gone before you is a good place to start with the cultural revolution.

Overcoming Resistance

We come now to a somewhat unpleasant topic. Resistance. You're going to encounter some when you start bringing up these new ideas. Not just inertia or foot-dragging. Or petty conflicts. Or knee-jerk reactions due to a lack of understanding. Or apathy. You can deal with all of these through the techniques we've mentioned. We're talking about honest-to-goodness hard-nosed serious resistance to what you're proposing. People who actively oppose your efforts.

What kind of people do we mean? Generalizing is always dangerous, but there are certain characteristics that tend to appear in people who don't want to change with the changing world. The people say they believe in individual effort. They got to the top or to their current positions through talent, skill, and hard work. There is nothing that can't be accomplished through perseverance. External influences aren't important. What counts is the "fire in your gut." Other people aren't important, although this person frequently refers to himself or herself as a team player. However, the "team" consists of people that are under his or her thumb, whose lives are directed by this individual. It's a team like the army is a team—it works only as long as everybody knows their places and takes orders unquestioningly.

Along with these characteristics goes an abiding faith in the U.S. business techniques that have always worked, i.e., "made this country great." You've met people like this. So have I. They've often risen far in organizations. Their drive and determination are admirable. But they've frequently been unable to deal with change. They've gone off the tracks and are spinning their wheels in sand. If the wheels spin fast enough, they'll make a little progress, which they will immediately misinterpret and redouble their efforts.

Not all people with drive, determination, etc. will oppose you. Most of them, like most of the population at large, have an uneasy feeling that something has gone terribly wrong with U.S. business. They'll be relieved and glad to assist you when you start making moves in the right direction. But you will encounter stiff resistance from the small minority who don't want to admit that we live in a different world than earlier generations of business people.

What can you do about these people? You can convert them. It's worth the effort to try. A fanatic on your side is ten times better than a fanatic opposing you. But what if conversion fails? Then you have three options. One: use their talents in areas of the company that are low on your list for improvement because change has not yet impacted them. In other words, the areas where the traditional ways of doing things are still working. A perfect fit for the individual who loves the traditional ways.

Two: Put them on the shelf in a job where they can't do any damage, or ask them to leave the company. An imperfect solution, but possibly the best that you have. You can't let a few people ruin an entire company.

If it's more than a few, or if the few are in charge of the company, then Option Three prevails. You have to go elsewhere. Maybe the company will welcome you back with open arms when its decline makes it obvious that you were right. Not likely. The world doesn't work that way. In fact, you shouldn't worry about it. Just do all you can to make the necessary improvements and if you can't succeed, fold your tent and move on. Maybe you'll be able to help another company.

Other kinds of opponents are also possible. Perhaps the devotees of office politics who have carried the game to such an intense degree that it's all that matters to them. Or the company owners who are milking it before liquidating it. Or many others. Your options are the same. Convert them, use them, force them out, or give in to them. It's your choice. But you have only one life to live and you'd better think about how you want to spend it.

Taking One Thing at a Time

Let's say that none of the really bad things has happened. You've been able to get people signed up and to start making plans to improve things. There's one last thing to bear in mind. Beware of grandiose plans. You can have ambitious dreams, but don't share them with a lot of people. Concentrate on one thing at a time.

Try to avoid setting targets very far into the future. For one reason, you don't want to be disappointed when things don't work out exactly as you would like. And they won't. The complexity and changing nature of the world will see to that. But there is a better reason. Dealing with the changing world is not an activitity that has a definable end to it. It's not a project that you start and plan to complete at some time in the future. You'll be doing it for the rest of your life. The only long-range goal that you need to set is the development of the ability to integrate change into your company's way of doing business. A plan to address an existing problem in two years makes no sense. The problem and the timing for fixing it will change by the time you get around to it. You have to understand what all the problems are, of course, but you don't need a five-year master plan to get to them. You need to work on one thing (not literally, but the key is not to overburden the organization) and then go on to something else. Be patient. Rome wasn't built in a day, and neither was Japan. Just make a good beginning, finish things that you start, and keep your eye on the future. You'll get there in fine shape.

Good luck!

Notes

Where financial and operating data on specific companies are available in annual reports, it is excluded from the following notes.

Chapter 1

1. The "brown lung" case (cotton dust exposure). *AFL–CIO vs. Marshall*, Court of Appeals, District of Columbia Circuit, 1979.
2. For example, 1980 survey "Strategic Planning for Human Resources," Opinion Research Corporation (ORC), Princeton, NJ, (confidential details available through subscription from ORC); also Lodge, George C., and Martin, William F., "Our Society in 1985—Business May Not Like It," *Harvard Business Review*, November–December 1975.
3. Drucker, Peter F., *Managing in Turbulent Times*. New York: Harper & Row, 1980.

Chapter 3

1. Study by a group of economists headed by Irving Kravis of the University of Pennsylvania, reported in *The Wall Street Journal*, 1 May 1979, p. 40.
2. 1981 American Insurance Association data, reported in *The Wall Street Journal*, 16 June 1981, p. 46.
3. *United States vs. Park*, decided by Supreme Court in 1975.
4. For example, Opinion Research Corporation survey, "Strategic Planning for Human Resources."

Chapter 4

1. For example, "How Lawless are Big Corporations." *Fortune*, December, 1980.

Chapter 5

1. For one study, "The Changing Board," Heidrick & Struggles, Inc., Chicago IL, January 1982.
2. Ibid.
3. 1980 study by *Directorship* magazine, reported in "The Law of Supply and Demand," *TEMPO* magazine, Touche Ross & Co., vol. 26, no. 2, 1980.
4. For one study, see "Board of Directors—Tenth Annual Study," Korn/Ferry International, New York, February 1983.

5. Ibid.
6. For example, *Harvard Business Review's* "From the Boardroom" series.
7. For two examples, see *Business Week's* "Annual Survey of Executive Compensation," and Arthur Young & Co.'s annual "Executive Compensation" reports.
8. Korn/Ferry, Board of Directors study.
9. 1979 data from American Society of Corporate Secretaries reported in *Harvard Business Review,* September/October 1979, p. 25.
10. Korn/Ferry, Board of Directors study.

Chapter 6

1. Study by Robert H. Hayes and Associates, reported in "The Group Executive: Power Figure or Gray Marshmallow," *Management Review,* March 1979.

Chapter 7

1. Details available in *Business Week,* 1 January 1981, special issue on U.S. economy.
2. Ibid.
3. "The Largest Industrial Companies in the World," annual report by *Fortune.*
4. Ibid.
5. "Annual Report on American Industry," annual report by *Forbes.*

Chapter 8

1. "Population Estimates and Projections," Series P–25, Bureau of the Census, 1982.
2. Motion Picture Association of America data, reported in *The Wall Street Journal,* 19 August 1981, p. 1.
3. Motion Picture Association of America data from study "Incidence of Motion Picture Attendance," by Opinion Research Corporation, Princeton, NJ, July 1980.
4. "U.S. Automotive Industry Trends for the 1980s," Arthur Andersen & Co., Chicago IL, 1981; also 1982 Ford Motor Co. study, reported in *Forbes,* 22 November 1982, p. 165.
5. 1981 study by Chase Econometrics as part of their industry forecasting service.
6. Ibid.
7. Ibid.
8. "Annual Report on American Industry," *Forbes.*
9. Ford study, as reported in *Forbes.*
10. "Annual Report on American Industry."
11. Survey by Needham, Harper, & Steers, "Life Style Study," Needham, Harper, & Steers, New York, 1982.
12. *Road & Track* owner survey available from *Road & Track,* Newport Beach, CA.
13. Studies by Harvard University and Sanford C. Bernstein & Co., reported in *Business Week,* 14 September 1981; studies by James Harbour reported in *Fortune,* 8 February 1982; studies by William C. Roney & Co., reported in *Business Week,* 1 March 1982.
14. 1983 report from Motor Vehicle Manufacturers Association (MVMA), "MVMA Facts and Figures," Detroit MI.

Chapter 9

1. "Employment and Earnings Statistics," Bureau of Labor Statistics, 1982.
2. Ibid.

Chapter 10

1. 1981 study by Bureau of Labor Statistics, reported in *Computerworld,* 2 November 1981, p. 1.

2. "VLSI Capital Equipment Outlook," Technical Ventures, Inc., San Jose CA, 1981.
3. "R&D Scoreboard," annual survey by *Business Week*.
4. For example, Freeman, Christopher, *The Economics of Industrial Innovation*. Baltimore: Penguin, 1974; Mansfield, Edwin, *Research and Innovation in the Modern Corporation*. New York: Norton, 1971; Schon, Donald, *Technology and Change*. New York: Delacorte, 1967; also see "The Strategy-Technology Connection," *Harvard Business Review*, July–August 1980.
5. Ibid.
6. For example, Bruno, Albert V. and Cooper, Arnold C., "Patterns of Development and Acquisition in Silicon Valley," University of Santa Clara, January 1982.

Chapter 11

1. Mitchell, Arnold, *The Nine American Lifestyles*. New York: Macmillan, 1983; also 1981 survey by Consumer Network and 1981 survey by BrainReserve and Leber Katz Partners, reported in *The Wall Street Journal*, 15 October 1981, p. 25.
2. 1982 confidential survey, reported in *The Wall Street Journal*, 26 August 1982, p. 1.
3. 1983 survey by Ward's Communications, reported in "Japan Still Tops in Quality," *Ward's Auto World*, March 1983.
4. Survey by *Fortune*, reported in "Ranking Corporate Reputations," *Fortune*, 10 January 1983.

Chapter 12

1. Needham, Harper, & Steers survey, "Life Style Study."
2. Survey by J. Walter Thompson Inc., "Brand Utility Yardstick," J. Walter Thompson, New York, 1981.
3. "Annual Report on American Industry," *Forbes*.
4. For example, Brookings Institution analyses, reported in *The Wall Street Journal*, 21 December 1981, p. 1.

Chapter 13

1. 1980 European Community (Common Market) data, reported in "The Japanese Juggernaut lands in Europe," *Fortune*, 30 November 1981, p. 108.
2. Ibid.
3. 1981 survey by *Fortune* and Twain Braxton Asia, "How We See Each Other," reported in *Fortune*, 10 August 1981.

Chapter 14

1. For example, Booz, Allen, & Hamilton study reported in *The Wall Street Journal*, 12 November 1981, p. 25.
2. Annual salary and position surveys by *Datamation*, for example, "Room at the Top," March 1976.
3. 1983 survey by Dun's reported in "The Computer and the Top Honcho," *Dun's Business Month*, May 1983.

Chapter 15

1. "Current Population Reports," Series P–25, Bureau of the Census, 1981.
2. Ibid.
3. "Employment and Earnings Statistics," Bureau of Labor Statistics; "Current Population Reports" Bureau of the Census, all years since World War II.
4. "Population Estimates for Standard Metropolitan Statistical Areas," Series P–25, Bureau of the Census, 1981.
5. Census Bureau data, reported in "Take Another Look at Regional

U.S. Growth," *Harvard Business Review,* March–April 1983.

6. 1973–1981 data from Organization for Economic Cooperation and Development (OCED), reported in *The Economist,* 14 August 1982.

7. "Current Population Reports," Series P–25, Bureau of the Census, 1981.

8. For example, 1982 Doyle Dane Bernbach survey, "What Does the Future Hold and Who's Worried About It?" New York, November 1982.

9. "Employment and Earnings Statistics" reports, Bureau of Labor Statistics, 1981.

10. Ibid.

11. For example, see 1980 study reported by John F. Runcie, "By Days I Make the Cars," *Harvard Business Review,* May–June 1980.

12. For example, 1979 study by Yankelovich, Skelly, & White, reported in "Yankelovich on Today's Workers," *Industry Week,* 6 August 1979.

13. "Employment and Earnings Statistics," Bureau of Labor Statistics, years from 1940.

14. "Employment and Earnings Statistics," Bureau of Labor Statistics, 1981.

Chapter 16

1. Yankelovich, Skelly, & White, "Yankelovich on Today's Workers."

2. Ibid.

3. For example, Opinion Research Corporation study, "Strategic Planning."

4. For example, 1979 study by Program on Neighborhood and Regional Change at MIT, reported in *The Wall Street Journal,* 5 February 1982, p. 1.

5. "Country Business Patterns" reports, Bureau of the Census; also

"The Largest Industrial Corporations" annual report by *Fortune,* 1960–1970.

6. For example, 1979 study by Program on Neighborhood and Regional Change at MIT.

Chapter 17

1. Miller, William B., "Motivation Techniques: Does One Work Best?" *Management Review,* February 1981.

2. 1980 survey by MNO Programs International, reported in *The Wall Street Journal,* 18 July 1980, p. 21.

3. For example, 1980 *Wall Street Journal*/Gallup survey, reported in *The Wall Street Journal,* 19 and 20 August 1980.

4. For example, 1980 survey by Doyle Dane Bernbach, "What Does the Future Hold?"

5. For example, 1980 *Wall Street Journal*/Gallup survey, reported in *The Wall Street Journal,* 14 November 1980.

6. For example, 1979 survey by Korn/Ferry International, reported in "A Career Profile of the Senior Executive," *Management Review,* July 1979.

Chapter 18

1. For references to other researchers, see annual "Productivity Perspectives" and "Productivity Indexes" publications of the American Productivity Center, Houston, TX.

2. "Science Indicators–1978" publication of the National Science Foundation, Washington, DC.

3. 1980 analysis based on Business Roundtable data, reported in *The Wall Street Journal,* 28 October 1980, p. 1.

4. Judson, Arnold S., "The Awkward Truth About Productivity," *Har-*

vard Business Review, September–
October 1982.

Chapter 19

1. "Economic Outlook and Issues,"
Data Resources, Inc., 1982;
"National Policies and the Deteri-
orating Balance Sheets of Ameri-
can Corporations," Salomon
Brothers, 1981.
2. "National Policies," Salomon
Brothers.
3. "National Policies," Salomon
Brothers.

Recommended Reading

YOU may wish to increase your general knowledge in some areas. For this reason I have provided the following sample of books on various topics of interest to management. Textbooks and other books of an instructional nature regarding basic business functions, such as accounting or production control, are excluded.

Andrews, Kenneth R., *The Concept of Corporate Strategy,* Homewood, Ill.: Dow Jones-Irwin, 1971.

Anshen, Melvin, *Corporate Strategies for Social Performance.* New York: Macmillan Co., 1980.

Ansoff, H. Igor, *Corporate Strategy.* New York: McGraw-Hill, 1965.

Anthony, Robert N., *Planning and Control Systems: A Framework for Analysis.* Boston: Harvard, 1965.

Argyris, Chris, *Management and Organizational Development.* New York: McGraw-Hill, 1971.

Beer, Stafford, *Decision and Control.* New York: John Wiley & Sons, 1966.

Beyer, Robert, and Trawicki, Donald J., *Profitability Accounting.* New York: Ronald Press, 1972.

Bower, Marvin, *The Will to Manage.* New York: McGraw-Hill, 1966.

Burton, John C., ed., *Corporate Financial Reporting.* New York: AICPA, 1972.

Chandler, Alfred D., Jr., *Strategy and Structure.* Garden City, N.Y.: Doubleday-Anchor, 1966.

——, *The Visible Hand.* Cambridge, Mass.: Belknap Press, 1977.

Cornuelle, Richard, *De-Managing America.* New York: Random House, 1975.

Dale, Ernest, *Management: Theory and Practice.* New York: McGraw-Hill, 1973.

Davis, Stanley M. and Lawrence, Paul R., *Matrix.* Reading, Mass.: Addison-Wesley, 1977.

Deal, Terrence E. and Kennedy, Allan A., *Corporate Cultures.* Reading, Mass.: Addison-Wesley, 1982.

Dowling, William, ed., *Effective Management and the Behavioral Sciences.* New York: Amacom, 1978.

Drucker, Peter F., *The Practice of Management.* New York: Harper & Row, 1954.

——, *Management: Tasks, Respon-*

sibilities, Practices. New York: Harper & Row, 1974.

———, *Managing in Turbulent Times.* New York: Harper & Row, 1980.

Durant, Will and Ariel, *The Lessons of History.* New York: Simon and Schuster, 1968.

Ewing, D. W., ed., *Long-Range Planning for Management.* New York: Harper & Row, 1972.

Galbraith, John Kenneth, *The New Industrial State.* Boston: Houghton Mifflin, 1967.

Gyllenhammar, Pehr G, *People at Work.* Reading, Mass.: Addison-Wesley, 1977.

Herzberg, Frederick, *Work and the Nature of Man.* Cleveland: World, 1966.

Jones, Landon Y., *Great Expectations.* New York: Ballantine, 1980.

Jones, Reginald L. and Trentin, George, H. *Management Controls in Professional Firms.* New York: American Management Association, 1968.

Leavitt, Harold J., *Managerial Psychology.* Chicago: University of Chicago Press, 1978.

Likert, Rensis, *The Human Organization.* New York: McGraw-Hill, 1967.

McGregor, Douglas, *The Human Side of Enterprise.* New York: McGraw-Hill, 1960.

Morrison, Samuel E., *The Oxford History of the American People.* New York: Oxford Universtiy Press, 1965.

Ouchi, William, *Theory Z.* Reading, Mass.: Addison-Wesley, 1981.

Pascale, Richard T. and Athos, Anthony G. *The Art of Japanese Management.* New York: Simon and Schuster, 1981.

Patton, Arch, *Men, Money, and Motivation.* New York: McGraw-Hill, 1961.

Peters, Thomas and Waterman, Robert, *In Search of Excellence.* New York: Harper & Row, 1982.

Porter, Michael E., *Competitive Strategy.* New York: The Free Press, 1980.

Pyhrr, Peter A., *Zero Base Budgeting.* New York: John Wiley & Sons, 1973.

Ross, Joel E. and Kami, Michael J., *Corporate Management in Crisis: Why the Mighty Fall.* Englewood Cliffs, N.J.: Prentice-Hall, 1973.

Shirley, Robert C., Peters, Michael H., El-Ansary, Adel I., *Strategy and Policy Formulation: A Multifunctional Orientation.* New York: John Wiley & Sons, Inc., 1976.

Simon, Herbert A., *Administrative Behavior.* New York: The Free Press, 1976.

Skinner, B. F., *Beyond Freedom and Dignity.* New York: Alfred A. Knopf, 1971.

Sloan, Alfred P., Jr., *My Years with General Motors.* New York: McFadden-Bartell, 1965.

Sloma, Richard S., *No-Nonsense Management.* New York: Macmillan Co., 1977.

Thurow, Lester C., *The Zero-Sum Society.* New York: Basic Books, 1980.

Toffler, Alvin, *Future Shock.* New York: Random House, 1970.

———, *The Third Wave.* New York: William Morrow, 1980.

Townsend, Robert, *Up the Organization.* New York: Alfred A. Knopf, 1970.

Vogel, Ezra F., *Japan as Number 1.* New York: Harper & Row, 1979.

Watson, Thomas J., Jr., *A Business and Its Beliefs: The Ideas That Helped Build IBM.* New York: McGraw-Hill, 1963.

Webb, James E., *Space Age Management.* New York: McGraw-Hill, 1969.

Wright, J. Patrick, *On A Clear Day You Can See General Motors.* New York: Avon, 1979.

Yoshino, M., *Japan's Managerial System: Tradition and Innovation.* Cambridge, Mass.: The MIT press, 1968.

Index

Labor. *See* Employees.
Labor law
beginnings, 11
1930s, 14
Labor shifts and productivity, 285
Labor unions, 27–28
beginnings, 11
and participative management, 267–268
Law of diminishing returns, 287
Lawyers
as board members, 75
and corporate relations, 62–63
Legal responsibilities and corporate goals, 210
Leisure industry, 132–133
Levi Strauss and Company, 184–185
Liabilities, corporate, 37–42, 306
Liability cases, 39
corporation reaction, 41
Liability of board members, limits
committee approach, 70
Liberal arts, as management background, 93
Lifestyles, 229–234
Likert, Rensis, 257–258
Line functions, 86
Liquidity, 306, 307
Long-range planning
foreign business ownership, 196
and special interest groups, 31
Low costs/low price maintenance, 122
Low growth industries, employee skills, 242
Low growth markets, 179
Loyalty to corporation, executives, 270

Management. *See also* Corporate executives;
Middle management; Top level
management.
awareness of customer desires, 122–123
board relations, 71
and change, 2–3, 302–303
high technology, 151–153
impact of technology, 252
labor unions as resource, 27–28
learning from others, 314–315
new positions, 80–85
of people, 255–275
and productivity, 287–291
and quality, 165
styles, 256–259
working with special interest groups, 30–32
Management reporting system, short-term
vs. long-term results, 169–170
Management systems, 217–220

Managers
career paths and demographics, 225
compensation, 270
of the future, 303–304
Manufacturing processes
and corporate goals, 211–212
and high technology, 144
Market expansion, as strategy, 122
Market saturation, 117
Marketing and international consumers, 189
Marketplace, 176–177
and new products, 153
profile development of needs, 183
Mass production, 13–14
and product variety, 36
Materials science, 149
Matrix management, 86–89
M.B.A. degree, 93, 303–304
McClelland, David, 259
McGregor, Douglas, 257
Measurement system, corporate, 214–217
Merit raises, 271
Metropolitan areas, 228
Middle management, 91–93
Military management model, 85
and job definition, 247
Minimum Wage Act, 14
Minorities in business, 23–24
Moral values, code of, 33
Moralists, 257–258
Motivation, 243, 259, 261
Motivational factors, 258
Movie theater industry, 116–117

National Highway Safety Administration
(NHTSA), 26
National Labor Relations Act (1935), 14
New products, 144, 151–153
and corporate goals, 212–213
Noise regulation, 28–29
Norris-LaGuardia Act (1932), 14

Obsolescence, broadcasting equipment, 138
Occupational Safety and Health
Administration (OSHA), 16
Ocean Spray Cranberries, Inc., 213
Office productivity, 292–293
Oil industry, statistics, 104
Oil problem, 103–106
Oil-producing countries, 104–105
Operating costs, control of, 305
Operating results, short-term vs. long-term
reporting, 168
Operational controls, high technology, 154–156